The Communist States and the West

The
Communist States
and
The West

EDITED BY
ADAM BROMKE
AND
PHILIP E. UREN

FREDERICK A. PRAEGER, *Publishers*
New York • Washington • London

FREDERICK A. PRAEGER, PUBLISHERS
111 Fourth Avenue, New York, N.Y. 10003, U.S.A.
77–79 Charlotte Street, London W.1, England

Published in the United States of America in 1967
by Frederick A. Praeger, Inc., Publishers

Library of Congress Catalog Card Number: 67-13865

This book is Number 185 in the series
Praeger Publications in Russian History and World Communism

Printed in the United States of America

Preface

MANY ORDINARY people, and perhaps some statesmen, look back upon the singleness of purpose of the war years with a certain nostalgia. The source of evil was then clearly identified, and men were confident where interest and duty lay. The end of the war brought brief confusion, but as old enemies became allies and erstwhile friends turned on one another, there emerged again a stark pattern of conflict. The rigid polarization of power between Moscow and Washington, and their mutual hostility, left little room for uncertain loyalties, but the sharp categories of this period were short-lived. Rebellion in Eastern Europe, schism in the Communist alliance, the recovery of Western Europe, the appearance of cracks in the NATO structure, and the emancipation of the colonies all contributed to the emergence of a more complex and uncertain world. As the familiar lines of the old pattern have begun to fade and as new lines have appeared, the murmur of conflicting opinion has mounted in volume.

The general objective of this book is to evaluate the impact of the Sino-Soviet split, the growth of polycentrism, and other recent developments in the Communist world upon East-West relations.

The problem is a complex one, for changes which are at present taking place are not confined to one side but cut across the ideological line dividing the world. What we are witnessing is not simply the weakening of the East and, in accordance with the doctrine of *divide et impera,* the strengthening of the West. Paradoxically, as a result of the weakening of the East, the West also tends to be internally weakened. Precisely because the Communist danger appears to be receding, the cohesion of the Western alliance is reduced. Feeling more secure, the various countries place their individual objectives over those of the alliance as a whole.

To examine and communicate the character of this new scene is no easy task. On one side is the confusion of fact and fiction, and, on the other, the mists of oversimplification. For editors the temptation is always to bully contributors into the framework of a particular model, to herd them onto one vantage point, and to discard those who insist on their originality. To do otherwise is to invite glib censure and to be reminded by the witty and witless that the King James Version of the Bible is the only successful book so far written by a committee. And yet, the too orderly analysis, stimulating as it may be as an intellectual exercise, gives but a poor picture of the current international scene.

For this reason, we have tried to present a range of views and to show something of the various approaches toward our present problems that may be taken by honest men. Too much consistency in a changing world is a dangerous hobgoblin and readers who seek the comfort of firm guidelines may be disappointed. They will find ideology downgraded to an almost decorative function and they will find it exalted as the main driving force of great powers. They will find recent history presented as a dismal record of error and held up as an epic of achievement. They will find nationalism encouraged, condoned, and condemned. And, in these paradoxes, it is hoped that they will catch something of the new international reality which a neater tale might not tell.

There is always, and properly, a certain tension between practitioner and analyst, between diplomat and academic, particularly in this era of "teach-ins." We are, therefore, fortunate to be able to present the views of a cabinet minister and of a diplomat, as well as those of men who have had experience in both the academic and diplomatic worlds. Eight of them delivered a series of public lectures at Carleton University during the winter of 1965–66. Other chapters have been added to give a more complete regional coverage.

We have been encouraged by many people at Carleton University, and we are particularly grateful to Dean D. M. L. Farr, Professor J. A. Porter, Professor R. A. MacKay, and Mrs. Judy Patterson. The interest and support of the Department of External Affairs has also been greatly appreciated. Finally, we are indebted to Mrs. Nona Bauer for her patient and efficient help in preparing the manuscript for publication.

A. B.
P. E. U.

Contents

ix

The Communist States and the West

1. Power and Ideology in East-West Relations

HENRY B. MAYO

ONCE UPON a time there was a man called Socrates. The Delphic oracle told him that he was the wisest man in Athens. He was puzzled by this—so we learn from Plato's *Apology*—and he went around to a number of persons who had a reputation for wisdom, starting with politicians (a curious first choice, you might think), and so on through poets and artisans. He concluded that they all thought they knew a lot but were mistaken, whereas he knew that he knew nothing; and so in a way the oracle was right, and Socrates was indeed the wisest man in Athens.

It is only in this sense of being uncertain about what I know that I make any claim to knowledge of this great subject, "Power and Ideology in East-West Relations." It is one, however, on which a great many other people seem to know a lot. Mention the word "Communism" in Mississippi, and white folks there will tell you the chief tactic of the "Reds" is to mix the races by integration and so bring about their ideological aim—the downfall of the West. In many small towns of North America people are convinced that the "Red" tactic is to put fluorides in our drinking water and so undermine us and make us an easy prey to Communist ideology.

These are extreme examples of the combination of certainty and invincible ignorance. Yet even eminent Sinologists and Sovietologists and international-affairs experts are susceptible to the disease of being confident about their guesses. There is something about Communism and the Cold War that leads people irresistibly to translate their fears or hopes into certainties and their guesswork into dogma.

There are, I think, two main reasons for this. One is that the study of international relations is often pursued as a way of finding solutions to world problems. That is, its exponents are partisan. Instead of pursuing an academic discipline that seeks knowledge about how states behave toward one another, they try to document the popular Cold War slogans.

The other reason is closely related, namely, an ideological and even conspiratorial view of international politics is easily held by those who fail to recognize that foreign policy is *foreign*. Let me explain. The study of the Communist part of the world is today one of our major academic industries. Sovietologists, for instance, do indeed know a good deal about the Soviet Union and its ideology, and some of what they know may even be reliable. But nevertheless, it is impossible to deduce Soviet policy, and still less the character of East-West relations, from a specialist knowledge of *one side*. In a similar way, experts on the United States may know a great deal about that country, but this alone does not enable them to predict or understand U.S. foreign policy.

The point here is that foreign policy is a *relationship* (like concepts of power, or leadership), and other countries are part of that relationship. No country can alone determine its own role in foreign affairs, and most are not free to shape all their domestic policies. This is a lesson that is perhaps easier for smaller states than for great powers to learn. We must beware, however, of attributing any special virtues to small states, in the manner in which Marx foolishly idealized the proletariat. Small powers differ from the great powers only in having less capacity to do harm.

Two examples may serve to illustrate the point that other states and the world environment help to shape any foreign policy. First, the change in the role that Canada has played on the world stage since about 1958 is not primarily due to changes within Canada (say the replacement of the allegedly wise and skillful Liberals by the allegedly unwise and blundering Conservatives) but derives much more from the changing circumstances of the world scene.

Second, consider next the United States. Here is a nation that desperately wanted to stay out of two world wars, yet in spite of itself it participated. Not Americanism or the American way of life —whatever these wonderful expressions may mean—but the circumstances and events in international life, events from outside, largely determined American action—in any meaningful sense of "determine" as applied to human affairs.

The world is changing around us, and very great changes have occurred in what we used to call the "Communist bloc" and the "Western bloc," and consequently in the configuration of international forces. Succeeding writers will analyze what is happening inside Russia and China, and the relations between the different Communist countries, and whether the "capitalist" world and the "Communist" world are converging toward one homogeneous, antheap, global society.

My question is a somewhat different one: What sort of picture do we and should we carry in our heads of the Western countries and the Eastern countries and the relations between them? The question can be dressed up, to appear academically more impressive, if we ask: What model, or what framework of theory, should we use in analyzing East-West relations? In particular: How much are East-West relations simply a contemporary large-scale power struggle and how much a conflict of ideologies? This is a quantitative question, but the answer obviously is not precisely measurable. And before we can attempt any sort of answer we must sharpen the question.

For one thing we can no longer speak simply of the "East," that is, the Communist countries, as a monolithic bloc. Even when this language was in vogue, Western attempts to explain the Soviet Union consisted of at least "Ten Theories in Search of Reality."[1]

[1] Daniel Bell, "Ten Theories in Search of Reality," *World Politics*, Vol. X (April, 1958).

There have long been differences between the Soviet Union and Yugoslavia—some have called Tito the Luther of a Communist Reformation—between the Soviet Union and its so-called satellites, and now of course the most dramatic of all, that between the Soviet Union and China. There is not, so far as we can see, any sign as yet of an Ecumenical Council to start bridging the schism between the divided faithful, and it seems unlikely that the lost unity can ever be restored. Still less can we speak of a Western monolith. The nearest we came to Western unity was in the NATO alliance, and this has been splitting at the seams over military policy, and even more over other foreign policy matters.

For another thing, all political relationships are power relationships, in the sense that power is needed to make and carry out public policies, both foreign and domestic. Jacques Barzun tells of a talk he once gave on politics. When he asked, at one point, what politics was about if not about power, the audience stared at him with horror, as if he had proposed polygamy.[2] To speak of power politics does not of course entirely answer our question, because power can be used for many purposes, and among these might conceivably be ideological purposes. And, of course, the kind of world we live in now may make communication between states almost as important as—or at any rate greatly modify—the relationships of power.[3]

We can profitably reframe our question once more: In all this complex and interacting East-West relationship, which is the more reliable picture to carry in our minds today—a picture of great powers on both sides pursuing such traditional aims as national strength, security, and expansion, or one in which they are pursuing unique ideological aims?

Let us look at the question first from the point of view of the Soviet Union. Ordinary national interests or Communist ideology, which is more important in accounting for Soviet foreign policy? I do not think this question can be answered conclusively one way or another. As Rousseau put it, "not every man can make the gods

[2] Jacques Barzun, *Teacher in America* (Boston: Little, Brown and Co., 1945), p. 111.

[3] Cf. John W. Burton, *International Relations: A General Theory* (Cambridge and New York: Cambridge University Press, 1965).

speak, nor will everyone be believed when he declares himself their interpreter." No one knows for sure how Marxist theory influences Soviet foreign policy. But I am inclined to think we shall keep closer to reality if we look at national interests rather than ideology, i.e., if we think of the men in the Kremlin giving priority to what they conceive to be their interests and those of the Soviet Union rather than world revolution in an ideological, Marxist sense.

It would be out of place here to expound at any length the Marxist-Leninist-Stalinist (and Maoist) doctrines. We cannot fail to note, however, that there is almost nothing on foreign policy in the original Marxism, and very little in the early Lenin. When Lenin became effective head of state he did not find in Marx much guidance on how a Communist state should behave, and so he had to work it out as he went along.

As everyone knows too, the original Marxism itself is a many-sided and ambiguous set of doctrines, philosophical, social, economic, historical, and more besides. The Leninist contribution added a further set of aims, abstractions, tactics, and strategies, often quite inconsistent with those of Marx and Engels. The end result is a smorgasbord from which a Communist state can select material to justify any one of a large number of foreign policies. One can advocate revolution in industrial countries or in peasant economies; one can be democratic or dictatorial; one can fight the social democrats or preach a popular front with them; one can wait for the dialectic of history to make one's grandchildren Communist or (as Mr. Khrushchev believed) one can rely on the science and productivity of the Soviet Union; or one can give history a shove either by promoting class war through party and propaganda or by making Leninist-type "revolutions from above." The methods and the timing are almost infinitely flexible.[4] But one cannot find in the mixed bag of Marxist theories any support for the idea of world conquest by Russia. This idea is mainly a Western invention.

My thesis is that Communist theories give very limited clues to the aims and methods of Soviet policy, and that ideology is adjusted

[4] As George Kennan put it in his famous article "The Sources of Soviet Conduct," *Foreign Affairs,* Vol. XXV (July, 1947): "the Kremlin is under no ideological compulsion to accomplish its purposes in a hurry. Like the Church . . . it can afford to be patient."

to practice and policy, rather than the other way around. One cannot "prove" this thesis in any strong sense of "proof," but politics, both domestic and international, is not the kind of subject that lends itself to proof and Euclidean demonstration with a Q.E.D. at the end of the theorem. Measurement is only for things measurable, as Aristotle pointed out long ago.

Nevertheless, my thesis does, I think, explain the facts, and that is as much as we can ask of any hypothesis. On what other thesis can we explain the treatment of Communist parties abroad as "expendable" whenever Soviet policy required it? How else account for the long phase of what Isaac Deutscher called Stalinist "isolationism," and which is more commonly known as "Socialism in One Country"? How else explain the emphasis on military espionage in Western countries? Or the emphasis at times on patriotism, even xenophobia, in the Soviet Union, and even more so in China? Or the willingness to make friends with states such as Egypt and Syria, which suppress their native Communist movements? The list of examples could be much lengthened, but the multiplication of instances would not strengthen the case. Adverse examples would, however, seriously damage it, in accordance with the well-known rules of inductive logic. But I have not been able to find any plausible adverse instances.

Perhaps it will not be thought out of place in a nonpartisan article if I quote the Prime Minister of Canada. He once wrote: "A study of the lives and times of Russian czars and Chinese emperors is, I think, as valuable for the understanding of our difficulties with Moscow and Peking as an expert knowledge of dialectical materialism."[5] I cannot vouch for the truth of the first part of this quotation, but I do endorse the fact that a knowledge of dialectical materialism does not help much in predicting or understanding Soviet foreign policy.

Let me not overstate my thesis. I am not saying it has always been one or the other—Soviet national interests versus purely ideological policies. It is a question of emphasis and degree, like most politics. My point is that where two policies have been mutually exclusive—nationalist or Marxist ideological—the nationalist pol-

---

[5] Lester B. Pearson, *Democracy in World Politics* (Princeton, N.J.: Princeton University Press, 1955), p. 85.

icy has generally been chosen. Where, of course, a nationalist policy can run in harness with this or that part of Marxism, it does so. The two do often coincide, or can be made to coincide with a little ingenuity, and Communist countries tend to blend national interests and ideology.

The ideological component of Communist policies, in particular the idea of world revolution, seems always to catch our attention, for an obvious reason. The international power politics of the Soviet Union, or now of China—like the internal politics of these countries—is almost always couched in ideological terms. We ought to expect this, since it is a common enough occurrence in politics everywhere. Politicians of most parties everywhere like to talk principles, to show that their every policy is derived from, or at any rate compatible with, their political philosophy, and sometimes indeed with the basic principles of the universe. This is a Germanic trait even more than a Russian, as Engels once noted. One could also argue, with much truth, that the language of Chinese Communists is more militant and alarming than their actual deeds. We ought not to let the ceremonial and the ritual language deceive us. Politics, especially international politics, is usually more pragmatic than the language used, and the world is fortunate that this is so. Surely we are not so ingenuous that we take ceremonial speeches seriously.

If now we turn to the "West"—the other side of the equation of "East-West" relations—then *a fortiori* ours has clearly not been primarily an ideological struggle. In the first place, what do we mean by the "West"? We can perhaps speak of the NATO alliance —a group of smaller nations led by a superpower, the United States. It is difficult to speak of "their policy," however, since they so often disagree on their relations with Russia, or China, or Cuba.

In the second place, it would be a rash person who claimed that a diverse set of something called "Western" policies could be deduced from something amorphous called "Western" ideology. It is hard enough to identify and speak of the ideology of any one Western country and to link it in some necessary way with its foreign policy. How much more difficult it is to find an ideology common to the fifteen NATO powers. They have a variety of religions, and some have virtually no religion; some are socialist and some are capitalist; some are democratic and some are not, and so the tale goes on. The original NATO Treaty speaks of the "common heritage and civilization of their peoples founded on the principles of democracy, individual liberty, and the rule of law." This had some plausibility perhaps when applied to the original eight members in 1949, but it is absurd when taken as the literal truth about a mixed bag of states that includes West Germany, Portugal, and Turkey. And naturally if the meaning of "West" is broader than NATO, then the argument about the diversity of ideologies (and of policies) is even more self-evident. NATO is (or should one say was?) a military alliance—why be ashamed of it? It was not originally designed, and does not continue, for the purpose of spreading *our* ideology and exterminating that of Communism.

It is high time we stopped dressing up the traditional political aims and policies such as defense and conquest, prosperity and power, isolationism or internationalism, the *status quo* or "bought" revolutions, coexistence or prolonged hostility, etc., in the trappings of high-minded rhetoric. The countries that opposed Nazism and the Axis states in World War II were certainly not united in any ideology; neither are those who today, rightly enough, reject Communism united in any ideological crusade or Holy War, and it is a good thing they are not. "Above all, no zeal" is a wise motto for international politics, because it tones down the evangelical and immensely dangerous enthusiasm of ideological fervor. Edmund Burke, a much overrated political philosopher, was entirely wrong when he wrote (in another context): "It is with an armed doctrine that we are at war."

What I have said conflicts to a large extent with the conventional wisdom of recent years. The picture of the world constructed for us has often been that of two titans, the United States and the Soviet Union, each the leader of a number of smaller states—allies or satellites as the case may be—locked in an ideological struggle, a battle for men's minds all around the earth, and since Sputnik, in the heavens above. Uncommitted nations, on this view, are at best spectators of this cosmic battle of political philosophies, and at worst mere pawns in the game.

Slogans like the "Cold War," or what Isaac Deutscher called the

"Great Contest," encourage this ideological fantasy, this drive to make international relations simple for the man on the street, this urge to impose a simple pattern upon the disjointed and inconsistent world of experience. (This of course is not a full account of why the "West" has tended to construct an ideology.)

Bits and pieces of the picture of international relations as a clash of ideologies may be accurate enough, but the focus is wrong and some things are left out. Mr. Churchill is often quoted as saying in 1943 that "the empires of the future are the empires of the mind." This was in a convocation speech, and it is hard to be sure what he meant by it, and perhaps he himself was not always sure what his superb rhetoric meant. But he was too practical a politician to subordinate politics to ideology. Who can fail to remember the 1941 invasion of Russia, the welcome and support which he extended to a fortuitous ally?

I have cast doubt on the clarity and unity of Communism as an ideology, but even more on the close connection between such a flexible ideology as Communism and the foreign policies pursued by Communist states in relation to the West. I have suggested further that something called a "Western" ideology is largely a myth, and that consequently we in turn have not pursued ideological aims in foreign policy. I have thus invited you to look at a picture of East-West relations which is more accurately described as a clash of alliances, a struggle for strength, security, expansion, and advantage. East-West relations are thus brought where they belong, into a historical tradition and hence they become understandable and, I think, more manageable. Coexistence, even competitive coexistence, is a more sensible and far safer policy for the world than the pursuit of global ideals.

No simple picture of the world or of international relations is likely to be true. So some qualifications must be added to my thesis. First, our age is certainly unique in some ways, even if not in ideological ways. The really indisputable difference between today and earlier periods is that we are scientifically and technologically more advanced. We can kill each other off more easily now that we have nuclear weapons and, one supposes, a further terrifying arsenal of biological and chemical weapons. The risks are higher today if we do not keep the peace.

Second, there are of course ideological overtones to the main international political conflicts. The Russians and Chinese in particular are more given to talk about political doctrines than we are. It is hard to tell whether this helps them or not. I am inclined to think it gives the non-Communist world the advantage, on balance, because it means that Communist states often misread reality when they view it only through the blinkers or distorting mirrors of ideology.

Walter Lippmann, writing in 1948, attributed the failures of American foreign policy up to that time to the wrong ideological image of the world that Americans carried in their heads. The special failures of policy he spoke of were the attempts to stay out of two world wars, the fact that in the interwar period the United States did nothing to prevent World War II, and that a few years after World War II its policy was merely one of reacting to Russian and Chinese initiatives. The wrong image he mentioned was derived from the refusal to recognize and admit the facts of international life, the conflict, the strife, the rivalry, the need for compromise. The situation was, he said, like "using a map of Utopia to find your way around New York City." The Americans have of course long since lost their political innocence. Their unilateral and successful action over missiles in Cuba was a useful lesson here, and so is the Vietnam experience.

Third, someone may say, have not the Communist states made many advances in gaining adherents in the postwar period? Have they not brought a number of countries into their sphere of influence? Yes, that is perfectly true. But that is not the same as saying that their ideology was the aim or even the motive for their actions or success. It requires no Marxist ideology to explain the occupation of the Baltic states, the coup in Czechoslovakia, or the occupation of those countries of Eastern Europe which have satellite status since World War II. Moreover, if ideology binds Communist states together, what shall we say of the rifts between these satellites and Russia, or the yawning chasm between Russia and China? One can resort to many kinds of explanations—personal, historical, national, economic—but ideology is the one thing we cannot resort to. The union of theory and practice—a wonderfully flexible Marxist axiom —can be, and is, more easily kept intact by adjusting theory to policy than the other way round. Those who are ambitious, who want to get or retain power, to consolidate their hold on office, to govern, to make a social revolution, to industrialize, to build national strength, to secure reliable allies, can always find the appropriate texts with which to justify their actions. Man is a rationalizing rather than a reasoning animal in his political life.

Politics is a universal phenomenon that will not disappear even in the Marxist Utopia. Nor is it absent, though driven underground, in Communist states. We are familiar with the main features of politics—with business politics, with university politics, yes and even with ecclesiastical politics, while in public life we have public politics. The rules of the political game are different in these different spheres just mentioned, but the activity is the same: the use of influence and power to get and retain office or advantage. And so is the social function of politics—so often the by-product: the making of policies for an organization or a state. Ideology is an auxiliary helper, often called into service by all parties to a dispute, but seldom if ever the prime mover or chief aim. Abstractions do not rule men or politicians, in spite of the remarks of Lord Keynes to the contrary. These considerations apply with equal force to international and to domestic politics. Marx did not invent politics or international conflict, and in fact spent his life vainly trying to transmute politics into a class "war."

Before he came to office, Lenin was indeed in many respects a fanatical ideologue rather than politician. A reading of his utopian book *State and Revolution* shows this in embarrassing detail. It is always easier to adopt an ideological stance when out of office, and the further from office the more ideological a party tends to be. Lenin held on to office once he had seized power and constructed a theory *ex post facto,* or more accurately *en courant;* so did Stalin and so now do his successors. I have seen many analyses of the Soviet Union, of the Khrushchev and post-Khrushchev regimes, many discussions of the prospects for democracy in the U.S.S.R. Nearly all of these analyses base the prospects for change or "ideological erosion" on the changing nature of Russian society, thus—

in classical Marxist fashion—giving priority to the social and economic environment.

Please note that I am not saying that ideas and beliefs do not matter. Indeed, the burden of my argument is that they are so important and their influence so far-reaching that we must get them right, because out of them we build our models or images or pictures of world affairs. But I am also saying that reality breaks in and modifies the most rigidly ideological picture.

Let me restate my position by asking, rather belatedly, what do we mean by an "ideology"? Karl Marx did not invent the notion of ideology, but he did popularize it. In Marxism, "ideology" meant the set of general ideas by which the bourgeois class justified its class rule. An ideology was thus essentially like the process that psychologists call rationalization. The bourgeois ideology consisted of such general ideas as the beneficence of economic competition, the rightness of private property, and so forth.

Nowadays, "ideology" is usually thought of as roughly equivalent to a social or political philosophy—a set of general propositions, more or less systematic, about man, society, and the state, and the relations between them. It contains elements of both empirical and normative theory, including as a rule a statement about ultimate ideals. Some ideologies, such as Marxism, are very comprehensive, embracing philosophy, economic theory, a theory of human nature, a goal for history, and so on. Others are more limited in scope, like nationalism, which is best regarded as a sentiment, without specifying much practical content. (Ideologies, in their empirical component, are of course often false.) Other ideologies are more elusive.

The relevant feature, here, of ideologies is that they are composed of *general,* often highly abstract, beliefs and propositions. Their very generality and abstractness gives them their flexible application. That is why John Plamenatz could rightly say, after considering utilitarianism, almost "any practical construction can be put upon any theory." Or, to the same effect, Justice Holmes could say that general principles do not determine particular cases. That is why too I can argue that the Marxist ideology, and more especially the ultimate goal which it enshrines, being general, is usually not a very useful guide to the way Communist states will behave in world politics. Marxism, like most ideologies, has a further advantage: that of being loosely knit and, one may argue, often inconsistent. No wonder therefore that Marxist theory has been appealed to in order to support the quite different policy proposals of Karl Kautsky or Eduard Bernstein, of Stalin or Trotsky, of Khrushchev or Tito, of Brezhnev or Mao Tse-tung, to say nothing of Fidel Castro, Tim Buck, Uncle Tom Cobley, and all. Most ideologies and political philosophies are subtle creations, and no wonder, since they are usually constructed by learned men. But only simple people believe they are easy to apply to the everyday life of politics, and that the relation of philosophy and politics is easy to trace and understand.

But, someone may retort, is not an ideology sometimes specific in its prescriptions? Yes, sometimes that is so. In that case is it not a reliable guide to policy-making? Not always, and for this reason: Sometimes a specific and practical proposition is stated, e.g., in Marx, that the revolution will come first in industrial countries; or in Stalin, that capitalist states will suffer a severe slump, even a collapse, after World War II. Later, when the propositions turn out to be in error—as these two did—then the propositions are demoted from ideological status to that of nonessential details. The general doctrines or articles of faith are preserved at the cost of losing touch with reality and practical politics. The phenomenon is common enough, in religion, politics, and everyday life. It is the usual method by which the true believer insulates himself from a disillusioning reality.

One hesitates to get bogged down in disputes over definitions since, although lively, such disputes are often sterile. One cannot avoid mentioning, however, Professor Carl Friedrich's definition of ideology in his recent book *Man and His Government*—a large, frustrating, and fascinating volume. He stipulates that "political ideologies are ideas in action."[6] Naturally this leads him to such strange remarks as that "Franklin Delano Roosevelt was an ideologist of high caliber."[7] This is an extraordinary conclusion, since by all ordinary word usage and political standards, Mr. Roosevelt was, on the contrary, the least ideological and most pragmatic of men.

[6] Carl Friedrich, *Man and His Government* (New York: McGraw-Hill Book Co., 1963), p. 11.

[7] *Ibid.*, p. 92.

When, indeed, he was asked about his social philosophy, he could only reply in some puzzlement: "I am a Christian and a Democrat."

The picture of East-West relationships or, if you like, the framework of theory, which I started with, was one of two ideological blocs locked in mortal combat from which one or the other ideology would emerge triumphant and the other defeated.

I went on to cast a cold eye on this picture, and to substitute another, of a more traditional international configuration where traditional (and even legitimate) national objectives are pursued, though sometimes in odd ways, and with ideological overtones. This modified image of East-West relations is not that of a world without conflict. There are still friction and rivalry and alarms and excursions. But the picture is a slightly more hopeful one than that seen through the spectacles of ideology, since interests can be compromised and accommodated.

I am content if I have raised doubts about the truth of the cosmic ideological struggle. One does not expect to persuade anyone except those who already believe the thesis. I am enough of a Platonist to think that man learns nothing new: He merely rediscovers what he already knew.

2. Soviet Policy Toward the West

BERNARD S. MORRIS

THE TOPIC of this chapter—Soviet Policy Toward the West—was, I am confident, simply designated to distinguish it from Soviet policy toward other areas and has no further significance. Yet in this volume, which takes as its point of departure the major realignment of political forces in the international arena, the author is well advised to reexamine traditional concepts, however serviceable they may have been in the past. Surely, both the Russian and Soviet concepts of what the West constitutes, defined in geographical, institutional, and cultural terms, have changed over the years. Thus, for the nineteenth-century Russian intelligentsia, the West meant Europe west of Vienna and Berlin and clearly did not include the Americas. In our day it is not so difficult, however, to define the West in Soviet terms: It constitutes that group of advanced industrial countries centered in Europe but scattered throughout the world and headed by the United States. The Soviet Union sees itself as separate from the West because of its differing social system,

17

which it regards as an advance over that in the capitalist countries. The Soviet position is paradoxical precisely because it holds its social system to be an advance over the West, that is, the historically logical successor to capitalism, thereby placing itself squarely within the Western tradition. For its part, the West regards the Soviet Union as a backward, alien social formation defined by its nationalization of property and its undemocratic political institutions. The image of the Soviet Union as an outsider has been fostered equally by the West and by the Russians.

Viewed from a historical and objective standpoint, however, the Soviet Union *is* a Western power, construed both in terms of its developing socio-economic structure and its strategic imperatives. Although its territory covers a vast expanse of Asia and terminates on the Pacific Ocean, and occurrences in the Asian states bordering on its territory cannot be a matter of indifference to it, it is less a Pacific or Asian power than the United States. Its focus technologically, culturally, and strategically is Western. Its strategic interests are defined primarily in terms of Europe and the United States, or in terms of the Atlantic alliance. As a great power, it is European-oriented, aspiring to global importance in an attempt to match the United States as a global decision-making power. Yet whatever influence its old culture patterns may have, and whatever the exigencies of policy on its eastern or southeastern flank, the decisive factor is the socialization that effectively Westernizes it, in spite of political institutions that are at variance with the Anglo-Saxon and Scandinavian traditions and, hopefully, with those developing in Germany and Italy.

Despite its expansion eastward, its large non-European population and its Orthodox Church, Russia has been progressively Westernized since the time of Peter the Great, not the least by its involvement in European wars. Marxism, generally regarded as the root cause of Russia's differentiation from, and hostility to, the West, has performed precisely the opposite function. A profoundly Western idea and movement, Marxism has in the long view served as a vital factor in integrating Russia with the West. Despite the argument that Bolshevism represented a sharp break with the Marxist tradition—and the argument has cogency—and that the political institutions developed in the Soviet Union had more in common with revolutionary Jacobinism or Oriental despotism, in historical perspective it was the modernizing impulse of Marxism that was decisive in shaping the underlying structure of Soviet society. Marxism, even in its Bolshevik version or, more accurately, perhaps precisely in its Bolshevik version of forced industrialization, accelerated the process of Westernization.

It may even be argued that the authoritarian political institutions developed by the Bolsheviks did not themselves set off Russia against the Western countries. What aroused the early enmities were fortuitous circumstances, for example, the withdrawal of Russia from World War I at a strategically disadvantageous juncture for the Entente. But more importantly, the break was precipitated by the West, which saw in the developments in Russia an implicit threat to its own social system. The efforts of the Western powers at first to throttle the Bolshevik regime and then to isolate it were a product of fear engendered by the breakdown of the European balance of power and the falterings of capitalism in the interwar period. Hostility toward the Soviet Union had no basis in the existing power relations: Russia was no threat; that it survived was a miracle. The fear was rather that Bolshevism would develop an appeal as an alternative way of ordering Western society. Both the West and the Bolsheviks proved to be wrong, but what was not so apparent in the interwar period was that both were parts of an entity called the West and that their destiny was closely intertwined. Although the Soviet Union appeared as an alien growth in the European body politic—and still does to a large extent—the appearance was what the Western eye wished to perceive. That the appearance was enhanced by certain activities conducted by the Communists, such as those of the Comintern, goes without saying, yet in large measure the appearance was justified only by Comintern pronouncement and not by its behavior.

The political aftermath of World War II, notably the creation of Communist states in Eastern and Central Europe, once again reinforced the appearance of East against West. The merits of the postwar arrangements aside, what was at stake was the traditional problem of the balance of power in Europe, now with global implications. But once again the process of socialization in Eastern Europe and renewed efforts in the Soviet Union itself served precisely to move these states, some of which could be designated as precapitalist formations, into the mainstream of the West European community.

The most significant and paradoxical event that sealed the Soviet Union's "Westernization" was the emergence of China as a Communist state, exercising great influence in Asia and ambitious to acquire a global role. Forced into a statement of position during the course of its split with China, the Soviet Union opted for the West, so to speak, favoring evolution over revolution, peaceful construction over violent eruption, and peace over war. Compelled to choose between its allies and its interests, it chose its interests, which lay with the *status quoism* and regularities of the Western system. The development and perfection of its social organism was its chief preoccupation, meaning the attack on problems faced by the advanced capitalist countries for some time and problems still outstanding, such as rates of growth, equitable distribution, automation, leisure, and alienated youth.

In short, it is erroneous to talk about Soviet policy toward the West in the sense that it represents an undifferentiated hostility whose resolution lies in revolutionary overturn or subversion of the Western order. It is even doubtful that operative Soviet policy toward the Western countries constitutes anything more drastic than American or German policy toward the Soviet Union. The Soviet Union is part of the Western order faced by many similar problems, which may be solved only in concert with the Western countries in an interrelationship that pervades all of society up to the formation of high policy.

None of the foregoing should be construed to mean that we have no further problems with the Russians—or they with us. These introductory remarks are designed merely to take the problem of Soviet-Western relations out of the Cold War and to provide them with a more objective and contemporary setting. The problems that do arise between the Soviet Union and the other countries of the West—one can no longer properly speak of East-West relations— are those which have traditionally made up the content of international politics, that is, the establishment of power arrangements that are mutually acceptable and the conduct of global political, economic, and cultural activities within that framework. A residue of ideological confrontation exists, but the ideological factor may affect the conduct of policy more consciously in the United States than in the Soviet Union. One does not have to look to ideology for the key to conflict; conflict exists in the very structure of contemporary international politics.

Conflict is inherent in the nation-state system. Temporary stabilization of relations is achieved by a shifting balance of forces. As the two great military powers, the United States and the Soviet Union are constantly engaged in protecting their perceived interests and in maximizing their power positions; in a negative sense they are engaged by other powers who try to use them to further their own particular interests. Each has a global sense of mission: the U.S.S.R. in principle hoping to see its form of social organization extended throughout the world; the United States, pursuing its assertive ambitions cloaked in a free-world ideology. Conflict in this sense is abstract, built into the system as it were, perpetuated often without apparent cause or rational objective. Temporary accommodations are reached when interests coincide, as with the partial test-ban treaty, or when the conflicts of other powers threaten a situation that both powers prefer for the moment to see unchanged, as in the case of the Indian-Pakistani flare-up in 1965.

Conflict between the United States and the Soviet Union is also a function of their individual readings of their respective military capabilities and their willingness to employ them. The Soviet Union, with few exceptions, has employed its military force as a defensive arm to maintain its security sphere and to assure itself of both a defensive and retaliatory nuclear capability. The United States, feeling itself the stronger power and reading the Soviet defensive position accurately, has been less inhibited in employing its military and subversive arms globally. Conflict in this sense is engendered in areas outside the immediate security spheres of both but necessarily provokes suspicion of motives and risk of war, and concomitantly deters efforts at accommodation.

But the center of conflict, the point at which the Soviet Union meets the Western countries, is in Europe. If there is a Soviet-West confrontation, it is on the Continent. The two world wars were bred on the Continent and rightly or wrongly the Russians pinpoint

Europe as the breeding ground for another possible conflict. They feel that the United States reneged on postwar European agreements; they have never accepted the tacit *status quo* that developed in Europe; and they are uneasy about the potential revival of Germany as a great power out of the changing circumstances developing in Western and Eastern Europe. The measure of security the Russians desire apparently entails the removal of the American military presence from Europe and a guarantee against the resurgence of a powerful German nuclearized military force. In policy at least, Europe remains the core security problem, and the United States figures as the key element in Soviet policy toward the West.

At the present juncture of events, Soviet foreign policy seems to have entered into a state of Nirvana. The Brezhnev-Kosygin tandem is enmeshed in the coils of problems, partly bequeathed them by Khrushchev and partly the consequence of fortuitous developments, which inhibit the conduct of a vigorous policy. The pursuit of accommodations with the United States along the general lines of Khrushchev's policy is frustrated by the undeclared war in Vietnam, which no Communist state can condone. The removal of Khrushchev may have forestalled his attempt to read China out of the international Communist movement, but it did not result in the improvement of Soviet-Chinese relations, even to the extent of stopping the polemics. Thus Soviet policy is further complicated by the need to maintain or, at least, salvage its position in the international Communist movement by carefully avoiding policies that would alienate other Communist parties and states. It is additionally beset by the need to maintain its authority in Eastern Europe as the Communist states there move toward the independent exercise of sovereignty as they perceive it to be in their interests. The Brezhnev-Kosygin regime may also be under internal pressures—this is more difficult to establish—which may contribute to the bind in which they find themselves. At any rate, there would seem to be a parallel between the Johnson and the Brezhnev-Kosygin administrations in the sense that both wished to occupy themselves with domestic matters from which they were, nevertheless, diverted by external events. There is a distinction with a difference to be made, however, since Johnson deliberately escalated the war in Vietnam, automatically engaging the Russians in an affair in which they had no desire to become embroiled. In short, whatever hesitancies and cautions may have been introduced into the conduct of Soviet policy by the assumption of authority of the new leadership, the direction of Soviet foreign policy has been obscured by the overriding importance of the Vietnamese war. Therefore, a backtracking is in order to reconstruct the main lines of Soviet policy from the Khrushchev era and to attempt to gauge to what extent these lines still exist in the present period.

Stalin had bequeathed the Soviet Union a foreign policy that was essentially European-oriented and "insular." This was as true of his conduct of policy in the interwar period as it was in the last years of his life, though the international environmental factors were different. In the earlier period, Soviet Russia was merely one of many so-called great powers whose military prowess was not highly regarded by the West. The primary preoccupation of the Soviet leadership was the construction of a modern industrialized state conceived along socialist lines together with a military force that was congruent with its new situation. The Soviet posture was essentially defensive and even the avowed revolutionary arm of Soviet policy, that is, the Comintern, functioned primarily as a tool of Soviet foreign policy interests.

Soviet policy after World War II was similarly inner-directed, preoccupied with the consolidation of the enlarged security sphere it had obtained as a result of the fortunes of war. With Russia militarily inferior to the United States and economically devastated as a result of the war, Stalin was primarily concerned with the rehabilitation of his country and the construction of a dependable security sphere. The latter was denied him by American policy in Germany, which Stalin tried to counter by shifting general Communist policy into a more aggressive course, the notable event being the Berlin blockade of 1948–49. This together with the rather special case of Korea exemplifies the outward thrust of Soviet policy. By the Nineteenth Soviet Party Congress, in 1952, Stalin's policy had, however, reverted to form: the development and consolidation of the Soviet Union and Eastern and Central Europe, on the one hand, and the containment of the Western thrust, on the other.

It was also characteristic of Stalin's conception of policy that the

Soviet Union did not consciously assume the role of a world power during his lifetime. There is an interesting parallel with American policy which may help clarify this point. In 1939, both the United States and the Soviet Union could be characterized as isolationist powers that sought to avoid entanglement in war, though the U.S.S.R. did attempt for a time to devise collective-security measures against the Nazi threat. In spite of themselves, both the United States and the U.S.S.R. were shot into the war, emerging from it as the two leading powers. Yet, for a time, neither consciously undertook a global mission. The United States began withdrawing troops from Europe; the Soviet Union was prepared to abdicate to the West in so far as extra-European arrangements were concerned. Even when the United States launched the Marshall Plan, the ostensible rationale was that the rehabilitation of Europe would enable the West European countries to fend for themselves, thus permitting the United States to retire across the Atlantic. It was only with the Truman Doctrine and the Korean war that the United States consciously took up its global mission in the sense that it now was prepared to play a vital role in political and security arrangements in all areas of the world. The Soviet Union under Stalin never did make the global commitment, never did consciously assume the role of a global power. It was, for whatever reasons one cares to adumbrate—economic and military weakness, absence of a colonial tradition, lack of imagination, or what have you—European-oriented. It was left to Khrushchev to make a radical break with the Stalinist tradition.

The new departure in Soviet diplomacy may have been a deliberate attempt to distinguish the new leadership from the old, to win support in the struggle for succession, or to respond in some way to domestic pressures. We do not know and this is no place, moreover, to discuss the relation between domestic and foreign policy. The interrelationship is as obvious as its precise workings are obscure. In the case of Khrushchev, his domestic concerns were initially paramount but the measures he took influenced the course of events both in the inter-Communist sphere and in the area of foreign policy itself. How much was conscious and deliberate on his part is uncertain, but the evolution of Khrushchev's policy took it into the nuclear age, so to speak, giving a new cast to Soviet relations with the West, with the former colonial areas, and with the Communist parties.

The general orientation of Soviet policy was formalized by Khrushchev's revision of the Leninist doctrine of the inevitability of war—one of the few instances in Soviet history when a major tenet was in effect scrapped. It was a dramatic gesture conceived in operational terms to reduce tension with the West and lessen the threat of a nuclear war. The policy was sloganized as "peaceful co-existence of different social systems." Reference to Leninist antecedents for purposes of legitimization and propaganda by the Soviet leadership was irrelevant. What was important was that Khrushchev took as his point of departure a policy of peace, or avoidance of war with the United States. Whatever service such orientation performs as propaganda, it is primarily significant as a value orientation. There is an enormous gulf between those who calculate policy primarily on an intention-capability spectrum in a context of undisguised enmity and inevitable conflict and those who calculate policy in terms of the preservation of peace even while the factors of capability and hostility are not ignored. Unless Khrushchev's formalization of peaceful coexistence at the Twentieth CPSU Congress in 1956 is dismissed as sheer propaganda, it is obvious that the Soviet leadership internalized, so to speak, the dangers of a nuclear war earlier than the United States, which for some years refused to take the Soviet position seriously and continued with its prosecution of Cold War politics.

A second area in which Khrushchev broke with Stalin was in defining the character of the relationship between the Soviet Union and the various Communist states and parties. The Twentieth CPSU Congress solemnly affirmed the doctrine of separate and national roads to socialism and the possibility of achieving a socialist revolution peacefully. Once again the writings of the masters could be cited for precedent: Marx for the possibility of peaceful revolution, and even the programs of the Western Communist parties of Great Britain, the Scandinavian countries, and others in the early 1950's, which had focused on the possibility of peaceful transition. The reaffirmation of the doctrine in Khrushchev's time, however, was substantial, responsive as it was to the actual conditions that had developed after the war in the Communist movement. It was first of all designed to accommodate Yugoslavia into sympathetic cooperation with the U.S.S.R. and also to reach an accommodation with Communist states that could no longer be controlled in the old manner. The doctrine of equality of parties and national and peaceful roads to socialism reinforced the central position on peaceful coexistence and gave a more permissive and peaceful cast to Soviet policy in general.

A third area in which Khrushchev made a dramatic break with the Stalinist tradition was his commitment of the Soviet Union to world-wide economic diplomacy. Again, while there was precedent in the Stalinist past, the relatively massive program of economic aid —loans, grants, technical and military assistance—coupled with a series of high-level personal visits, opened a new era in Soviet diplomacy. The new departure reflected the growth of Soviet economic capabilities, now in a position to exploit the coming-to-independence of the former colonial areas. It was also a sign of the Soviet Union's maturity that enabled it to enter into the type of activity that had been almost exclusively a preserve of the Western powers. Its new confidence based on its military power, economic resources, and breakdown of Western influence in the former colonial areas at last seemed to cast the Soviet Union in the role of a global power. Its involvements jumped borders—the so-called law of expansion by contiguity no longer held—and the U.S.S.R. became intimately involved in the politics of the Near East, the Congo, and Cuba, where it succeeded for the first time in history in establishing a *point d'appui* in what the United States considered to be its immediate security sphere. Viewed in conventional terms, the Sovet Union had entered into a new phase of competition with the West far more dangerous than anything that could have emerged from the Communist parties themselves. Yet the striking characteristic of the new Soviet diplomacy was less its hostility and competitive character than its bid, if unstated, for a codetermining role with the United States in the regulation of the world's important political affairs.

The Chinese Communists have bitterly characterized the implicit thrust of Soviet policy as Khrushchev's and his successors' "line of

Soviet–U.S. collaboration for the domination of the world."[1] The Chinese may exaggerate a bit and the Americans may recoil from the suggestion that they have enough in common with the Russians to join them in a working *entente* to patrol the world; yet the idea is neither as unprecedented nor as outrageous as it seems. Franklin Delano Roosevelt's conception of the postwar international security organization, for example, was based squarely on the idea of great power hegemony, with Soviet-American cooperation as its cornerstone. Whether there was virtue in this policy or whether it was conceived in error may be left to the judgment of history. But Roosevelt's policy aside, the environment in the world of the 1960's contained the objective conditions for a generous measure of Soviet-American cooperation, even if a tacit agreement for codetermination appeared to be premature, or, for domestic reasons, impossible. First of all, the possibility of a nuclear war made it incumbent on the two great nuclear powers to achieve the measure of understanding that would minimize the possibility of a conflagration. Of priority concern was agreement on the use of the weapons. The avoidance of nuclear war implied that outstanding issues involving the security of the United States and the U.S.S.R. be resolved. The one area in which there was a direct Soviet-American confrontation fraught with tension was Europe, and it was one of Khrushchev's primary interests to arrive at a new political settlement. In other parts of the world, Soviet-American security interests were secondary and could be handled if there developed a strong feeling of cooperation. Khrushchev's abortive attempt to install missiles in Cuba was significant in defining the limits of Soviet *Weltpolitik* and, paradoxically, in contributing to a greater measure of understanding between him and President Kennedy. Khrushchev's "competitive coexistence" meant that the United States and U.S.S.R. could conduct clashing—competitive—policies in areas of secondary concern without risk of war, if understanding had been attained at the highest level. The Russians made a point of down-

[1] "Refutation of the New Leaders of the CPSU on United Action," *Jen-min Jih-pao* (*People's Daily;* Peking) and *Hung Ch'i* (*Red Flag;* Peking), November 11, 1965. The article is studded with references to alleged Soviet-American collaboration for world domination on matters ranging from nuclear agreements to the Vietnamese war.

grading the use of violence by Communist parties and called attention to the need for containing local wars, a position running against the Chinese grain.

The Khrushchev era then may be regarded as a transitional phase of Soviet society moving from an insular, semi-industrial stage into that of a modern, advanced industrial society with global pretensions to power. Khrushchev himself symbolized the transition: a shrewd country bumpkin decked out in the custom clothes of an Italian tailor; an older-generation Communist bent on modernizing the economy though still conditioned by doctrinal, institutional, and political practices of the old school. Whatever his place in history, Khrushchev bequeathed his successors a set of most difficult problems, many of which derived from policies which they profess to hold as their own. His policy of peaceful coexistence and *détente* with the United States has cost the Soviet Union the Chinese alliance, the loyalty of a number of Communist parties, and has generally undermined its authority in the Communist movement. The Sino-Soviet rift has served to accelerate the assertion of sovereignty in the Communist states, encouraged by Khrushchev's doctrine of equality of Communist states and by the growing confidence of the Communist elites of the various countries in their indigenous support. The impact of Western ideas on the economic, scientific, and technical cadres in Eastern Europe was significant in the Khrushchev era—and remains so. On the face of it, it appears that Khrushchev's policy, resulting in a large measure of autonomy for the East European countries, has worked against the interests of the U.S.S.R., or, at the very least, requires the Soviet leadership to revamp its concept of security on its Western border. As far as China is concerned, Khrushchev's policies have produced a hostile neighbor or even an enemy where there was once a friend and has required a revamping of security policy in Asia, particularly with reference to India.

An unforeseen consequence of Khrushchev's policy toward accommodation with the West was the development of a more aggressive policy on the part of the United States. Its escalation of the war in Vietnam was based in part on the assumption that the Sino-Soviet breach was too wide to permit the Soviet Union and China to join hands for the defense of Vietnam; in part it was escalated on the assumption that Soviet national interest would not be so vitally at stake as to involve it in the fray in force. In short, for some purposes, the American administration has come to accept at face value the Soviet protestations of peaceful coexistence. As a result, Khrushchev's successors were unable to follow up the main line of his policy of improving relations with the United States, even though they had given every indication that they were interested in doing so. The professed willingness of the United States to continue to reach agreements with the U.S.S.R. while it carried on daily bombings in Vietnam may be politics in the best Machiavellian tradition, but the Russians must feel like the cuckolded husband whose friendship is solicited by his wife's seducer.

In Europe, Khrushchev's attempt to legalize the *status quo* was unsuccessful. It has been consistent Soviet policy to press for a treaty that would recognize the territorial situation which resulted from World War II, formalizing the existence of two German states and the Oder-Neisse as Poland's western border. The desirable consequences of such a treaty from the Soviet point of view are obvious. Germany would remain divided, the eastern part in the Soviet sphere of influence. The Western hold on Berlin would be weakened, even though new arrangements were negotiated for a Western presence and access. Presumably large contingents of American troops would be withdrawn from the Continent. Any revisionist aims of the Federal Republic of Germany would be contained. The Soviet Union could rest easier in its security. Peripheral benefits would accrue through the absorption of Soviet theater forces into the civilian economy.

The Soviet objectives in Europe can plainly be seen and, on the face of it, conflict with American interests but not necessarily with the interests of all the European powers. If Khrushchev's attempt to redress the balance of forces in Europe in the Soviet's favor were unsuccessful, his general policy of peaceful coexistence did induce an atmospheric change that contributed directly to the unfreezing of political initiative in Europe. The growth of European economic and military power, on the one hand, and the attenuation of the Soviet threat to Europe, as perceived by the Europeans, combined to call into question America's hegemonic role in Europe. De

Gaulle's assertion of sovereignty was predicated on the assumption that the Soviet Union did not represent a direct and immediate threat to France or to Europe. De Gaulle's long-range purpose envisaged the reconstitution of a European system that would explicitly include the Soviet Union, against which the Western alliance is now directed. But the assertiveness of De Gaulle merely reflects the changed relationships of the European powers toward the United States in the context of their estimate of Russian intentions and their own capabilities. If De Gaulle is regarded the thorn in the side of American policy, the greater potential threat is Germany, that is, precisely the European force on which the United States has built its Western defense. De Gaulle's idea of a "constructive *entente* from the Atlantic to the Urals" is, France's role on the Continent aside, directed at containing Germany.[2]

All in all, the weakening of NATO seems to play into Soviet hands. Merely by politicking for the end of the alliance, the Russians win a political victory by seeing it disrupted and perhaps scrapped. They can also claim some credit for the course of events by virtue of a conscious policy of accommodation and *détente*. Yet does the disruption of the alliance or even its demise remove the primary cause of Soviet concern in Europe? What, if anything, changes in so far as the German question is concerned?

If Soviet fear of German revisionism, implying the forcible reunification of the two Germanys and the emergence of a united Germany as challenger to Soviet power on the Continent, can be taken at face value, Soviet opposition to the Western alliance and to the American presence in Europe is ambiguous. Although Germany is the linchpin of American European policy, at the same time Germany is subordinate to the United States, which acts, or can act, as a brake on German ambitions. Although American policy is formally committed to the reunification of Germany, it has not given any evidence of implementing the commitment. In other

---

2 "We do not hesitate to envisage that the day will come when, in order to achieve a constructive *entente* from the Atlantic to the Urals, all of Europe will wish to settle its own problems and, above all, that of Germany, by the only means that will make it possible to do so—that of a general agreement." (President de Gaulle's press conference, September 9, 1965, "Speeches and Press Conferences" [New York: Press and Information Service of the French Embassy], No. 228 [September 9, 1965].)

words, the tacit *status quo* in Europe, maintained by American presence in force, coincides with Soviet policy to maintain the present division of Germany and to restrain West Germany's ambitions in Europe. It may even be argued that NATO's primary purpose of a military counterpoise to the Soviet Union is now obsolete and its essential, if unspoken, function is to contain West German ambitions. The original purpose of NATO was to pledge American nuclear power against superior Soviet ground forces, thereby containing the Russians while the Continent bought time to rebuild its industrial and military power. For some time, however, NATO's military function has been replaced, if not explicitly, by political functions, that is, the organization has justified its continued existence through the various political advantages that it affords its members. The substitution of goals, once the original ones have outlived their usefulness, is characteristic of the morphosis of organizations. In any case, the dismantling of NATO, to follow this line of reasoning, could theoretically work against the interests of the Soviet Union.

Soviet insistence on a postwar settlement may possibly be explained by its penchant for the observance of precise and legal forms in its international dealings. The legalization of the *status quo* in Europe may serve as a reassurance to the Soviet Union in the way that a tacit arrangement, inherently maintaining tension, does not. Presumably, the Soviet leadership might also regard the legalization of the *status quo* as an entering wedge for the removal of American power in Europe. Yet the formalization of a European settlement might not automatically work in favor of the Russians, as suggested above, and it might in addition give impetus to the Communist states' assertion of independence of Moscow. Soviet motives, then, must have deeper roots, which may lie purely and simply in their distrust of American policy and fear of an American-German combination against them. Despite the argument that American hegemony in Western Europe serves to contain the West Germans, the fact of the matter is that U.S. policy not only relies primarily on West Germany, but that the Americans have gone so far as to supply it with nuclear warheads. Although these weapons are under the ultimate command of the Americans, this can be but small reassurance to the Russians: It is at the very least psychologically unacceptable. Nor can the thrust of German ambition to attain the status of a nuclear power be discounted. Why should the Germans be denied the status the French have sought and in part have gained, especially when their own capabilities are so much greater?

Thus far the discussion has been concerned only with a putative Soviet fear of German revisionism, without regard to the question of whether there is an objective basis for the Soviet feeling. There exists a considerable amount of literature contending that the re-unification of Germany is not in the cards; that the Western powers, including the United States, prefer to see Germany remain divided —despite their public pronouncements—and that the West Germans themselves, rolling in prosperity, similarly display little interest in uniting with their brethren, despite some evidence to the contrary from public-opinion polls, whatever their reliability. There is admittedly no strong evidence of a sentiment for unification existing in West Germany. But to let it go at that ignores history and politics. The fact that the European powers prefer to see Germany remain divided does not mean that it will remain so. The smaller members cling to NATO in part because it gives them some hold over the Germans, who remain suspect. The past fate of free cities and corridors is no reassurance for the future. The existence at the present of a number of divided countries is no cause for complacency—this is the way things are—first because of what is actually occurring in these countries (*vide* Vietnam) and secondly because only a relatively brief period of time has elapsed since the end of World War II. The final returns are not yet recorded. Moreover, within West Germany itself, the temptation to exploit nationalist and irredentist issues and to have Germany play a role on the European scene commensurate with its power is always present.

What this argument amounts to is that German revisionist ambitions cannot be discounted simply because they are unpleasant to contemplate. Given the realignment of world forces at the present time, the Sino-Soviet split, the fragmentation of the international Communist movement, the weakening of Soviet authority over the Communist states, and in the West, the weakening of NATO, France's challenge to American hegemony, and the emergence of

West Germany as the key factor and, in a sense, determining factor in the Western alliance, the possibilities of bargaining have been opened up to an extent that did not exist in the stark bipolar confrontation. If there is any substance to this argument, it follows that in this one great area of potential conflict, there is also substantial basis for Soviet-American cooperation.

A resurgence of German nationalism would subsume a thrust toward unification and the reacquisition of the eastern territories lost to Poland. In meeting the thrust, the Russians have a range of options from peaceful concessions to the application of violence. The Russians—not the Americans—hold the trump cards in any bargaining that might develop with Germany. Berlin is a hostage to the Soviet Union, and East Germany is subject to massive Soviet pressure. The conditions of Rapallo may not repeat themselves, but in some circumstances a new Soviet-German arrangement, arrived at peacefully, may be preferable to the Russians to the prospect of another war. (What was on Khrushchev's mind in his last days of power when he was entertaining a visit to West Germany?) A Soviet-German agreement would effectively reduce American power and influence on the Continent. Alternatively, if the Russians were uncooperative, Germany jockeying for a place in the sun would raise the threat of a new war, unavoidably involving the United States.

The prospect of a resurgence of German nationalism cannot be viewed with equanimity by either the United States or the Soviet Union. The tension implicit in the present disintegration of alliances, the breakdown of tacit agreements and the maneuverings of the various states require the devising of a new framework of relations. Events of the past twenty years have made the Cold War obsolete. Objective bases exist for Soviet-American cooperation: first and foremost the mutual desire to avoid a general nuclear war; the embourgeoisement of the Soviet Union which gives it a stake in the *status quo;* the attenuation of ideological politics in the West; and the emergence of the underdeveloped areas, including China, as the source of revolutionary motion. Soviet and American response to the revolutionary challenge of China or to the revolutionary ferment in the underdeveloped areas may differ, but their destinies are intertwined and dependent on the preservation of Western power and influence. The Soviet Union, the United States, and the Western powers have a vital stake in arriving at arrangements that would minimize tension among them and permit the explosive politics of the underdeveloped countries to develop in a framework of peaceful change. Yet, the depressing fact is that the conduct of foreign policy appears to have a logic all its own, which may change in form but not in substance. The pursuit of the national interest all too often appears to be a flight into irrationality directed against the interests of humanity.

3. Eastern Europe and the West

H. GORDON SKILLING

For many centuries, the peoples of Eastern Europe have been passive subjects rather than active participants in the drama of world politics. Throughout its entire history in fact, this unfortunate region, due to its lack of political unity and its general weakness, has been a power vacuum, and hence a dangerous crossroads of intersecting national interests and a breeding ground of conflict and war. Even between the wars, when independent states existed throughout most of the region, they were in many respects mere pawns of the great powers and were unable to play an influential role in world affairs. Their independence was in a sense an illusion, the product of a temporary and transient correlation of forces, and was shattered by the return of Germany and Russia to power in Europe. After World War II and the subsequent Cold War, the partition of Europe into "East" and "West" and the strict Soviet control of the East consigned the Communist states, with the exception of Yugoslavia, to a new powerlessness. As a Czechoslovak commentator, Jaroslav Šedivý, recently expressed it, in retrospect, "A world shut in on itself by Cold War gave little opportunity to the diplomacy of smaller states."[1] "Both camps," he said, "were powerfully centralized around their own chief great powers and on both sides of the dividing lines the power of decision was in the hands of hard dogmatists." In this situation, he admitted, Czechoslovakia was "at best a co-creator but in the main a mere supporter of a foreign-policy effort determined first and foremost by the Soviet Union."

It is against this background of traditional impotence that the events of the past two or three years stand out in sharp perspective. As a result of the "process of disintegration," which took place in both world blocs, it became possible, wrote Šedivý, for the individual Communist states to conduct their own diplomacy and, within the unity of the socialist camp, to develop their own initiative. Moreover, as international tension declined, the character of diplomacy itself changed. "Foreign policy," he continued, ceased to be "a mere calculation of the economic or military strength of one's opponent" and has become "a political and sociological probing of the contemporary world." It thus resembles more and more "diplomacy in the classic sense of the word, giving increasing prominence to the subjective elements—the degree of experience and skill of those forming and implementing it." "If it is to be effective," he argued, "it is not possible always to say 'no' to the proposals of the other side. It is necessary to seek the path of compromise—sometimes to say 'maybe,' 'perhaps,' and sometimes 'yes,' too."

Although some of these propositions may be challenged, there can be little doubt that in very recent years, most of the states of Eastern Europe have stepped on to the stage of world politics as increasingly independent factors, capable in some degree of relating their foreign policies to their own national interests, and in some spheres of taking independent diplomatic initiatives. Three major shifts in the shape of international politics have made possible this altered role of Eastern Europe, especially the lessening of its isolation from Western Europe and the rest of the world, and the

[1] Jaroslav Sedivy, "How Do We Make Foreign Policy?," *Veda a zivot (Science and Life; Prague),* No. 9 (1965), pp. 513–19.

manifestation of the distinctive national interest of each of the states of the region. One is, of course, the previously mentioned breakup of the postwar bipolar system, under which two major powers, Moscow and Washington, had a near monopoly in the fashioning of the course of international relations, and the emergence, on both sides, of what is generally called polycentrism, i.e., a multitude of centers of decision-making. This has meant the assertion of independence mainly by countries such as China and France, but has resulted in the desire, and the ability, of even small states, such as Romania, to follow, within limits, a line of their own. The second factor has been the moderation of the mutual hostility between the two camps and their leading powers, the United States and the U.S.S.R., an acceptance in principle of peaceful coexistence, and on both sides the recognition, sometimes explicitly, sometimes only implicitly, of common interests. Even in Vietnam, for instance, in spite of intense and continuing conflict, there has been some evidence of a kind of silent understanding between Moscow and Washington on the desirability of the peaceful settlement of a controversy that threatens the possibility of common actions in other regions and in other areas of mutual interest. And finally, as a third major factor, in the Communist world Stalinism, with its totalitarian claim to control all aspects of life of all members of the bloc and its apparently inherent drive toward a permanent revolution in every sphere of society, has given way, in most of Eastern Europe, to a lessening of total control and to a slackening in the tempo of change. Parallel with this, there has also been a certain decline in the importance of ideology and a rise in significance of more rational aspects of policy-making.[2]

These fundamental transformations produced a favorable climate for normalizing the relations of East and West. Certain Western governments took initiatives leading in this direction, as for instance President Johnson's proposals for the "building of bridges" of trade and cultural communications with Eastern Europe,[3] and President

[2] See Skilling, *The Governments of Communist East Europe* (New York: Thomas Y. Crowell Co., 1966). Another recent book on this area is by J. F. Brown, *The New Eastern Europe: The Khrushchev Era and After* (New York: Frederick A. Praeger, 1966).

[3] Speech at Lexington, Virginia, May 24, 1964.

de Gaulle's concept of a "Europe from the Atlantic to the Urals," embracing the Soviet Union and its East European allies.[4] Even Germany evinced a strong desire to improve its relations with Eastern Europe.[5] Western intellectuals urged even more far-reaching measures of "disengagement," or "peaceful engagement," which would help to reknit the threads binding Europe, East and West, and would perhaps prepare the way for the eventual restoration of a united Europe.[6] These moves have been greeted in Eastern Europe with mixed feelings but with some degree of sympathy, and have produced counterinitiatives, mainly for cooperation in the field of trade and commerce.

Events in Vietnam have, however, cast an ominous cloud over this emerging "dialogue" between East and West, threatening to disrupt it completely.[7] The paradox—which must of necessity often obtrude in this discussion—is that events in distant Asia, especially in Vietnam, threaten to block the advance toward a greater degree of European unity, and in the worst event might reverse the more fundamental trends in world politics, described above, which created the climate for the progress thus far made. This analysis will, however, mainly concern itself with the attitude of Eastern Europe toward the West, although some consideration of the policies of the West toward Eastern Europe must be included.

George Kennan coined an illuminating phrase when he wrote that the members of the bloc, in its new polycentric form, are

4 Press conference, February 4, 1965.

5 Gerhard Schröder, "Germany Looks at Eastern Europe," *Foreign Affairs*, XLIV, No. 1 (October, 1965), 15–25.

6 See, for instance, Zbigniew K. Brzezinski, *Peaceful Engagement in Europe's Future* (New York: School of International Affairs, Columbia University, Occasional Papers, 1965); Andrzej Korbonski, "U.S. Policy in East Europe," *Current History*, XLVIII, No. 283 (March, 1965), 129–34, 181–82; and George F. Kennan, in his addresses to the Pacem in Terris convocation in New York, February 18, 1965, and at the "European Talks," Vienna, June 15, 1965, and his Walter E. Edge Lecture, Princeton University, February 25, 1965, all available in mimeographed form. See also several articles on the theme of European unification in the issue of *Survey* entitled "Foreign Policy in a Polycentric World," No. 58 (January, 1966), especially those by Raymond Aron, K. A. Jelenski, George F. Kennan, and Jacques Freymond.

7 P. Winkler, "Our Foreign Policy and European Security," *Nová mysl (New Thought;* Prague), No. 11 (1965), p. 1288.

caught in "a great crisis of indecision" on the proper attitude that a Communist country should take toward non-Communist ones, in this case the Western powers.[8] Each country in Eastern Europe has been confronted not only with a painful choice between Moscow and Peking, but with the equally difficult decision, closely related to the former, of the position to be adopted toward Washington, toward the major West European countries, and to one another. In the situation created by the Sino-Soviet split and polycentrism in both West and East, they must face up to questions that did not pose themselves in the time of monolithism and Cold War. As might be expected, their response has not been uniform, and in particular has varied greatly in regard to each of the major Western powers.

At the two extremes are Albania and Yugoslavia, the former strongly anti-Western, the latter more pro-Western than any member of the Communist bloc. Albania clearly and definitely opted for Peking in the Sino-Soviet conflict and broke almost all its links— diplomatic, political, and military—with the U.S.S.R. and the other states of the bloc. She has, however, continued, and even broadened trade relations with the latter and has maintained a diplomatic connection with, and a certain degree of polite cordiality toward, Romania.[9] In all major political questions, Albania has adopted the extreme anti-Western (and anti-Soviet) line of her giant partner, but economically has turned increasingly to the Western powers, especially France and Italy. At the other end of the spectrum, Yugoslavia broke with Moscow and veered to the West as early as 1948, and rejected Peking's political and ideological viewpoint long before the other European Communist parties. Military and economic assistance from the United States and the West made possible her independent stand vis-à-vis Moscow and has been welcomed. Yugoslavia has often rejected American policies and has supported many Soviet positions in world affairs, but has claimed to be following a course of independent nonalignment and has not associated herself with the Warsaw alliance. In recent years she has

---

8 George F. Kennan, "Polycentrism and Western Policy," *Foreign Affairs*, XLII, No. 2 (January, 1964), 175.

9 The return of a Polish ambassador to Tirana in February, 1966, was followed almost at once by a renewed break, when the Albanian ambassador was expelled for conducting anti-Polish activities.

swung back somewhat toward Moscow and has begun to play an important role in Soviet-bloc politics. Although still not a member, she is linked with COMECON as an observer and even participant in some activities and has sought to recover some of her lost trade with the bloc countries, but has also maintained her economic and cultural ties with the West.[10]

Between these two extremes, the other states of Eastern Europe have taken up varying positions, reflecting their own conceptions of their national interests. All except Romania have fully supported the Soviet Union in the dispute with China, although most of them have sought to moderate Moscow's views toward Peking and to avoid a final and open break. Yet the stance taken by each state toward Moscow and the West has not been uniform and must be clearly distinguished. East Germany, for instance, has maintained the most intimate, if not subservient, relations with Moscow, and has persisted in being almost as hostile toward the United States as Albania. Bulgaria, while remaining strongly pro-Soviet, has shown signs of initiatives in foreign policy, especially in her improved relations with Greece and in an effort to achieve the same end with Turkey. Romania, on the other hand, while continuing to remain in the East European bloc, has adopted what has been called a position of nonalignment, at least as between Peking and Moscow, and has defended a strongly independent policy within COMECON and the Warsaw alliance.[11] At the same time she has intensified her economic relations with the West, including the United States, and in this respect has come closer than any of her partners to a kind of "Yugoslav" course.[12] Poland has remained loyal to the Soviet Union and the bloc, but since 1956 has insisted on her freedom of action vis-à-vis Moscow and has enjoyed limited Western

[10] In recent years, 50 per cent of her trade has been with the West, and only 25 to 30 per cent with the Soviet bloc. See John C. Campbell, *American Policy Toward Communist Eastern Europe: The Choices Ahead* (Minneapolis: University of Minnesota Press, 1965), p. 44.

[11] See Ghita Ionescu, *The Break-up of the Soviet Empire in Eastern Europe* (Baltimore, Md.: Penguin Books, 1965), chap. IV; and my article, "The Rumanian National Course," *International Journal* (Toronto), vol. XXI, No. 4, Autumn, 1966.

[12] By 1962, Romania's trade with the "Free World" had risen from less than 20 per cent in 1958 to almost 35 per cent. See Campbell, *op. cit.*, p. 51. This ratio has remained largely unchanged since then.

economic aid and broad cultural relations. The high tide of Polish-Western collaboration has, however, receded, and criticism of the United States and West Germany has become more and more vigorous. Two other states, Czechoslovakia and Hungary, are as thoroughly anti-Peking and pro-Moscow as Poland, but have not in the past gone quite as far in cultivating friendly relations with the West: Czechoslovakia because of the slowness of de-Stalinization, and Hungary because of the legacy of hostility to the West left after 1956. Both countries have recently evinced less antagonism toward the West and a desire to expand economic and cultural relations.

The use of the term "West" conceals the diversity that exists within the Western world and the wide difference in East European attitudes toward the individual Western states. The posture toward the United States, for example, has been restrained and suspicious, especially since the escalation of the war in Vietnam. With some exceptions, the regimes have resorted to increasingly bitter attacks on U.S. aggression and have openly wondered whether good relations were possible as long as American intervention in Vietnam continued. The chief exceptions, Yugoslavia and Romania, have not been so shrill in their condemnation of U.S. policy and have not let Vietnam stand in the way of maintaining their friendly relations with Washington. Romania, for instance, is the only East European power whose foreign minister has visited Washington (in October, 1965).

In other states, the verbal opposition toward the United States has steadily mounted. The Czech scholar, Šedivý, for instance, argued that, as far as the United States was concerned, "peaceful coexistence" was "more or less only a tactic, and a still inconsistent tactic at that."[13] In particular, Johnson's concept of "building bridges" has been characterized as a subtle device for implementing a policy of hostility toward the Communist states and for undermining their unity. The tactic of bridge-building was recognized as having some positive aspects, embodying as it did "a certain political realism" and the abandonment of earlier hopes of "liberation." "We are not against bridges connecting the East and the West,"

13 Sedivy, *op. cit.*, p. 516.

wrote a Czech commentator in March, 1965. "We are primarily interested in knowing the intentions of the people walking across these bridges from the West."[14] Another Czech later found "a common denominator" between "the building of symbolic bridges into the socialist countries of Europe" and "the physical destruction of bridges in Vietnam by bombs." Both were parts of "the global strategy of the imperialists against socialism and the national-liberation movement."[15] An equally critical view was expressed at the end of 1965 in the Hungarian Communist Party paper, which wrote of "a far-reaching shift in American policy" since the assassination of Kennedy, and of Johnson's "harder line," with "honeycake" giving way to the "whip."[16] Hungarian policy had been harmed it was said, by "certain illusions" and by a "naïve optimism." "The struggle against imperialism had been seen as simpler than it is in fact." There were "false views," for instance, "that the leading circles of the imperialists had perceived the senselessness of military actions." Although the Hungarians had not accepted the Chinese view of the "paper tiger," they had tended to think of imperialism as "a dying lion which had lost a large part of its military, political, and economic strength." The main enemy, however, remained "international imperialism," and to meet this, Communist unity and a more militant version of peaceful coexistence were required.

The posture adopted by the East European states toward most of the other states of Europe has been markedly different. It has been generally assumed that the latter's belief in coexistence and their desire for increased economic and cultural contacts were sincere and lacked the ulterior motives of American diplomacy. The East European regimes have therefore manifested a keen desire to reciprocate these attitudes and to broaden and deepen their contacts with non-Communist neighbors. There has been an especially vigorous exchange of visits by high-level representatives, and a rash of commercial and cultural agreements, for instance with Austria and with other smaller states, and also a growing official cordiality with larger countries, such as Great Britain and Italy. Each Communist coun-

---

[14] Emil Sip, *Předvoj (Vanguard;* Bratislava), March 25, 1965.
[15] D. Rozehnal, "Vietnam, Europe, and Peaceful Coexistence," *Nová mysl,* No. 9 (1965), pp. 1052, 1058.
[16] *Népszabadság (People's Freedom;* Budapest), December 4, 1965.

try, too, has sought to encourage closer relations with its own particular neighbors, as Bulgaria has done with Greece and Turkey, or Poland with Sweden, and to expand their contacts with certain African and Asian states. Not without significance, too, is a deliberate policy of promoting more friendly contacts with fellow-Communist countries, including Yugoslavia, through frequent Party and government visits and commercial and other exchanges.

In this context, France occupies a special place, largely because of the peculiar features of President de Gaulle's policy toward East and West. In the past two years, the Foreign Ministers of Czechoslovakia, Hungary, Poland, and Romania have all been to Paris. The French Foreign Minister has visited Moscow, as has De Gaulle himself, whose vague and romantic conception of "a Europe from the Atlantic to the Urals" has been greeted with interest, although with some doubt and uncertainty as to its real meaning. We must determine, said János Peters, Hungary's Foreign Minister, whether this position is "ideological, historical, or geographical."[17] Certainly if De Gaulle is considering, as sometimes seems to be implied, the liberation of Eastern Europe and even the Soviet Union from Communism, and still more if he is thinking of allowing China to control the U.S.S.R. east of the Urals, the concept of a "European Europe" can hardly have any appeal to the Communist regimes. No doubt the special sympathy for France is engendered by the fact that De Gaulle condemns American policy toward China and Vietnam, and that his actions in Europe tend to undermine and reduce American influence and to divide and weaken NATO and the Common Market. Moreover, his plea for a role for the former satellites in a revived Europe appeals to both governments and peoples. The Hungarian leader, János Kádár, speaking in the Budapest parliament on February 11, 1965, indicated this when he declared: "The classic struggle has not invalidated geographical concepts." He recognized that Europe did in fact extend from the Atlantic to the Urals, and from the Arctic to the Mediterranean, but voiced the reminder that "Europe" today embraced nine countries of the socialist camp, including the U.S.S.R., that Hungary was located in its center, and warned that any *rapprochement* between two countries must not be

[17] *The New York Times*, February 1, 1965.

directed against a third. Noting that there were "many possibilities for useful cooperation offered by geographical proximity," Kádár proclaimed Hungary's readiness "to establish normal and good relations with any country but only as a socialist nation belonging to the Warsaw Treaty Organization, and maintaining close relations with every other socialist country."[18]

The position of Eastern Europe toward Germany, as an integral part of Western Europe, is conditioned by vivid historical experiences and present fears of a renewal of German expansion. Peaceful coexistence with this part of the West is hampered, in their view, by the unwillingness of the Bonn government to recognize with finality the Oder-Neisse line or the existence of an East German state, or to agree to the unification of the two Germanys along lines acceptable to the East. The West German refusal to recognize diplomatically the states of Eastern Europe, and her ostentatious breach of relations with Yugoslavia several years ago, pour salt on the wounds. Behind all this, they believe, lurks the desire to absorb the German Democratic Republic in a united non-Communist Germany, and to recover the lost territories to the East. This fear, based in part on a very real danger, but exaggerated by a massive propaganda campaign, is shared by all the East European nations, including Yugoslavia. It is felt and voiced most acutely by East Germany, who considers her very existence at stake, and by Poland and Czechoslovakia, who believe their territories are threatened by German *revanchism*. These fears reinforce East European suspicions of the United States, which is regarded as fully supporting West German ambitions and planning to arm her with nuclear weapons, and which pointedly excludes East Germany from its policy of building bridges. All the more welcome is the attitude of France, which through the mouth of De Gaulle has indicated a willingness to recognize the Oder-Neisse Line and has suggested the settlement of German unification by the European states, including the U.S.S.R. Paradoxically, the countries of Eastern Europe have shown a readiness, indeed an eagerness, to expand their commerce with West Germany, and this has been reciprocated by the latter. Bulgaria, Poland, Romania, and Hungary have concluded economic agree-

18 Official English translation of speech (Budapest: mimeographed).

ments with her, usually including West Berlin in the trading area involved. In most cases, too, West German trade offices have been established in states that Bonn does not recognize diplomatically. Only Czechoslovakia has so far been unable to come to terms with her, because of Prague's refusal to include West Berlin in the stipulations of the proposed treaty and Bonn's unwillingness formally to proclaim the Munich boundaries as invalid.

It is in this context of kaleidoscopic differentiation that the relations between Eastern Europe and the West must be examined in somewhat greater detail in three major fields: economic, cultural, and political. In each sphere there is additional evidence of diversity of viewpoints, both in the East and the West; of uncertainty and ambivalence of attitude of the governments, again both in East and West; and sometimes of differing views between the Communist regimes and influential social groups among the intelligentsia.

In the economic realm, the East European states have all shown a keen anxiety to emerge from their previous isolation and to participate more actively in the world market. The desire of Western industrialists to tap the markets of East Europe, and the desire of Western governments, including the American and German, to make trade with the Communist world an important element of their diplomacy, have together created a favorable environment for increased economic cooperation. There is a constant exchange of visitors, both official and private, between East European and other European capitals, usually with the object of negotiating commercial arrangements. As we have noted, the regimes have been willing to do business even with the less popular states, such as West Germany. In fact, the latter is the leading trading partner (outside the Communist bloc) of some of them. There has also been a readiness to develop with Western firms, including German, joint production schemes, involving close collaboration and joint use of resources for the manufacture or distribution of specific products.[19]

The desire of the East Europeans to trade with the West is a product of many factors. It is in part the result of growing anxiety

[19] M. Gamarnikow, "Eastern Partners for Western Businessmen," *East Europe*, XIV, No. 9 (September, 1965), 17–24.

concerning the harmful effects of the European Common Market on their export trade, and it is in part a result of the failure of COMECON to fulfill its potentialities in increased mutual trade within the bloc, and of the desire of each member of that body to preserve freedom of maneuver to promote its own national economic objectives. Romania was the pacesetter in resisting the Soviet plan of economic integration through COMECON and in developing extensive commerce with Western countries. Even states more sympathetic to the objectives of COMECON have been seeking to lessen their economic dependence on the Soviet Union. The recent suicide of Erich Apel, East Germany's chief planner, followed the negotiations for a trade treaty with the U.S.S.R. and may have been motivated by the continuing subjugation of the East German economy to Soviet interests. In the case of Albania, there are special reasons for her resumption of trade with the West, mainly the ending of her exclusive reliance on Soviet economic support and the inadequacy of Chinese assistance.

In general, however, the turn to the West, apart from Albania and Romania, has been closely linked with a fundamental re-examination of the economic systems, stimulated by serious crises, and the introduction of reforms which often go beyond those proposed in the Soviet Union.[20] The aim of economic policy has more and more become greater efficiency of production and improvement in the quality of goods, and efforts to achieve this have been made by relaxing the strictly centralized planning system and reintroducing elements of a market economy such as enterprise independence and profits. This has led to a more realistic appraisal of the value of foreign trade, as well as of its requirements. The regimes recognize the need to produce commodities salable in the West. Even within the bloc complaints about the poor quality of merchandise provided by their trading partners have increased. The resort to a market mechanism, the introduction of profits as criteria of efficiency, and the effort to set more realistic prices are all factors that facilitate foreign trade and are required by it. Moreover, trade with the

[20] Even in Albania suggestions of reforms in the planning system have been raised. See *Christian Science Monitor*, February 15, 1966. Vague indications of impending reform were also given by the Romanian Vice Premier, Barladeanu, at the Party congress held in July, 1965.

West makes it possible to secure specific goods required, such as wheat, in a lean crop year; or needed raw materials; or elaborate machine tools or equipment, even whole factories; and to take advantage of Western expertise and experience through these deals and through joint production enterprises. The motives are not altruistic, needless to say, nor even mainly political, but are primarily based on realistic economic considerations of improving the Communist economy and aiding it in meeting the requirements of its present phase of development.

There are still major obstacles in the way of cultivating these sprouts of economic cooperation between Eastern Europe and the West. The former still find much to complain of, in particular the strategic embargo maintained by the United States and its allies; the lack in most cases of most-favored-nation treatment and the existence of other barriers to their exports; and the absence of adequate credit facilities. The East European states would like to see these hindrances modified or eliminated. The Western governments are anxious to encourage trade with Eastern Europe but are often reluctant to remove the impediments mentioned and are confronted, especially in the United States, with bitter public resistance even to the present extent of trade. Moreover, trade with Eastern Europe faces difficulties in the form of some of the traditional features of the Communist economies themselves, such as their state monopoly of foreign trade and their preference for bilateralism. Yet there is a strong desire among business interests in the West for an expansion of trade with Eastern Europe, and there is general consensus among the governments that politically this would contribute to a growing independence of action by the individual Communist states and to a moderation of their foreign and domestic policies. Without doubt the trade of Eastern Europe will continue to be predominantly with the bloc and the U.S.S.R. (except in the case of Yugoslavia), but the balance will tip somewhat to the West and may have the political advantages mentioned. A strengthening of the economies, and therefore of the governments, may also result, but in a manner, it is hoped, that will lead them away from the totalitarian and doctrinal patterns of the past toward a more rational and welfare-oriented system in the future.

In the cultural sphere, it is the West that has been pressing for the expansion of relations between East and West, hoping not only to provide Western scholars with firsthand knowledge and experience, but also to broaden the horizons of East European scholarship and the creative arts, and thus to loosen the hold of Communist ideology on the intellectuals. The intellectual thaw associated with de-Stalinization, which has occurred in varying degrees in almost every East European state, has created a favorable atmosphere for greater intercourse with the West.[21] The intelligentsia are keenly aware of the damage done by the years of isolation and by enforced imitation of Soviet patterns and have been most anxious to see the opening of doors to the West.[22] The regimes themselves have seen the advantages of cultural exchange, especially as a means of acquiring knowledge of Western economic methods and scientific and technological processes, and as a *quid pro quo* for economic agreements with the West. Some countries, for instance Poland, and more recently Hungary, have taken advantage of the Ford Foundation program to send large numbers of scholars to the United States. In 1964, Yugoslavia agreed to an exchange of professors and students under the Fulbright program. Other states, such as Czechoslovakia, Bulgaria, and Romania, have concluded cultural agreements with the United States. The tourist trade has also been fostered by almost all the countries of Eastern Europe, mainly for the purpose of acquiring foreign currency, but also in order to relax the widely condemned restrictions on travel characteristic of the Stalinist period. The jamming of foreign radio broadcasts has, with the exception of Bulgaria, ceased.

The risks of these openings to the West have been clearly recognized officially, although they are not regarded as sufficiently serious to warrant an abandonment of the program. President Novotný, for instance, welcomed the idea of "world perspectives" in the following terms:

> We are in favor of making use of all the positive aspects of capitalist society for the good of our society, as long as they do not violate the

21 Klaus Mehnert, "West Wind over East Europe," *Osteuropa* (*East Europe;* Stuttgart), XVI, No. 1 (January, 1966), 3–17.

22 For instance, R. Selucky, "We and the World," *Literární noviny* (*Literary Gazette;* Prague), September 5, 1964; and J. Hajek, "The East-West Dialogue in Vienna," *Rudé právo* (*Red Justice;* Prague), July 11, 1965.

socialist principles of life; we are in favor of getting acquainted with the cultural values originating in the capitalist countries as long as they are progressive. We want to make use of all the scientific and technical knowledge which is a positive contribution to the advance of society as a whole, and to the advance of man. We want to make use of it and learn from it. In this respect we don't want to shut ourselves off from the West.

But he asked the advocates of "world perspectives" whether they wished to "open the door to capitalist principles and the destruction of the socialist order," and declared firmly that "the ideas of socialism and those of capitalism are incompatible."[23]

Indeed the common theme, oft repeated, of Communist spokesmen has been that "peaceful coexistence" should not extend into the ideological realm. It has not been thought of as permitting a cohabitation or toleration of rival systems or doctrines, and still less as envisaging their interpenetration and ultimate synthesis, but as involving a bitter and unrelenting struggle against bourgeois ideology. In every country of Eastern Europe, the penetration of alien ideas from the capitalist world is deplored and resisted. In Hungary, for instance, there has been public discussion of some of the dangerous implications of widened cultural relations: the harmful influence of Western tourists, the defection of Hungarian tourists abroad, and the propaganda of Radio Free Europe and the Voice of America.[24] Although the risks are thus recognized, peaceful coexistence has also been considered as offering an opportunity for Communists to penetrate the Western intellectual world and to combat Western ideas, in an open confrontation or dialogue, with more confidence, tact, and frankness than in the past.[25]

Another striking, and yet equally ambivalent, aspect of the cultural and intellectual thaw in Eastern Europe has been the changing attitude toward religion and the churches. The regimes have not, of course, abandoned atheism, but the campaign against the churches has lost some of its extreme bitterness. The Ecumenical

---

[23] *Rudé právo*, December 5, 1965.
[24] See the speech of I. Szirmai, in *Társadalmi Szemle* (*Social Review;* Budapest), November, 1965.
[25] M. Bauer, "The Struggle of Ideas and the Tactics of the Imperialists," *Nová mysl*, No. 1 (1965), pp. 29–30.

Council and its evidence of the Roman Catholic Church's changing policy toward Communism was welcomed by Communist commentators. Many Catholic dignitaries were permitted to go to Rome. Concurrently certain religious leaders, such as Archbishop Beran in Czechoslovakia, were released from internment or prison. In 1964, an agreement was signed between the Hungarian Government and the Vatican. Although Cardinal Mindszenty continues to be confined in the American Embassy in Budapest, it is likely that the Hungarian Government would grant him his freedom if he would leave Hungary. Even in Poland a *détente* in Church-State relations seemed to be developing, and the possibility of a more open and friendly dialogue between Catholics and Marxists appeared to exist.[26] There was even serious talk of a possible visit by the Pope for the millennium of Polish Catholicism. Then came the thunderbolt of the Polish Catholics' invitation to German bishops to attend the millenniary celebrations, the regime's bitter attack on this action, and the refusal to let Cardinal Wyszinski visit Rome. Although this crisis has many causes and is closely related to internal politics, it has its foreign-policy aspects too, notably with reference to the German question. More generally, however, it reflects the Polish regime's fears that the Church sought a *rapprochement* between Poland and the West. Gomulka, in explaining the refusal of a visa to the Cardinal, charged him with this and reportedly declared that the Polish nation could not be won over to the West.[27]

It is in the political and military realm that the least progress has been made in East-West relations, and that few, if any, new initiatives have been taken by either side. The idea of peaceful co-existence originated, of course, in this very sphere, as a product of the mutual recognition of the danger of nuclear war and the necessity of seeking the peaceful settlement of disputes and a consensus in areas of common concern. This in turn became a central issue in the Sino-Soviet dispute, with the Chinese denying the possibility of serious agreements with the United States and condemning efforts

26 See the speech by Archbishop B. Kominek, *Tygodnik powszechny* (*General Weekly;* Warsaw), November 22, 1964.

27 *Trybuna ludu* (*People's Tribune;* Warsaw), January 15, 1966. See *The New York Times,* January 15, 1966.

by the U.S.S.R. in this direction. Apart from Albania, the states of Eastern Europe supported the more moderate Soviet view of East-West relations and rejected Chinese extremism. As *Nová mysl* expressed it in January, 1965, the "sectarian" view that it was "an illusion to talk of the possibility of any improvement of relations with the United States" had been refuted by practice.[28] The crisis in Vietnam has therefore created a real dilemma for Moscow and its supporters, apparently casting doubt on the feasibility of peaceful coexistence and vindicating the Chinese position. Most, including Romania, have rallied to the support of Vietnam, as a fellow-socialist nation under attack by imperialism, and some (Czechoslovakia, East Germany, and Hungary) have accepted permanent representatives of the Vietcong in their capitals.[29] Yet there is still little or no sympathy for China in Eastern Europe, and the gap between these states and Peking has not closed. Apart from Romania, they have all given full backing to the Soviet proposal of Communist unity in support of Vietnam and have condemned the Chinese for opposing this solidarity of action. The Chinese in turn have denounced the Soviet Union and her allies for giving too little aid to Hanoi and for secretly trying to reach a peaceful settlement.

The Vietnam crisis has therefore not brought the East European states nearer to China, but it has pushed them closer to Moscow and further away from Washington. Moscow has kept in close touch with Eastern Europe, especially with its most reliable partners, Czechoslovakia, Poland, Hungary, and Bulgaria, by frequent meetings with their top leaders. The most serious effect of Vietnam, however, has been the setback to the improvement of economic, cultural, and even political relations with the West, especially with the United States.[30] There is still a desire in Eastern Europe for improved relations with Washington, but a cooler, even hostile attitude has developed, and economic and cultural cooperation has not advanced as rapidly as once expected. Peaceful coexistence has not been abandoned but has been given a more militant connotation. This doctrine has always been regarded as a form of class

---

[28] Bauer, *op. cit.*, p. 27.

[29] Poland and Romania have also agreed to the opening of Vietcong offices.

[30] See the testimony of George F. Kennan before the Foreign Relations Committee of the U.S. Senate, *The New York Times*, February 11, 1966.

struggle—"a peaceful method for the international strengthening and expanding of the position of Socialism and Communism."[31] This did not, however, exclude cooperation with "imperialist" governments on specific matters of common concern, and subordinated the use of violence to peaceful competition, at least in relations with the Western world. A more belligerent version now prevails, as expressed in the important speech in November, 1965, by the top Hungarian ideologue, Szirmai: "We have always preached that it is necessary to fight for peaceful coexistence. We desire peaceful coexistence; the aggressive circles of the imperialists do not want it. Therefore, by mobilizing all the adherents of peace, we have to pursue a constant struggle against the imperialists and have to force peaceful coexistence on them. This struggle is under way now, despite the explosion of bombs in Vietnam. This struggle is made up of several components: our efforts to induce the United States to withdraw from Vietnam as well as our endeavor to localize the war in Vietnam, if we are unable to persuade the United States to withdraw its forces."[32]

In Europe proper, it is the unresolved German question that remains a standing obstacle to East-West cooperation. Evidence is accumulating that opinion in West Germany has been shifting away from the rigid and inflexible course of the past and moving in the direction of establishing diplomatic relations with the East European states, relaxing the Hallstein Doctrine (which condemns the recognition of East Germany by other states), and even accepting the *fait accompli* of the Oder-Neisse Line. Still less doctrinaire views, abhorrent in official circles in Bonn, are reflected in the policy of France, and concrete initiatives for relieving tension have been suggested by private individuals in the West.[33] The East European states have greeted most such moves with suspicion and have not offered any original ideas of their own for a solution of the German problem. They have stood firmly on their traditional positions, insisting on the unconditional recognition of the Polish-German and Polish-Czech frontiers, the acceptance of the two Germanys,

---

[31] Cf. D. Rozehnal, "Peaceful Coexistence or Nuclear Catastrophe?," *Nová mysl*, No. 3 (1962), p. 272.

[32] Szirmai, *op. cit.*

[33] See Brzezinski and others cited above, note 6.

and the denial of nuclear weapons to West Germany. Older proposals for nuclear disengagement and a nonaggression pact between NATO and the Warsaw bloc have been reiterated. In the summer of 1966, the Communist bloc in Bucharest proposed a conference on European security open to all interested parties.[34] There has been some sympathy for these views in unofficial circles in the West but no favorable official response. The storm in Poland over the invitation by the Church to the German bishops, which expressed a willingness to "forgive" the crimes done by Germans in Poland and implied, some felt, the possibility of a compromise on the Polish-German border, indicates how sensitive the frontier question remains and how far the two sides are from a meeting of the minds.[35]

There is little doubt that for the East European states, apart from Albania, improved relations with the West, including the United States, are far more important than total victory in Vietnam, and that a peaceful settlement of the conflict there is a matter of urgent concern. Behind the façade of verbal hostility, there is much evidence of a desire to limit their own military commitment and to maintain the links with the United States and the West, at least to the extent already achieved.[36] If a peaceful outcome of the conflict were achieved, the channels of communication between Eastern Europe and the West, now somewhat obstructed, would again be opened, and a renewed effort at East-West cooperation in Europe, perhaps going far beyond what has so far been envisaged on either side, made possible. This would certainly strengthen the ability of the East European states to follow a more independent course and facilitate the building of more authentic and genuine bridges of friendship between them and the West.

[34] See my article in *International Journal* (Toronto), Autumn, 1966.

[35] Statements by the Catholic hierarchy and the Communist leadership suggest that an end of the rift is not excluded. See *Trybuna ludu,* March 17, 1966, and *The New York Times,* March 18, 1966.

[36] See *Christian Science Monitor,* March 28 and 29, 1966, and *The New York Times,* March 28, 1966.

4. The Atlantic Alliance and the International Strategic Equilibrium

HARALD VON RIEKHOFF

THE CREATION of the North Atlantic Alliance in 1949 was a response to the evolution of a global bipolar international system.[1] NATO in itself may be regarded as representing a system governed by a set of principles with distinct, though changing, patterns of behavior. Thus the alliance is at one and the same time a system and a subsystem in a wider international context. Because of this integral interrelation of systems, any diagnosis of ailments and recommendations relating to NATO's cure should be preceded by an examination of changes in the macroenvironment.

[1] Morton Kaplan, in his *System and Process in International Politics* (New York: John Wiley & Sons, 1957), differentiates between the characteristics of a loose and a tight bipolar system. In application, however, the Cold War at its hottest incorporated features from either system, while increasingly shifting toward the former after 1954.

Perhaps the psychological trauma of the Cold War between the two camps of a bipolarized world accounts for the rapidity and eagerness with which statesmen and analysts have accepted the concept of an accomplished shift from a bipolar to a polycentric international system. The term polycentrism, as it was first coined by Togliatti in an interview of June 16, 1956, in the paper *Nuovi Argomenti,* was entirely applicable within the specific context of the argument, insofar as it referred to the emergence of new centers to which Communist parties, emerging nations, and even committed allies could turn for ideological guidance, economic assistance, and cultural contacts. Polycentrism in this sense means a proliferation of interstate dealings and contacts, but it would be inaccurate to equate this with the emergence of centers of power which in terms of military and economic strength could rival the existing bipolar hegemony of the two superpowers. In the bipolar world of the Cold War, international dealings followed strictly vertical channels between allies and their respective bloc leader; moreover, it was largely a downward flow of communication from the leader to the ranks. In the West this took the form of dynamic, though democratic, leadership by the United States within a multinational alliance framework. For the Kremlin it involved the use of absolute directives to its satraps, which displayed the normal predilection of imperialist powers for parallel bilateralism instead of multilateralism. Interbloc communication was the exclusive prerogative of the superpowers, and room at the top for summit contacts was extremely sparse.[2] Alliance members on either side of the Iron Curtain, who had been reared in the same historical and cultural cradle, were condemned to monastic vows of silence and abstention from direct contacts.

However, to interpret this proliferation of contacts among political centers, which has received the label polycentrism, as the emergence of new centers of power that could challenge the superpowers and the consequent return to a modified version of the "balance-of-power" system that regulated the behavior of the European

2 Because of the nonhierarchical nature of the Western alliance and the early emergence of European institutions such as the Brussels Pact, the European Coal and Steel Community, and the European Economic Community, Washington never became the switchboard for intra-alliance communication that Moscow was.

powers in the eighteenth and nineteenth centuries,[3] seems to represent a disregard for the existing power relationship. In order to avoid the association of polycentrism with the emergence of new centers of power, it might be preferable to describe the present process of proliferating contacts, which is emerging under the impact of the superpower nuclear equilibrium, as centrifugal pluralism.

Those interpretations which see in French diplomatic recognition of Communist China, or in President de Gaulle's cordial state reception for Premier Cyrankiewicz of Poland, or in friendly champagne toasts exchanged between Foreign Ministers Couve de Murville and Gromyko—none, to be sure, devoid of political significance —a return to the historical Paris-Warsaw axis or the renewal of the Sazanov-Poincaré alliance system in the framework of the classical "balance-of-power" system, reveal a mesmerization with conventional models whose application, under present conditions, must be viewed with serious reservations. In the first place, the existence of strong ideological barriers, despite the recent willingness to accommodate political intercourse to persisting ideological cleavages, would grossly impair the facile and flexible operation that characterized the "balance-of-power" system under its common monarchical-aristocratic ascriptive basis. Secondly, the "balance-of-power" operated under the explicit assumption that war constituted a rational instrument of policy that enabled actors to make whatever adjustments were required for maintaining the equilibrium. Elaborate conventions and chivalrous codes that were being reinforced by the primitive state of military technology limited the destructive impact of war and thus perpetuated the rationality of war as an acceptable option for policy. The existence of nuclear weapons, the gross increase of the destructive power of conventional weapons, as witnessed in two world wars, the unpredictable outcome, and the unacceptable penalties for miscalculation have virtually ruled out preplanned war against each other as a rational policy option for the decision-makers of the major powers. Finally, it required five or more states, relatively comparable in power, to support the "balance-of-power" system, like a group of caryatids, against bipolar tendencies or aspirations for universal hegemony.

[3] For a very lucid analysis of the rules governing the behavior of members of the "balance-of-power" system, see Kaplan, *op. cit.*, p. 23.

Votaries of the polycentric doctrine tend to diagnose present trends in international relations as an indication of the depolarization of power and the restoration of multiple centers of power. In terms of military power, however, the United States and the U.S.S.R., each having an impressive nuclear second-strike capability, remain supreme and unchallenged. This supremacy could only be enhanced by the creation of an antimissile system. The discrepancy of power between the two superpowers and any others, singly or collectively, is greater than ever, and no *force de frappe* style of power can redress the imbalance of the equation. It is questionable whether a comparable rival will emerge within a generation. China, while enjoying the strategic advantages of size required for weapons decentralization and warning time, lacks economic resources. A united Europe may provide the latter, but with its overpopulation and space problem at the periphery of a continent, it suffers from inherent strategic disadvantages.[4]

The bipolar concentration of military power has increased, is increasing, and will hardly diminish. It cannot be discounted by the argument that nuclear weapons will never be used, and thus, so to speak, they do not exist. Certainly the most elaborate safety and control mechanisms have reduced the chances of accidental nuclear war to microscopic dimensions. Furthermore, both superpowers have demonstrated by their behavior that they have excluded nuclear war as a rational instrument of policy. Nevertheless, escalation from crisis or war situations, neither possibly corresponding to the choice or plans of the superpowers, cannot be excluded altogether. More important still, if nuclear weapons are to be regarded as means for deterrence rather than for actual military use, the opportunity of manipulating the delicate balance between nuclear threats and deterrence has placed into the hands of the superpowers a political and diplomatic weapon of very considerable dimensions—an adapted Clausewitzian version of diplomacy by intensified means—against each other and *a fortiori* against smaller powers. This is a factor that no rational decision-maker can afford to

4 The economic sacrifices that would be demanded for the construction of a European nuclear second-strike force, in addition to the problems of control and management, would tend to impair rather than stimulate the process of political integration in Europe.

ignore. Khrushchev's Cuban Canossa in response to limited conventional operations and gently executed but unmistakable nuclear alerts testify to this.

From this it may be concluded that we still live under an international system that is characterized by the bipolarization of power. What has emerged is not polycentrism, if this is to imply the formation of new centers of power, but what the German journalist Theo Sommer describes as the creation of new centers of ambition within a bipolarized world.[5] In the same manner, Henry Kissinger observes that "polycentrism is on the rise not because the world has ceased to be bipolar, but because with respect to nuclear weapons it essentially remains so."[6]

This does not mean that events have been static and that bipolarity in 1966 reveals entirely the same characteristics as bipolarity in 1954. It has been a decade of immense transitions. The principal event in this evolution, namely the emergence of the superpower nuclear stalemate, has been strategic-technological in nature. By responding to the Cuban missile crisis in the manner they did, Soviet decision-makers renounced their own experiment of trying to outflank the stalemate. They thereby demonstrated their willingness to make the necessary political and ideological adjustments and sacrifices to accommodate themselves to this strategic reality. The Sino-Soviet conflict, which preceded the stalemate and which reveals a much wider spectrum of causes, has, nevertheless, become an integral, even subordinate,[7] function of the stalemate and is gathering increasing momentum as the result of the superpowers' continuing necessity for accommodation to this strategic reality.

While present-day international relations may still be said to operate within the power context of a bipolar system, the existence of the nuclear stalemate has created such far-reaching transformations in the patterns of international behavior that the unqualified use of the term "bipolarity" may no longer suffice. One analyst

[5] Wilhelm Cornides, "German Unification and the Power Balance," *Survey,* No. 58 (January, 1966), p. 141.

[6] Henry Kissinger, *The Troubled Partnership* (New York: McGraw-Hill Book Co., 1965), p. 17.

[7] The term "subordinate" should not be interpreted in a manner that discounts the very serious risk that the Sino-Soviet dispute poses to the continued operation of the present superpower nuclear equilibrium.

defines it as "partially neutralized bipolarism."[8] Since the term "neutralized" may create the wrong impression of a reduction rather than a proliferation in international dealings, one might perhaps characterize the present system as a *three-tiered multidimensional system within a bipolar setting*. The first tier consists of the two superpowers. The second tier is composed of states in Western and Eastern Europe which are characterized by a high level of economic development and industrialization, and an intimate interdependence with the United States and the Soviet Union, even though some countries in the first category, like Sweden and Switzerland, and Yugoslavia in the second, do not participate in the formal alliance framework that links the second tier to its respective superpower. Countries like Australia, New Zealand, and Canada, though lying outside Europe, would qualify for second-tier membership by virtue of their high economic development and close links with the United States. From the strategic point of view, Canada may even be regarded as forming an integral unit with her first-tier neighbor. Countries of the third tier, despite their wide diversities and the fact that some are nonaligned and others associated with first- and second-tier powers by formal alliance ties, have in common a much lower degree of industrialization and economic development and, strategically and economically, a less immediate interdependence with the superpowers than that which exists in the relations between first- and second-tier powers. The term "multidimensional" refers to the recent proliferation of East-West contacts and transactions, both between the two superpowers and between the different members of the second tier, either horizontally with their counterpart on the same tier or diagonally between second-tier powers and the opposite superpower.[9]

8 Wilhelm Cornides, *op. cit.*, p. 142.

9 The model suffers from obvious crudities and oversimplifications. One problem arises from the attempt to accommodate China in this system. Despite her dispute with Moscow, Peking has never formally abrogated her alliance with the Soviet Union, thus like other second-tier powers she still operates under the shadow of the Soviet nuclear umbrella and claims whatever other alliance benefits, such as consultation, may still be harvested from its ruptured framework. On the other hand, China actively combines her quest for superpower status with leadership aspirations in the ranks of the third tier, of which she is a member by virtue of her experience as an exploited power, her economic state of development, and her strategic location vis-à-vis the superpowers.

The two superpowers at the apex of this multitiered system are no longer engaged in a situation of pure conflict. With the appearance of the nuclear stalemate their relations have assumed aspects of what Thomas Schelling would classify as mixed-motive games, involving elements both of conflict and cooperation. The continuing ideological conflict; the jockeying for preferred positions in the developing countries; the cleavage between East and West Europe, which refutes the experience of history and the logic of geography; the enforced partition of Germany and the presence of the Berlin Wall, which frustrate most genuine human aspirations, are all tangible symptoms of continuing conflict. Even in the absence of ideological differences, the existence of conflict between the two unchallenged centers of economic strength and military might must be regarded as normal. Until the emergence of a rival of equal power dimensions, it therefore seems to be idle—Chinese accusations notwithstanding—to talk of a Moscow-Washington alliance, for power seeks protective alliances against power; power does not form alliances with power against nonpower, as Herbert Dinerstein correctly concludes when he states that there can only be a *détente* between the United States and the U.S.S.R., not an *entente,* for "they can only become friendly; they cannot become friends."[10]

The nuclear equilibrium has not terminated superpower conflict, but it has introduced a novel and significant element of cooperation into their relations. Both parties are interested in preventing their own conflicts from reaching a level that might culminate in the breakdown of the ultimate control mechanism, of which the "hot line" is a direct, if symbolic, reflection. Even more so, superpower cooperation is a security precaution against involuntary entanglements in direct confrontations arising from situations that are neither instigated by the superpowers nor related to the time and place of their choosing. Their common antiproliferation platform, which was given tangible form in the signing of the test-ban treaty, complies with this principle.

This superpower cooperation is not so much an alliance directed against another power or group of powers as an insurance against undesired eventualities. American-Soviet policy approximates alli-

[10] Herbert S. Dinerstein, "The Transformation of Alliance Systems," *The American Political Science Review,* September, 1965, p. 596.

ance characteristics most closely in its posture toward China. For here the mutual desire to strengthen India against an eventual Chinese attack; the efforts at pacifying the dispute between India and Pakistan in order to prevent the latter from slipping into Peking's direct sphere of influence; the apparent Soviet shifting of support toward the neutralist forces in Laos; and possibly an eventual U.S.–Soviet cooperation in solving the Vietnamese crisis, all point in the direction of a parallel policy for the containment of China. Peking's charges are, therefore, not entirely unrealistic. On the other hand, German apprehension lest the *détente* be consummated at her expense has proved unfounded. The improvement of relations has not led to the sacrifice of the Western position in Berlin but has enhanced the latter's security, while those concessions relating to the control of the access routes to Berlin which the United States proposed in 1959 and 1962, despite considerable opposition from Bonn, have now been deposited on the shelves of diplomatic archives.

The strategic balance of the superpower equilibrium, the economic recovery of the two sectors of Europe, and the general ideological relaxation have fundamentally altered intra-alliance relations. In the various capitals of Europe the quality and value of superpower leadership is now being analyzed more objectively and critically. Strategic doctrines emanating from the planning staffs of the Kremlin and Pentagon are being subjected to a new and more sophisticated scrutiny. In short, the allies in Western Europe, and to a lesser degree those in Eastern Europe, have regained the power of veto and counterproposal. A bilateral flow of intra-alliance vertical communication and bargaining has replaced the erstwhile passive doctor-patient relationship between the United States and her NATO allies and the master-tributary status of the Warsaw Pact.

Complementing this transformation of intra-alliance relationships has been the gradual horizontal restoration of the telephone lines between the two European partitions, implementing, as it were, a direct dialing system without requiring the services of the Moscow and Washington central-switchboard operator. Second-tier East-West horizontal relations have largely proceeded along bilateral lines. Britain's continued effort at retaining a more flexible approach vis-à-vis Eastern Europe, both in matters of trade policy and diplomatic contacts, has been duplicated by De Gaulle's recent cultural and political engagement, especially in countries such as Poland and Romania, and is now being followed by German economic overtures in that area, thus, in part at least, outflanking the so-called Hallstein Doctrine in actual practice. At this early and delicate stage, a network of bilateral engagements may not only be the sole option available to the West in order to avoid a massive counteroffensive by the Soviet Union in the direction of renewed rigidity, but it may also entail distinct tactical advantages, which allow Germany to manipulate her tantalizing economic assets and let France bargain with her cultural prestige and the appeals that Gaullist nationalism carries in East Europe. One might even be tempted to speculate whether these partial engagements could not, within the superstructure of the existing nuclear stalemate, duplicate in microform the mosaic of European alignments and spheres of influence of the interwar period, with strong French involvement in Poland and Czechoslovakia, matched by German strength in Hungary, and overlapping ties in Romania.

Despite the growing pattern of engagements, relations between the two parts of Europe reveal some aspects of the competitive-cooperative behavior of the superpowers. Europeans want to exploit the regained freedom accruing from the nuclear stalemate without incurring the risks of political "licentiousness" within their own ranks and without the threat of escalation from third-tier crisis situations. Consensus in this area does not, however, exclude the continuation of conflict in the horizontal relations among second-tier powers, as shown by the importance of ideological cleavages in the intellectual fabric of European life and culture; the unacceptability of the Rapacki Plan; the lack of agreement over boundaries; and the acrimonious relations, or officially the state of "nonrelations" between Bonn and Pankow.

The growing diagonal contacts between France, a second-tier power, and the Soviet superpower should be interpreted not in "balance-of-power" terms but largely as having Western-oriented goals, namely those of enhancing the French position in the Atlantic region. Occasionally these diagonal engagements can play a useful role of initiative and mediation between the superpowers, as was seen by the important British contribution to the successful conclusion of the test-ban treaty. Vietnam may be another area for useful diagonal engagement. Moscow has welcomed the emergence of these bilateral diagonal contacts with Western powers, probably less for their mediating function than for their catalytic effect on the disintegration of NATO.

Despite President Johnson's policy of 1964 of "building bridges" to Eastern Europe and the generous economic agreements with Romania of that year, the reciprocal diagonal engagement process between the United States and East Europe has not achieved the same significant dimensions as the parallel process between the Soviet Union and Western Europe. The war in Vietnam is one reason for this lag, as is the still-restricted international maneuverability available to the Soviet allies in Europe. This is enhanced by the discrepancy in the relative ratio of power of France, Britain, and Germany, individually, vis-à-vis Moscow, as compared to that of Poland or Romania vis-à-vis the United States. Nor may historical and cultural factors be excluded. While American economic and technological strength exercises a magnetic appeal in Eastern Europe, her political and academic involvement in that region has never reached the degree of priority that has been accorded to areas such as Western Europe, Latin America, or East Asia. Twice within this century, the United States has remained notoriously immune to East European crisis situations which immediately plunged the rest of Europe into war and delayed her entry until such time that her priority interests in Western Europe and East Asia were being challenged.

The third tier represents the most heterogeneous of the three layers in this model, displaying great power differentials, cultural and ideological cleavages, and varied states of political and economic development. The nearest common denominator within the third tier is its distinct difference from the other two tiers, as shown by the lower degree of economic and technological development, a greater degree of political instability, and thus a greater propensity for sudden rather than gradual change. This is the area in which superpower competition is most visible, but because of the less immediate strategic interdependence with the latter, the nuclear stalemate has been less successful in imposing conditions of immobility and stability in the third tier.

Horizontal dealings within this tier follow very diffuse and noncrystallized forms of bilateralism, and organizations for multilateral transactions, such as the Organization of African Unity and the Arab League, are more aspirational than functional in nature. Conflicts tend to follow the trend of pure-conflict or zero-sum games, without the ameliorating factor of mixed-motive games or conflict-cooperation statesmanship, which characterizes the behavior of the superpowers and to a lesser degree that of second-tier powers.

Relations between second- and third-tier powers used to be conducted in a vertically downward direction along the bilateral channels that existed between the European colonial powers and their overseas colonies, protectorates, or satellite states. With the liquidation of Western colonialism, bargaining situations have assumed a reciprocal nature, and despite the heavy colonial legacy there has been no disengagement of the second tier. The political, economic, and cultural involvement of Britain and France continues in the third tier and is now joined by German economic participation in that area. In certain situations, Britain and France can draw considerable benefits from their colonial experience, while it constitutes a liability in others. In some of the latter cases, Germany, lacking a recent colonial tradition, may play a useful role, although her scope is severely restricted as the result of her own political division and her consequent vulnerability in international ventures. It cannot be denied that second-tier involvement has helped stabilize relations among third-tier powers by providing mediating services and the bare framework for multilateral dealings through such organizations as the Commonwealth. On the other hand, engagement by the second-tier powers of Eastern Europe in the third tier has been minimal. This may be explained by their inferior economic development and the absence of a colonial tradition. Insofar as the primary characteristic of the "third world" is nonalignment, relations between the latter and the first and second tier can be said to follow strictly vertical channels rather than a combination of vertical and diagonal directions.

Neither the United States nor the Soviet Union is heir to a colonial tradition in the third world comparable to that of Britain and France. As has been indicated above, superpower rivalry in the third tier has recently displayed certain elements of cooperation, especially in regard to those countries in Southeast Asia which are faced with the Chinese menace. Conversely, third-tier powers have criticized the superpower conflict situation as being a threat to peace and a hindrance to the expansion of foreign-aid commitments. At the same time, however, there is deep suspicion lest superpower cooperation assume the nature of an oligarchical collusion of the "haves" against the "have-nots." The ability of the third-tier powers, even on the rare occasions that they have acted in accord, to function as mediators in superpower conflict situations, whether in the forum of the United Nations or the Geneva Disarmament Conference, has to this date been minimal.

Now that under the impact of the nuclear equilibrium the international conflict-cooperation situation has permeated even to the lowest level of the multitiered bipolar system, and as we seem to have reached a *modo perpetuo* mechanism for creating international stability, can we still justify the continued need for NATO and other alliances? The affirmative position, which is advanced here, can be sustained only by allowing for the broadest interpretation in defining the role of alliances and by assuming that present alliances are capable of adjustment to changing international conditions. Under the "balance-of-power" system, when war constituted a legitimate instrument of policy, the mechanism of flexible and shifting alliances was required as a means of preserving members against hegemonic ambitions and supranational aspirations. The postwar bipolar system with its inherent threat of war, at a time when advanced military technology made the prevention of total war imperative, created the need for a tightly organized alliance system as a means of fortifying the deterrent. The present situation, which has been created by the nuclear equilibrium, demands new approaches and alliance functions. American alliance participation in the Western hemisphere, in SEATO, and in NATO, as a continuing asset to international peace and stability, will depend on a capacity to transform these alliances to meet the different needs of our age.

Distinct transformations can already be witnessed in the American hemispheric alliance and in SEATO. Although the Rio Pact provides the legal formula for a military alliance, moreover one which was adopted by NATO, the original concern was less with foreign aggression than with the creation of a multilateral mechanism to prevent intra-alliance conflicts and to promote good-neighbor relations. Its aim was to establish an internally oriented "security community," to use Karl Deutsch's definition, by developing formal and informal practices and institutions to allow for the expectation of peaceful change within the community over a long period.[11] The emergence of an extrahemispheric threat, which appeared subsequently and then mainly in the form of Communist subversion, provided the hegemonic power with a stimulus to transform this alliance, designed for internal peaceful adjustment, into an "Alliance for Progress" in the social and economic sphere.

The present role of the United States in SEATO reveals certain similar features, although the process of alliance formation followed from diametrically opposite directions. SEATO and CENTO members displayed neither the degree of cultural homogeneity nor the common political exposure that applied to Latin America. Their joint participation in a tier of containment that stretched from the Bosporus to the Pacific was in response to a direct threat of Communist aggression and not for reasons of forming an internal "security community." The waning of the threat of Communist aggression, as it is being interpreted, has removed the previous inhibitions and constraints of these allies and has accorded them virtually the same range for independent action, including the establishment of friendly ties with the U.S.S.R. and China, that is presently enjoyed by nonaligned third-tier powers. Yet the alliance affiliation of these powers has been retained, less for the original purpose of deterring or combatting Communist aggression than for the aim of improving their respective bargaining position for a bigger slice from U.S. foreign-aid appropriations, and possibly also with a view to enlisting American assistance in the event of bilateral conflicts with their neighbors. Thus, while the original purpose of SEATO and CENTO has all but vanished, these organizations have played an important role in furthering economic and social prog-

11 Karl Deutsch *et al., Political Community and the North Atlantic Area* (Princeton, N.J.: Princeton University Press, 1957), p. 5.

ress in the third tier. At present it would be too optimistic to foresee
the emergence of a "security community" among this diverse collection of powers whose primary focus of contact may be the competitive process of seeking the most favorable access to the American
Treasury. However, the effects of continuous exposure within an
established multinational organization, and the possibility of American mediation, cannot be discounted as a stabilizing and progressive factor in the relations among third-tier powers.

The Atlantic Alliance and the Warsaw Pact, which link the
superpowers with the majority of second-tier states, play a very different and more significant role than alliances with third-tier groupings. Certain analysts believe that the present nuclear stalemate has
removed the rationale for NATO, or, to cite the title of a recent
work, has created the End of Alliance.[12] They regard its dissolution
both as an inevitable as well as a desirable consequence. Such a
conclusion, it would seem, tends to view American and Soviet
involvement in Europe strictly in terms of their formal alliance
commitments and the presence of their military forces in the European theater. As long as there is a nuclear equilibrium between the
superpowers, Europe will continue to be regarded as the most valuable piece of strategic "real estate" next to their own territory. The
intimate strategic, economic, political, and ideological involvement
with Europe will therefore neither cease with the physical military
disengagement of American and Soviet troops from the European
area, nor will it be terminated by the formal dissolution of the alliance structure. In view of this fact, it will be necessary to examine
the possible benefits that may be drawn from the continuation of
a transformed and reformed North Atlantic Alliance, for if a *de
facto* "presence" of the superpowers in Europe is inevitable, it
would seem preferable to accommodate them in some regulated
system.

As the consequence of the nuclear stalemate there can be no
major European settlement without superpower consensus, and in
all probability it would require an even more active engagement
in the form of Soviet and American guarantees. On the other hand,
the equilibrium is of such a delicate nature and the superpowers

---

12 Ronald Steel, *The End of Alliance: America and the Future of Europe*
(New York: Viking Press, 1964).

themselves too vulnerable to allow a bilateral Soviet-American settlement of the major European issues—another Tilsit or Yalta—
without the consensus of their major European allies.

Even though the urgency of the Communist military threat and
the gravity of its ideological appeal is no longer felt in Western
Europe, as was previously the case, the enormous discrepancy in
military power between the West European states and the Soviet
Union remains constant. The European attempt to counterbalance
this discrepancy by seeking to link its military forces with the superior power of the United States represents a normal, almost intuitive
pattern of international behavior. This need to counterbalance the
superior force of their immediate Soviet neighbor would continue
to exist even if the Soviet Union should sacrifice its expansionist
Communist ideology and revert to the status of a "normal" state.
In terms of the factors of power it is therefore highly questionable
whether "with the disappearance of Communist ideology the necessity for the [NATO] pact will also disappear, and the free play of
diplomacy between nations might once again be manifest, in the
fashion of pre-1914 Europe."[13]

The West European states may already enjoy the full protective
custody of the American nuclear deterrent by virtue of the latter's
security involvement in Europe without requiring a formal alliance
framework. The latter, however, may be said to enhance the credibility of the American deterrent, as applying to Europe, insofar
as it introduces an additional factor in the enemy's computation of
risks that would have to precede any preplanned aggressive move
or confrontation. It is precisely for this reason that President de
Gaulle, who has otherwise set into motion all levers for disbanding
NATO's military integration, has repeatedly pledged his loyalty to
an Atlantic Alliance along traditional lines of cooperation.

Apart from the far-reaching political consequences that would
arise if NATO's integrated military structure were to be sacrificed,
the Gaullist position, which settles for a minimum security insurance at the lowest political premium, suffers because it envisages

---

[13] Jean-Baptiste Duroselle, "De Gaulle's Designs for Europe and the West,"
in Arnold Wolfers (ed.), *Changing East-West Relations and the Unity of the
West* (Baltimore, Md.: The Johns Hopkins Press, 1964), p. 186.

war in Europe strictly in terms of a preplanned Soviet attack. In fact, this argument tends to focus on the least likely contingency. The relative stability of the nuclear stalemate might encourage the Soviet Union to exploit whatever limited sectors of strategic maneuverability remain. This could take the form of probing actions on NATO's flanks. More likely, however, confrontations in Europe will not arise as the result of preplanned military engagements that are being controlled and invoked by the superpowers. Military confrontations are more likely to arise out of local and spontaneous incidents, political emergencies such as unrest in East Germany, or a conflict precipitated by one of the European allies in the "licentious" spirit of its regained freedom of action.

Political stability is largely derived from a genuine settlement of issues and an appropriate adjustment of power. The Congress of Vienna stands as a model settlement of this nature. The political settlement of Europe has remained in a state of animated suspension since World War II. The image of stability has been sustained by the permafrost conditions of the Cold War, but it rests on a shaky political foundation, which has left unresolved the status of Berlin, the unification of Germany, the latter's frontiers with Poland, the boundaries and relations of the East European states with one another and with Moscow, as well as their future political and social structure.

Europe cannot therefore be pictured as a future conflict-free zone. Conflicts arising from the above-mentioned conditions would, at least in their initial phase, be limited and conventional. Western counter-response should therefore be in the same currency. The peace-time creation of allied forces-in-being and of an integrated planning staff represents one of NATO's greatest achievements. The integration of conventional military forces may be regarded as a concession to the demands of modern conventional warfare, since striking power and mobility have rendered obsolete traditional alliance behavior, which relied on a minimum of staff planning, while postponing the coordination or integration of forces, commands, and infrastructures until the event of hostilities. It is, indeed, an irony of history that the country that twice in a generation has been overrun by hostile forces, precisely because traditional alliance methods proved inadequate, should now be the principal advocate for the regression to traditional military patterns.

If integration of the conventional forces in the central sector of Europe were to be disbanded, this might either lead to a complete renunciation of a conventional military option despite the possibility of limited conflicts, and would be accompanied by mounting pressure from Germany and other allies to duplicate the French strategic rationale of treating an independent nuclear force as a substitute for an integrated conventional defense posture, or, in a specialization of functions, it could relegate to Germany exclusive responsibility for a conventional defense option in Western Europe. The latter would demand a considerable increase in the size of the present Bundeswehr. Both options would exert an extremely negative effect on the relaxation of tensions and on stability in Europe.

In this respect the continuation of NATO and of an integrated conventional defense option may be seen as fulfilling important stabilization and "control" functions in relation to Germany.[14] The term "controlling" functions should not be interpreted in the negative sense of keeping Germany under lock and key, although originally the realization of the potential controlling effects of military integration facilitated Germany's entry into NATO. Alliance thinking along these lines would nowadays be outdated and unwarranted. However, it cannot be denied that by playing an active role in the integrated planning and command functions of NATO, German strategic thinking and actions would tend to assimilate and reflect a collective or corporate rather than a purely national outlook. Furthermore, it should be realized that her division has made Germany politically the most exposed of the NATO allies, while her geography has left her strategically the most vulnerable one. The firm absorption of Germany within an integrated allied defense structure that can satisfy her very real security concerns, therefore, constitutes the best insurance against unilateral German military

---

[14] The use of alliances as a means of controlling or influencing the policy of other powers is a well-established principle which Bismarck applied with consummate skill. The value of the Triple Alliance to Germany lay less in Italy's military contribution than in the opportunity it offered to Bismarck to help prevent a conflict between Italy and Austria-Hungary. In the same manner, the Three Emperors' League served German diplomacy by helping to avoid a confrontation between Vienna and St. Petersburg.

measures that must appear provocative to her eastern neighbors and risky to her allies. The presence of integrated NATO forces on German soil acts as a *cordon sanitaire* that guards her against foreign threats and protects her against herself in the event of provocative developments in East Germany, where the human bonds might break the shackles of reason and thus create the temptation for a precipitate intervention.

In the same light, the joint Atlantic Alliance framework still seems to constitute the best means of satisfying the security and prestige needs of such allies as Germany and Italy. This could be achieved by providing for their legitimate and active participation in the formulation of strategy, in nuclear-planning functions, and in crisis management, without having to resort to physical proliferation. Whether the present selective-nuclear-study committee, which originated from the proposal that Defense Secretary McNamara made to the meeting of NATO Defense Ministers in May, 1965, will arrive at an acceptable solution cannot yet be predicted. It does, however, represent a more imaginative and realistic approach to the planning and control problem of nuclear weapons than MLF contraptions. A solution along these lines would deny to allies like Germany unilateral physical control over nuclear weapons and thus offers no absolute guarantee that nuclear weapons will be used in their defense. But it does considerably enhance the capacity of these allies to "condition" American strategic behavior to react along the desired lines. This is essentially a problem of strategy and should not be advanced as a legal test case for sovereignty, for in the nuclear age, "sovereignty, rather than [being] a reservoir which can be only full or empty, is a divisible nexus of powers of which some may be kept, some limited, some lost."[15]

If conceived along these lines, NATO loses its apparent attributes as an alliance with vested interests in retaining the Cold War climate and displays a capacity for stabilizing the nuclear equilibrium through its prospective proliferation control functions and for stimulating the dynamics of a relaxation of tensions between

[15] Stanley Hoffmann, "International Systems and International Law," in Klaus Knorr and Sidney Verba (eds.), *The International System* (Princeton, N.J.: Princeton University Press, 1961), p. 235.

the two parts of Europe by accommodating Germany's security needs, and in consequence those of Eastern Europe.

The superpowers cannot share the gains of the nuclear equilibrium while denying its benefits from affecting their European allies. Rather than trying to halt the process of change set into motion by the nuclear stalemate, the United States and the Soviet Union would be better advised to seek to influence and guide this process in a positive and stabilizing manner from within the existing, though changing, multilateral alliance forum. Second-tier stability is a precondition to the unimpaired function of the nuclear equilibrium, while the very existence of the nuclear stalemate produces centrifugal forces in the behavior of allies that exert a destabilizing effect on the former. This predicament could best be resolved through the continued cooperation and coordination of policy in a multilateral forum such as NATO, which can link first- and second-tier powers.

Some of NATO's functions stem from strictly internal alliance needs and may play no direct or visible role in East-West relations. One is the need for multilateral organizations and international clearing-house functions among a group of industrially advanced countries in the North Atlantic region which are experiencing a proliferation of contacts and transactions. This includes the need for the uninterrupted process of joint consultation, analysis, and information, as has evolved in the practice of the NATO Council. It is a requirement that exists even apart from security concerns and may be regarded as having "professionalized" the conduct of international affairs in response to the complexities of modern demands.

Secondly, the process of multilateral consultation and information as a matter of habit in place of the more formal ordinary bilateral interstate relationships has been helpful in ameliorating the political liability caused by the discrepancy of power that exists between the United States and her allies. While the multilateral approach has not always been successful, it has made the rank members better informed in addition to strengthening their capacity to exert influence on other members, including the United States, on East-West relations, and in the international community at large. Furthermore, this multilateral association with the United States within the NATO framework, by preserving their self-esteem and search for identity, has better satisfied distinct psychological needs of allies than purely formal bilateral contacts.

It must also be realized that the centrifugal forces released in the alliance as the result of the general political and military relaxation under the nuclear stalemate have evoked the specter of renewed intra-alliance conflicts and military confrontations, as for example between Greece and Turkey. The cohesive element of joint consultation and the Secretary-General's potential role as mediator give NATO an important function in preserving intra-alliance peace and stability, which is a prerequisite for general security in Europe.

In addition to satisfying some of the internal needs within the Atlantic region, there exists a very distinct demand for the continuation of the Atlantic Alliance within the context of changing East-West relations. For one, the multilateral framework of the alliance might eventually prove to be a fruitful source for devising and coordinating plans in the field of arms control in Europe. Whatever form an eventual arms-control agreement or military-safety mechanism for Europe might assume, superpower guarantees and inspection measures by members of both alliances will be required. Insofar as the core of such agreements would be anchored in the two parts of Germany, Poland, and Czechoslovakia, considerable benefit might be drawn from a solution that would involve as policing agents not only the countries most immediately concerned but which would aim for a degree of balance by introducing "alliance neutrals"—if that paradoxical term may be used—that is to say, countries like Canada and Norway for NATO and Romania for the Warsaw Pact, because of their ability to display a greater degree of psychological and geographic aloofness and objectivity.

The continuation of the superpower dialogue is a prerequisite for the continuation of the limited nuclear *détente*. At the moment this dialogue is being obstructed, though not entirely interrupted, by the conflict in Vietnam. A considerable responsibility, therefore, falls on other allies of the second tier to assist in bridging this gap. In relation to the predicament in Vietnam, countries like Canada and Poland, which combine the advantages of expertise in that area with those of military noninvolvement, can contribute substantially in preserving the fluidity of the superpower dialogue. However, their influence is very largely derived from their respective membership in NATO and the Warsaw Pact, combined with their special bilateral ties with the two superpowers.

Finally, there remains the very important alliance function of coordinating the recent proliferation of bilateral East-West contacts. The specialization of functions in East-West contacts according to the choice and capability of individual alliance members has achieved far more effective results than those which could have been reached by a corporate NATO advance. However, the continuation of NATO's clearing-house operations in the field of consultation, coordination, and information exchange remains imperative if these complex bilateral contacts and aims are to be brought to a fruitful synthesis without producing conflicting and counterproductive results or intra-alliance disputes and suspicions. To proceed otherwise by tackling the complex subject of an East-West *détente,* of arms control measures, and of an all-European solution in the spirit of competitive sovereign isolation without the benefit of alliance co-ordination would be self-defeating and dangerous. Joint participation in NATO's policy information and coordination or adjustment functions should be regarded as an automatic contrapuntal rather than an inhibiting factor in the process of bilateral specialization in East-West contacts, and should not be seen as a barrier to the emergence of selective multilateral undertakings that would involve some but not all alliance members. The latter might take the form of "a broadly-conceived proposal for an all-European economic cooperation plan [that] should be addressed to the East," with the aim of creating "an enduring fabric of international stability."[16]

Even without the unilateral initiative taken by General de Gaulle, the Atlantic Alliance is bound to be subjected to major conceptual and structural changes. The number of members is unlikely to increase and might well diminish. Countries like Denmark and Norway, which have normalized their relations with Moscow, may, in the light of diminishing East-West tensions and with fading memories of the failure of their previous policy of neutrality, prefer to exchange NATO membership for participation in a neutral

[16] Zbigniew K. Brzezinski, "American Globalism," *Survey,* No. 58 (January, 1966), p. 28.

Scandinavian bloc together with Sweden. In the same manner, other NATO flank powers, such as Turkey, perhaps in protest over Cyprus, may eventually prefer to substitute friendly bilateral relations with the Soviet Union for NATO membership. This need not, however, be interpreted as an inherent incompatibility of the two roles. Portugal was originally admitted to NATO for strategic reasons that no longer apply. Her colonial policy and the nature of her regime are often of considerable embarrassment to the other allies and constitute a distinct political liability in their relations with the third tier. While it might be difficult to demand Portugal's withdrawal in 1969, other NATO members might serve firm notice that in their relations with third-tier powers and their conduct in the United Nations they will feel under no compulsion to support or condone Lisbon's colonial policy. This in itself might lead to the voluntary withdrawal of the latter. On the other hand, it should not be overlooked that Portugal's separation would deprive the alliance of whatever influence it still enjoys in restraining Portuguese policy.

Secondly, under the impact of re-emerging diversities within the alliance, it may be necessary to sacrifice the present emphasis on the principle of universal consensus, which has been achieved at the price of finding it at the lowest common denominator, in favor of consensus within a smaller forum. In other words, within the otherwise loosening framework of the alliance, certain members might find it necessary to assume special commitments and to participate in selective engagements without insisting on universal participation. This trend may already be reflected in the voluntarily restricted participation in the present nuclear study subcommittees. This approach would duplicate NATO's own emergence from the ranks of the U.N., when the latter organization failed to satisfy the security needs of the Atlantic powers, and the process of crystallization of the "Inner Six" from the more universal but less cohesive Council of Europe. In neither case did the members of the new group withdraw from the parent organization, nor was the latter negatively affected by this process.

Under these circumstances, NATO might assume the shape of concentric circles of specialized-role functions. Countries in the outside layer, such as France, would retain their formal alliance commitments and the pledge to cooperate during a conflict, while continuing to participate in the political discussions of the NATO Council. But they would neither play an active role in the peacetime military integration of the conventional defense forces in Europe nor participate in multilateral nuclear-sharing agreements. The second circle would be composed of those allies who regard the maintenance of an integrated defense posture in the central sector of Europe as an essential strategic requirement.[17] Still other members might seek to gain greater influence over questions of nuclear strategy and crisis management, as well as greater access to American technological information, by joining a nuclear committee with planning and certain executive functions in that field. A concentric alliance participation is far from an ideal solution, but it does provide a degree of balance between the need for integrated defense forces and multilateral nuclear planning and the growing elements of diversity, while preserving the over-all political consultative mechanism of the alliance.

The necessity for changes in the concepts and functions of the Atlantic Alliance has been promoted by intra-alliance evolution, in the form of West European economic recovery and political stability, and by the altered pattern of East-West relations, as derived from the nuclear stalemate, the Sino-Soviet conflict, and the economic progress of the East European states. There is little evidence that NATO exists merely because its original founders see a vested interest in its perpetuation.[18] Similarly, the emergence of the East-West *détente* tends to contradict the claim that NATO willfully obstructs such a *détente* by preserving a Cold War climate.

Under the impact of the nuclear equilibrium, the North Atlantic

[17] Even if Canada were to withdraw her present ground- and air-force commitments from Europe, her continued role in the Allied Mobile Flank Force would still place her in this second circle. Furthermore, if she were to withdraw her forces from Europe, or if these were to be transformed to a denuclearized role, Canada might remain a member of the inner nuclear sanctorum as long as she maintained a nuclear role in the defense of the North American continent either by adopting responsibility for antinuclear submarine functions or by participating in an eventual large-scale antimissile program.

[18] Of the principal founding fathers, Prime Minister Pearson, whose creative leadership and flexible statesmanship in NATO policy can hardly be challenged, is the last one who still holds a major political office. The other founding members have either died, or they have retired from office and restrict their ventures into politics to writing memoirs and the occasional article in *Foreign Affairs*.

Alliance is faced with the enormous task of reconciling the requirements for stability with the dynamic and centrifugal tendencies in the behavior of allies, of finding a balance between allied demands for a larger role in nuclear decision-making without incurring the risk of proliferation, of satisfying Germany's political and security aspirations without violating the security of her eastern neighbors, and of reaping the fruits of bilateral contacts without sacrificing the benefits of joint consultation and cooperation. If NATO were to master this task, the benefits would not merely be restricted to alliance members but might even extend to the Communist states in Eastern Europe. So far, Soviet policy has taken no official recognition of this factor, and NATO continues to be the target of her most vitriolic attacks. In all probability Soviet policy in this respect does not follow so much from the dictates of her own pathological fear toward NATO as from the expedient of manipulating the latter as a means of retaining the loyalties of her East European allies and for justifying her own military presence in that area. Certain changes of attitude, however, may be discerned in a country like Poland, which could justly regard herself as the primary target of any aggressive move by NATO, if such a threat did in fact exist. Recently two Polish writers have critically examined that aspect of General de Gaulle's policy, which seeks to eliminate superpower involvement in Europe.[19] This policy was regarded as being detrimental to East European security and stability. The argument may be interpreted as implicitly approving of America's military presence in Europe and thus also of the existence of NATO, under whose multilateral auspices this presence may be retained.

Given the conditions of the nuclear stalemate and the altered context of East-West relations, the industrialized and interdependent first- and second-tier powers on either side can neither dispense entirely with the security payoff and the political functions of alliances, nor will they be able to assign to these organizations unrestricted freedom to dictate policy. The shift of emphasis from alliances whose function lay in the conduct of war to interde-

19 Edmund Osmanczyk, *Polityka* (*Politics;* Warsaw), May 5, 1965; and Ludwik Debinski, *Tygodnik powszechny* (*General weekly;* Warsaw), April 11, 1965, and August 29, 1965. Cited in Adam Bromke, "Poland and France: The Sentimental Friendship," *East Europe,* February, 1966, pp. 13–14.

pendent regional associations whose aim is the deterrence of war, coupled with the need to perform political clearing-house activities among a group of industrially advanced states, is transforming traditional military alliances into international communities. "What thermonuclear weapons have rendered obsolete," writes Raymond Aron, "are not alliances but alliances of the traditional type. . . . Alliances will either evolve toward communities or else dissolve altogether; they will certainly not revert to their pre-atomic prototypes."[20] The task of re-forming traditional alliances into communities is one of agonizing complexity. Drawing on his inexhaustible supply of epigrams, Raymond Aron notes that "this world of growing complexity promises to be a paradise for analysts and a hell for statesmen."[21] This may be so. More likely, however, both statesmen and analysts will jointly find themselves neither in paradise nor in hell but in the purgatory of restored reality. For the latter, this involves a confrontation with agonizing complexities rather than a scholastic redefinition of predetermined positions, while for the former, it means the exchange of a sterile political and ideological litany for the channels of laborious but creative diplomacy.

---

[20] Raymond Aron, *The Great Debate: Theories of Nuclear Strategy* (Garden City, N.Y.: Doubleday & Co., 1965), pp. 262–63.

[21] Aron, "On Polycentrism," *Survey*, No. 58 (January, 1966), p. 18.

5. Canada's Role in East-West Relations

PAUL MARTIN

ANY CANADIAN who is aware of the far-reaching changes in the nature of world politics taking place during this decade is bound to ask himself whether Canada's position is affected by them for good or ill. So far have these changes gone that it is even legitimate to ask whether there still exists such a thing as "East-West relations." Is there still a contest between two camps, each arrayed around one of the superpowers, with a mass of nonaligned nations looking on, sometimes on the sidelines, sometimes caught in the cross-fire?

A few years ago this was the world scene. The expression "East-West relations" in practice covered everything of real importance in international affairs. That bipolarity has gone, and we find ourselves today in a much more complicated political and economic and military environment. In such a situation of relative fluidity it is clear that the smaller powers, including Canada, have greater scope both for the pursuit of their own national interests, which

are unique by definition, and for the exercise of constructive initiative in search of solutions to problems of concern to the world as
a whole.

This scope I intend to explore. In doing so, I shall argue that the
growth of pluralism does not necessarily mean the dissolution of
"East" and "West" as we have known them, but rather the adoption
by the Soviet Union and the Communist states closest to it (China,
with its friends, is perhaps another matter) of a pattern of international relations similar to that of the rest of the world. This I
believe is likely to be accompanied by the gradual abandonment in
practice of world revolution as an instrument of the policy of Communist states. The end result of this tendency, if it is maintained,
would not necessarily be the disappearance of rivalry between the
Communist and non-Communist worlds, but the removal of that
rivalry from the sphere of ideology and related military moves to a
more rational and stable plane.

It is on such a plane that Canada can best play a creative role.
But how close are we to it? Clearly we have not yet reached a point
of stable international balance, let alone international harmony.
Evolution in that direction has gone perhaps far enough to demand
adaptation of our policies, but we must not confuse identification
of a tendency with its fulfillment.

Let us examine the nature of that evolution as it affects the Communist world. It is essential to define one's own view of that evolution before suggesting the policy implications for Canada and other
Western countries. The monolithic unity of the Stalin era is obviously long gone. The Sino-Soviet rift seems irreparable, short of a
profound change of policy amounting to a *de facto* surrender by
one side or the other to the ascendancy of its rival. The rift has
given leverage to certain East European Communist countries, notably Romania, and some non-ruling Communist parties, in enlarg-
ing somewhat the area of their independence from Soviet control.

This independence is real, if as yet sharply limited. It extends to
some national cultural expression, with affirmation of its distinct-
ness, especially from that of Russia; to some economic autonomy,
with assertion of national control over planning; to a degree of
divergency over political issues within the Communist world; and
to the development of intellectual and trade relations with the

West. But it is to be noted that this independence stops short of any significant departure from the general line of Communist policy toward the non-Communist world. The most that can be said is that, having fewer resources and fewer vested interests elsewhere in the world than the Soviet Union itself, the East European countries are able to reap many of the advantages of the strategy of peaceful coexistence in its positive aspects, while avoiding serious involvement in those aspects that entail risks of conflicts with the West, and specifically the strategy of wars of national liberation.

This is by no means the same as saying that the political unity of the Soviet camp has been seriously undermined. Neither the East European leaders, nor still less the Soviet Union, are prepared to allow that. The East European leaders seek to enlist for themselves the same support the regimes in the Soviet Union and Yugoslavia enjoy, through the same appeal to nationalist sentiment which those regimes can make. Originally imposed from outside by Soviet bayonets, they are trying within the limits of adherence to the basic tenets of Marxist ideology to legitimize themselves by identifying their regimes with national interests, as far as they can. Because of their economic insufficiencies the most pressing of these interests are economic. The profound differences between a highly industrialized country like Czechoslovakia and a relatively backward one like Bulgaria require a variety of economic policies; reform is dictated by economic necessity in one country, while another can continue with the same command machinery sanctified in the primitive prewar economy of the U.S.S.R. Variations of economic approach require elbow room, which is attainable only within a more flexible relationship with each other and with the U.S.S.R. But there is no necessary correlation between economic reform and political reform domestically, nor between variety of economic system and variety of political approach to the outside world.

Romania, for example, has led the movement against uniformity and coordination in the economic field, and remains the least tractable of Soviet allies in inter-Communist relations. But it is still among the more politically rigid of the East European countries, and has shown no inclination to embark on the extensive reconstruction of its economy which Czechoslovakia or East Germany have undertaken. East Germany, which remains in effect a Soviet colony, was the first Communist regime (apart from Yugoslavia) to launch such reforms. But in its attempt to create the illusion of a genuine identity it has emphasized above all those features of Communism that give it its bleak distinctiveness. Hungary and Czechoslovakia, loyal allies of the U.S.S.R. in foreign and inter-Communist affairs, have adopted internally a course of economical as well as political relaxation.

Clearly, therefore, polycentrism in the Warsaw Pact area has not destroyed either the cohesiveness or the essential Communism of the regimes. This is not surprising. The appeal to national sentiment was never intended to achieve this result. On the contrary, by attempting to strengthen the domestic position of the regimes its basic aim was to consolidate their existing alignment, and this because the ultimate endurance of those regimes depends upon the support of the Soviet Union. All the signs point to precisely this strengthening: the substitution of an elastic and therefore resilient form of unity for a rigid and therefore brittle discipline. The Council for Mutual Economic Assistance, which was visualized by Khrushchev as a supernational coodinating agency, approving plans and assigning tasks ostensibly in the general interest, has never achieved such authority. Instead there is a network of bilateral economic commissions linking each of the East European countries to the U.S.S.R. and to each other. In a comparable way, the political pattern of the past, when East European Party and Government leaders were summoned to Moscow to receive directives from the "leader of the Socialist camp," has given way to frequent exchanges of visits among the Soviet and other Party heads. By this means we may assume policy is carried forward through consultation. The Russians' own term, "socialist commonwealth," may perhaps be taking on substance.

Although we have no direct evidence on the subject, it is reasonable to suppose that the development of this process, however successful it may be in its results, has not taken place without a certain reluctance on the part of the Soviet Union. The U.S.S.R. is not only very much the most powerful of the Communist countries, having a background of authoritarianism in all spheres of life; it is itself the creator of the regimes allied to it, and bears the ultimate responsibility for the advancement of the cause on which to a greater or lesser degree they all depend for their credibility. An illustration of the continuing adherence of East European leaderships to the common cause appeared in the Czechoslovak Party organ *Rudé právo (Red Justice)* on the occasion of the 10th Anniversary of the Twentieth Party Congress of the CPSU. According to *Rudé právo,* the positive program of that Congress has been distorted by "revisionism and radical criticism." The West, which expected de-Stalinization to turn into liberalization, should have learned a lesson from the Hungarian events of 1956, but still hopes for "ideological erosion" to break down the commitment of Czechoslovakia to the principles enunciated by the CPSU. These hopes, it says, are vain.[1]

It is worth examining at this point the question of ideology and its importance in the Communist world. This is not purely an academic question, but is close to the heart of most of the problems with which the rest of the world must cope in its dealings with the Communist countries. It is sometimes held that ideology is some kind of blueprint according to which all Communist governments construct their policy, whether it be a subtle scheme of world domination or an exchange of chamber orchestras. At the other extreme it is (allegedly more realistically) argued that ideology is nothing more than a set of incantations, empty of substance and used only in *post hoc* justification of policies already adopted for more concrete reasons. Both views are equally misleading. The dichotomy between ideology and policy is false. In fact, ideology is a motive, an instrument, and a justification of the policy of Communist governments, but it is not the only one. At various times it may be more or less flexible, and its flexibility, the extent to which it will be adapted or revised, will be determined by a whole series of other factors, ranging from the psychological to the political, economic, and geographical circumstances in which a particular group of Communist leaders find themselves.

How does this relate to the external policy of Communist states? Among Communist states, the pluralism of which I have spoken is obvious evidence of the capacity of Communist ideology to adapt itself to changing circumstances. The acknowledgment that there is

---

[1] *Rudé právo* (Prague), February 16, 1966.

more than one road to socialism has been extracted from the Soviet leadership by difficult stages, and until recent years only painfully. Yugoslavia in 1948, and even more, Hungary in 1956, show just how painfully. The acknowledgment once made, however, its consequences have multiplied. The old concept of one universal truth good for all times and places has had to be abandoned where it can neither be maintained nor even, as in most of Africa and Asia, imposed in the first place. We have instead the situation, unbelievable ten years ago, of *Pravda* bestowing a blessing on non-Communist parties in the third world, on "African Socialism," which had been roundly denounced as recently as 1962 as a fraud, and of the imposition by the CPSU of a policy on Arab Communists at the end of 1964 which obliged them to accept the liquidation of their own parties and to join instead as individuals the ruling nationalist single parties in their respective countries.

But this policy does not represent a nonideological or anti-ideological departure as a result of some putative conflict between ideology and the national interest of the U.S.S.R. I shall not, except indirectly, go into the ideological justification for it. It is more instructive to look at the motivation, and the extent to which it may be adjudged ideological.

The West in general is well content if countries in Africa and Asia remain independent and nonaligned. After a few disastrous experiences the U.S.S.R. has decided that nothing is to be gained by direct attempts at communization. Its policy has evolved in at least three distinct phases during the post-Stalin era. In the first four or five years up to 1959, the major thrust was toward the exploitation of anticolonialism by direct external support of the new governments, without much concern about their domestic policies, in the belief that aid would have a decisive effect on their policies. Anti-Communist measures taken in 1958–59, both in the U.A.R. and in India were a clear demonstration that this would not work, and the sudden emergence of large numbers of independent African states in 1960–61 made it imperative to devise a new approach. This was that of the "national democracy," wherein the "most advanced section of the working class," i.e., the Communists, where they existed, should ally themselves and cooperate with the nationalist ruling party in order to press on with the revolution, which had only begun with the achievement of political independence.

Unfortunately for this line, only one or two of those countries in which the nationalists displayed really radical militancy were equipped with Communist parties, and they showed no particular anxiety to accept the Communists, who, as in Algeria, had done little or nothing to contribute to the achievement of independence, as allies. The others were certainly not prepared to allow the formation of Communist parties which would tend to divide a national unity that was often hard won. Accordingly the policy changed again. The third phase, which emerged during 1963, after the outlawing of the Algerian Communist Party, was that of liquidationism—the decision that Communists should work from within to promote the economic revolution, put their countries on the "noncapitalist path," and eventually succeed to the leadership.

Here we have an evolution away from a situation in which the U.S.S.R. worked in a largely nonideological fashion through the cultivation of direct contacts with Afro-Asian governments regardless of their internal policy. The present Soviet policy, although it was arrived at under the pressure of tactical necessity, is nevertheless based firmly on an ideological preconception: that social evolution of a noncapitalist kind is bound to be toward the Communist pattern; that the logic of history, in short, will lead the countries of the Third World one by one into the Communist camp.

I have dwelt on the ideological question because I wanted to bring out this point. Ideological presuppositions determine policy choices both in Communist countries and the West. The main difference is that our ideology—or ideologies—are a good deal less constricting in the choices they permit us to perceive, or to make when we do perceive them. Bound by their "scientific" world view, the Communists, whether Soviet or Chinese in orientation, are united in believing that nonalignment is a historical dead end. The U.S.S.R. holds that it is a way station on the road from colonialism to Communism. The Chinese reject it out of hand as impossible. In practice this does not prevent them from welcoming the rejection of Western alignment which it entails, but they do so *faute de mieux*. The difference between the two is an aspect of their different approaches to the question of peaceful coexistence.

Any discussion of relations between the Communist states and the West hinges on the meaning of peaceful coexistence. The Soviet Union is fond of saying that its policy has always been one of peaceful coexistence, ever since the days of Lenin. This is not helpful, since the claim that Soviet policy has been consistent over the last half century is hardly to be taken seriously. But if, as I have tried to show, pluralism among the members of the Warsaw Pact has stopped short of disrupting their political and ideological cohesion, and if, as the evidence of its policy indicates, the Soviet Union anticipates a continuing evolution of the Third World toward this united "socialist commonwealth," we have identified two of the pillars on which the structure of peaceful coexistence as it is now understood in the U.S.S.R. rests. The third is the struggle of the proletariat of the industrially developed countries of the West for the creation of a Communist system, a fantasy on which we need not waste time, since it is of no great importance to the theory of peaceful coexistence, although it is an ideological element in the Sino-Soviet dispute.

From the Soviet Union's point of view, therefore, it is meaningful to speak of "East-West relations" and meaningful to discuss the manner in which they should be carried on. I would like to explore what sort of relationship the Soviet Union and its allies (now they can no longer properly be called satellites) believe themselves to be conducting with us. A recent article in the main Soviet theoretical journal, *Kommunist,* stated:

> Peaceful coexistence of states with different social systems implies struggle but excludes war between states. Peace has been preserved and strengthened as a result of the growth of the might of the U.S.S.R., of the world system of socialism, the development of the international working class and Communist movement, and the strengthening of its alliance with the national liberation movement and all anti-imperialist forces.[2]

There are the three bases to which I referred. This is a familiar formula. Does it fit the pattern of Soviet policy as we see it unfolding now? Broadly, I think it does. The ingredients are all there.

[2] V. Golikov, "Vital Principle of Leninist Foreign Policy," *Kommunist* (*Communist,* Moscow), No. 18 (December, 1965).

Let me try to sort them out. The first point about peaceful coexistence is obviously that it excludes war *between states*. The Soviet leaders make much of their people's horror of war and their determination that the catastrophe of a third world war must be avoided. They are right to do so. The implication that these sentiments are somehow more their property than other peoples', and are not shared by "ruling circles" in the West, is a propaganda line not reflected in the policies they actually pursue. It is reasonable to say, then, that, like ourselves, the Soviet leaders will not knowingly embark on a course likely to lead to serious risks of nuclear war. We can, I think, discount such unpleasant voices from the past as that of Marshal Chuikov, Chief of Soviet Civil Defense, who declared as recently as February, 1966, that if a nuclear war took place, it would "lead to the final collapse of capitalism as a socio-economic formation and the victory of the new, progressive socialist system."[3] Such a collapse does not in fact seem to figure among the immediate objectives that Soviet policy is designed to promote.

We can take the Soviet formula at face value; war *between states* is to be avoided. Other forms of war, namely wars of national liberation, are not, and in fact form an integral part of the policy of peaceful coexistence. The reasoning behind this is that the power of the Soviet Union and its allies is now such as to deter any attack by the "imperialists" on them. The existence of this power, it is claimed, both encourages revolutionary forces elsewhere to struggle for their freedom and inhibits the deployment of the full strength of "imperialism" against them. The support of the Communist camp will ensure the success of that struggle and the magnetism of its economic success will draw the liberated peoples inevitably into the Communist orbit.

There is no reason to doubt that this is what the Soviet leaders expect to happen, indeed believe is happening. Their justification of the current form of the policy of peaceful coexistence against its critics, notably the Chinese, lays emphasis on its militant aspects, and the execution of the policy itself, paradoxically enough at present, requires a more militant approach marginally in order to buttress the central premise that the success of Communism in the long term can come about through peaceful means.

3 *Sovietskaya Rossiya* (*Soviet Russia;* Moscow), February 12, 1966.

The strategy of national liberation war is an integral part of peaceful coexistence, as the Soviet Union sees it. The success claimed for it justifies the policy whereby the Soviet Union can benefit from the advantages of a peaceful relationship (more or less close—as the years since 1960 have shown) with the West, while the cause of world revolution progresses more or less by its own momentum. The parallel with Stalin's policy, whereby the prime duty of all other Communists was to contribute to the defense and development of the U.S.S.R., comes readily to mind. There is no particular reason, however, to think that the U.S.S.R. has a consistent policy toward violent revolutionary outbreaks, or necessarily has a hand in them when they occur. This is a matter of tactics. Thus the support, measured though it is, which the Soviet Government has given to North Vietnam and the NLF of South Vietnam since the end of 1964 differs from the relative indifference shown by Khrushchev before his fall, and differs again from the apparent reluctance of the Soviet Union to encourage armed insurgency in Latin America. In each case, however, confidence in eventual Communist victory underlies the approach adopted. There is no disposition to exploit crises in areas where the U.S.S.R. might become directly and dangerously involved in the consequences, no inclination to force the pace in areas where Communist influence may be expected to grow without incurring the risks of a violent upheaval.

But whatever tactics the Soviet Union may employ in a particular situation, its present leadership asserts that "coexistence is indivisible." This slogan, used in criticism of U.S. Vietnam policy, is put forward as a warning that the United States cannot expect good relations with the U.S.S.R. while it is carrying on a war with another Communist country. Its meaning in fact goes beyond that. What the slogan means is precisely what it says: Coexistence is not an acceptable policy for the Soviet Union if "national-liberation struggles" as it understands them cannot be carried on.

It is reasonable to ask why the U.S.S.R. should want to tie itself to revolutionary movements in various parts of the world which it cannot always control and which might embroil it in conflicts with Western countries with which it is in its own best interests to cultivate normal relations. The question has the more force in terms of the Soviet leaders' own claim that the strength of the Soviet camp is the decisive factor in the world today, and that history is in any case carrying one nation after another toward a common Communist future. If they believe this to be the state of the world, and if, as I have argued, ideological formulations like this do reflect the basic attitudes of those making Soviet policy, why does not the U.S.S.R. employ its strength as a superpower in such a way as to lubricate the wheels of history, perhaps, but otherwise concentrate on the immediate advantages of peaceful coexistence?

In part the answer is that this is precisely what it is doing. The general line as at present pursued by the Soviet Union does give priority to the direct exercise of state power in international relations over its indirect exercise through support and manipulation of national-liberation struggles. Having greater power than China, the Soviet Union is less dependent on the exploitation of such struggles to promote its objectives than is China. It might be added that in view of the recent lack of success of Chinese policy, which gives priority to the national-liberation struggle as a weapon against "imperialism," and the general unpredictability and complexity of national-liberation movements, there seems in any case to be little incentive for the Soviet Union to put much reliance on them. The constructive and skillful exercise of diplomacy at Tashkent advanced the Soviet Union's cause in a manner that does it credit. If this approach were to come to typify Soviet foreign policy, we should have less to fear from its advancement. This is certainly the most striking example we have yet seen of the Soviet use of state power for peaceful purposes.

Another part of the answer is that official Soviet doctrine holds that as a corollary of the decisive strength of the Communist world in the present stage of international relations, the "imperialist" world has gone over to the counteroffensive. Seeing their power inexorably slipping away from them, the "imperialists" are said to be turning desperately to military means to retain it. It is in these terms that events in the Congo, the Dominican Republic, Vietnam, and sometimes Indonesia are accounted for. In these circumstances, the U.S.S.R. maintains that it has no choice, it is its "sacred duty" to give moral and material assistance to "peoples fighting for freedom and independence." The mix of moral with material, as we have seen, varies nevertheless according to the overriding interests of the U.S.S.R.

Finally, and this is a point of very special interest, the U.S.S.R. and its allies are inhibited from acknowledging the primacy of their national interests as states over the world-revolutionary role they have traditionally assumed. This inhibition goes very deep. In the words of Raymond Aron, the Soviet Union "does not wish to disavow the ideocratic nature of its state, nor can it do so. It will not admit to being a state 'like any other State,' with national interests, for this would undermine the foundations of the regime."[4]

Here we are back at the question of the role of ideology in Soviet policy. From the very beginning, its first and major function has been legitimization; the Soviet regime rests its claim to the exclusive loyalty of its people fundamentally on its revolutionary mission, and this has been preached incessantly for nearly fifty years. Unable to maintain with any hope of success that Soviet society is yet the best of all possible societies in a material sense, it has relied ultimately on its claim to moral superiority, and this has meant its claim to be fighting for the oppressed of all the world. The problem may become less acute as the material well-being of the Soviet people improves—and material incentives seem now to have won the long struggle with moral incentives as the main lever of economic growth inside the U.S.S.R. But this is another paradox. At precisely the time when the system no longer seems to require revolutionary zeal as a mainstay, it finds itself the more dependent on it. Without the revolutionary ethic, the maintenance of Party spirit and of ideological rectitude becomes an impossible task. And without these, the very authority of the Party, on which the whole structure of the regime is built, would be dangerously weakened. Hence the importance of what might be termed "surrogate revolutions" in Soviet domestic propaganda. As the revolutionary era of the U.S.S.R. itself slips into the past and popular ardor cools, the regime seeks increasingly to keep the spirit alive by identification first with Cuba, then with Vietnam.

It may thus be argued that the continuance of the Soviet system in its traditional form depends upon the maintenance of at least

4 Raymond Aron, "On Polycentrism," *Survey*, No. 58 (January, 1966).

the appearance of world revolutionary leadership. And appearance might be enough, were it not for the determination of the Chinese to expose what they consider the betrayal of the world revolutionary cause by the revisionism of the Soviet leaders. This challenge the Soviet Union finds intolerable, and this is the remaining reason, and some would argue the most compelling reason, why the U.S.S.R. at this time cannot consult only that national interest which seems to dictate an accommodation with the West, but must continue, in deeds as well as words, to try to make good its claim to leadership of a world revolutionary movement.

Returning to the Soviet Union and its allies, then, it is evident that the pluralistic but still basically united "East" is faced with a set of apparently contradictory choices in foreign policy. On the one hand, the perpetuation of its own social and political system and the retention of control over the international Communist movement, a weapon which has always been considered essential to the eventual triumph of that system, as well as a basic national interest of the U.S.S.R., seem to demand a continuing commitment to a strategy that entails a constant danger of collision with the West. On the other hand, the overriding need to avoid such a collision, with its danger of nuclear catastrophe, the need to find a solution to the problems of nuclear proliferation, and the necessity to resist the Chinese challenge—all these seem to demand accommodation with the West and therefore relinquishment of a revolutionary role.

The solution apparently being tried is interesting and could be both disturbing and encouraging from the Western point of view. I prefer on the whole to regard it as encouraging. This development, which is logical, and which would scarcely be remarkable in the policy of another country, is the increasing differentiation shown by the Soviet Union in its policy toward Western countries. In the past, when the Soviet Union could still speak of itself and its allies as a monolithic unit, it was prone to regard the West as something comparable and to treat NATO members—and even such other Western nations as Sweden—much alike, as imperialist powers, more or less under the domination of the United States. More recently, in seeking to reconcile the conflicting objectives it pursues, the Soviet leadership has come to take a more realistic view. If the revolutionary imperative prevents an accomodation with the West in general, it does not prevent accommodations with certain Western states in particular, and some of the benefits of *détente* can be retained even at a time when the most important *détente*, that with the United States, is in suspense because of the revolutionary imperative.

It would be a mistake to treat this development purely as a device to enable the U.S.S.R. to make the best of both worlds. There are clearly other advantages the U.S.S.R. may hope to derive from such a policy, most obviously, perhaps, to divide the Western alliance, "to take advantage," as *Kommunist* puts it, "of the contradictions in the imperialist camp in the interests of the U.S.S.R. and socialism."[5] It is in this respect that this Soviet policy may be thought disturbing. Being both more subtle and more realistic, and at the same time ostensibly no less antagonistic, we are confronted with a more complex problem of the best response. As I have said, however, I judge this evolution to be encouraging, not only because I do not believe the unity of the Western alliance will be subverted by it, and because I know we are capable of finding the appropriate response, but also for the simple reason that any increase of realism is a contribution to the long-term understandings we seek.

Let me be more specific about the differentiation of Soviet policy towards the West. The best known example is of course the manifest Soviet desire to cultivate the friendship of France. The Soviet Union is also cultivating friendly relations with the Scandinavian countries, Japan, and Canada. The significance of these efforts should not be exaggerated. They are thrown into greater relief by the relative coolness of the Soviet attitude toward the United States, Britain, and West Germany. They are nevertheless illustrative of Soviet recognition not only of the political but of the economic necessity of keeping its lines open to the other industrial nations of the world. This is yet another imperative, one which has come into play with greater force as it has become clearer that the Soviet economy is desperately ill-equipped to meet the social demands of the second half of the twentieth century.

[5] Golikov, *op. cit.*

It takes two to conduct friendly relations, and what is Canada's position vis-à-vis the U.S.S.R.? If the main lines of Soviet policy are formulated by leaders having a world view basically inimical to Canada's, if peaceful coexistence is a device to immobilize the West while national-liberation wars gradually consume the rest of the non-Communist world, would it be short-sighted for Canada to welcome the opportunity to establish relations on a sane and rational footing with the Communist world?

I have, I think, said enough about our judgment of the Soviet world view to demonstrate why we do not consider it immutable. Inimical to us it may be in its origins, but it is equally inimical to the real interests of those who hold it, and those interests are increasingly making themselves felt. I am not so naïve, of course, as to believe that the growth of contacts, and exchanges, rapid though it is, between East and West, will work any miracles. To quote *Kommunist* once again:

> As an ardent supporter of useful business contacts with capitalist countries, Lenin invariably warned against forgetting the class approach to these relations. He pointed out that the capitalists would seek in every way to undermine our system, to corrupt our people and to instill capitalist habits in them. It is necessary to watch closely each step of the enemy and to employ all means of control, supervision, and persuasion to paralyze bourgeois influence. Peaceful coexistence calls for the intensification of Party ideological work inside the country and decisive struggle against bourgeois ideology in the international arena.[6]

I need not emphasize that these are not idle words and that Soviet officialdom governs contacts with the West accordingly. But this is not the whole story. Those (and they exist both in Canada and in the U.S.S.R.) who believe the old days are gone forever, and nothing serious now stands in the way of eternal good will, may have overestimated the pace of change; but change there is.

Canada, like most other Western countries, has participated in these exchanges for a number of years, not only with the U.S.S.R. but with Poland, Czechoslovakia, Hungary, and other countries of Eastern Europe. Canada has sold great quantities of wheat to these same countries, as everybody but the people who eat it knows. The

[6] *Ibid.*

volume of private tourism from Canada to the European Communist countries is rising rapidly, and they have ceased to be entirely remote and mysterious regions. Intergovernmental relations are reasonably good, always allowing for the gulf on fundamental issues.

What, then, can we conclude from this about Canada's role in East-West relations? The examples I have given refer to Canada's own particular relations with the Soviet "East," an area with which Canada has common geographical and economic problems, and from which Canada has drawn a substantial part of its population. There is clearly ample room for cooperation with those countries, and there would be a great deal more which it would be in Canada's national interest to develop if the political obstacles were overcome. Purely from the Canadian point of view, therefore, and leaving aside the vital concern Canada shares with all humanity in finding the stable world order essential to our survival—a point I scarcely need to labor—Canada has a definite interest not only in the absence of hostility but in genuine cooperation. Moreover, despite the vaulting ambitions of some visionaries to see Canada take a prominent part in every international situation, it is subject to the same sort of imperatives as every other country. Canada acts in the world and is acted upon in two ways: as itself alone, pursuing its own unique national interests, and as an ally, a neighbor, or a member of one or another group. Obviously there is constant interplay, even tension, between these two aspects of our international being. In a pluralistic world there is far greater scope for interplay and sometimes greater occasion for conflict. This being so, can it reasonably be argued that Canada's commitment to a common Western cause runs counter to its true national interest?

A few years ago, it was not uncommon for fairly well-disposed people of Soviet sympathies to describe Canada as the "Poland of the West," meaning, presumably, a country allied to an overwhelmingly powerful neighbor, but showing encouraging signs of independence whenever it could. With all due respect to the Polish people, I have never been able to accept the analogy. But it throws light on the point I am trying to make: Canada's own conception of its place as a nation committed to the NATO alliance in defense of the West is different from that attributed to it by the Communist countries, and this difference has an observable effect on the sort of role it can play in relations with them.

That role is also profoundly affected by another observable fact —that as far as the Soviet Union is concerned there is really only one non-Communist country in the world whose policy is of vital significance to it—the United States. I do not discount the importance the Soviet Union attaches to its relations with other countries —India, Japan, France are all objects of special Soviet attention at present—but in Soviet calculations the United States is the ultimate interlocutor. And who is to deny the realism of this view? What it means is that in the absence of understandings between the two superpowers, no stable solution is possible of the key questions of world affairs: Germany and European security, disarmament, problems of underdevelopment. It does not mean, however, that the only worthwhile dialogue is that between the superpowers. The Soviet Union does not believe so, evidently, as the differentiation it makes among Western states confirms. But it is logical to suppose, and experience bears this out, that a dialogue with a lesser state is the more interesting to the Communist world to the extent that state may be, or may be thought to be, associated with a concentration of power greater than itself alone.

It is a matter of traditional wisdom that Canada's closeness in all senses to the United States has lent its views greater weight than they might always have received uttered in isolation. This is the positive aspect of our situation, on which I think it reasonable to lay greater stress at this juncture in East-West relations than on the negative aspect, that we owe our security in an age of superpowers to our great neighbor. But let that fact not be forgotten. I speak of "security" not in the sense that there would be anywhere to hide in the event of a nuclear war, but in the sense that the long-term prospects for a stable peace rest on the continued ability of the West to resist military pressure. We have not worked our way out of the Cold War, just as we did not survive the bitter confrontation of Stalin's day, by giving way to such pressure. And the West's ability to resist it is basically the ability of the United States. Having that power of resistance confers the freedom to seek constructive solutions. It has not been used by the West to exert such pressure in its turn. In Hungary in 1956, in Berlin in 1961, in Cuba in 1962, a response in kind to extreme provocation would at the least have paralyzed the process of internal evolution in the Communist world for years, even if it had not led to the ultimate disaster.

It is this engagement of the Soviet Union with the United States which enhances Canada's role in East-West relations. Clearly close relations with the United States, symbolized in the security field by Canada's active cooperation in NATO and NORAD, are essential if its views are to be taken into account in Washington—which they are. Similarly on the Soviet side, Canada is of interest less for what it is—a nation of 20 million people—than as a neighbor of the United States, sensitive to the movement of American public opinion and disposing of some influence in Washington.

Those who argue that Canada would be able to play a more effective role internationally if it withdrew from NATO fail to answer two arguments. They cannot demonstrate that it would gain new influence. Canada could not hope to lead the nonaligned states, whose principal concerns are different from its own. And it would lose the close association with the United States and the other major members of NATO, which is the source of much of its influence in the world, an influence that is greater than its population and economic power would alone support.

The Alliance confers on Canada both influence and the freedom to use it constructively. What is Canada to do with it? What it is doing is this: It is addressing itself to the central problems of disarmament—and specifically at present nuclear proliferation—in preparation for the time when genuine progress can be made. It is equally working on more immediate issues such as the war in Vietnam, which stands almost impenetrably across the road to profitable resumption of the Soviet-American dialogue. For reasons of its own, the Soviet Union has not yet seen fit to work openly for a peaceful settlement in Vietnam, but neither has it cut its lines to the West as a whole because of it. Indeed, the Soviet Union has specifically declared that the war in Vietnam should not be allowed to obstruct the disarmament negotiations at Geneva. Nevertheless, the manner in which the Vietnam war is ended will do much to shape the form of East-West relations in the future. Meanwhile, as long as no Soviet-American dialogue on the war and its attendant problems is taking place, Canada, with contacts in Washington and Moscow,

Saigon and Hanoi, has both the responsibility and the opportunity to help span the gap.

There are other matters which are not so immediate or difficult but which are still important; such matters as peace-keeping, another field in which Canada actively seeks to associate East and West, and in which the concept of national-liberation war makes understanding seem remote. They also include the bilateral exchanges and trade that it conducts with the Soviet Union and Eastern Europe, in increasing volume.

All such exchanges contribute to the same purpose of introducing elements of normality and stability into a world where rapid social change and the monstrous destructiveness of weapons produce too volatile an atmosphere for widely divergent views to be carried to their logical conclusions.

There is still an "East" and still a "West," and we are not yet done with polarization, but pluralism provides diplomacy with opportunities both to divert such dangerous logic and to narrow the divergencies. To quote Raymond Aron again in conclusion: "This world of growing complexity promises to be a paradise for the analysts and a hell for statesmen. In it the first can display their ingenuity and the second will discover the limits of their power."[7]

I take no particular delight in analytical ingenuity. My interest lies rather in the broad implications of our assessments for government policy. In this field, my conclusion would be somewhat different from Mr. Aron's so far as Canada is concerned. We may find the limits of Canada's role expanded rather than diminished by the growing complexity of the world. In that possibility lies Canada's hope for rational discussion, for constructive diplomacy, and for a determined attempt to ensure world peace.

[7] Aron, *op. cit.*

6. The German Problem

PEYTON V. LYON

ALTHOUGH COLD WAR crises are apt these days to break out almost anywhere, the "German Problem" remains the most intractable and dangerous of the international bones of contention. Failure to cope with this problem not only perpetuates tension in the heart of Europe, but impedes other measures of *détente,* especially in the field of arms control.

To most non-Germans, the "German Problem" means how to contain the "German Menace"—how to control 75 million Germans and prevent this virile, vigorous, and violent nation from embroiling Europe and the world in another holocaust. Any German, however, will tell you that the Problem is simply the problem of German reunification—how to liberate 17 million East Germans and re-establish the unity of the German nation.

The two versions are related. Most foreigners, especially the East Europeans, believe that the best way to control the Germans is to keep them divided. To permit 75 million Germans to reunite, they contend, would create alarm and intolerable instability. Recalling the experience of the interwar years, they would not be entirely reassured by security guarantees or provisions to regulate German military strength. European security, they contend, lies in German disunity.

The Germans, and a significant minority of foreigners, take precisely the opposite view. How, they ask, can a powerful nation be denied self-determination in an age when this right is being granted to the Gambians, the Cambodians, and the Congolese? To deny the Germans the right to form their own nation-state, they argue plausibly, could produce frustrations that would pose an even greater threat to the stability of Europe.

Such diametrically opposed views suggest that there is no solution to the German Problem. A study of the demands of the two alliance systems leads to the same conclusion. Unrealistic when first formulated, the NATO demands became even more so with the growth of Soviet nuclear power. The stipulation that Germany be reunited on the basis of free elections is a thinly disguised demand that the Soviet Union accept the repudiation of its puppet regime and the surrender of East Germany—a particularly valuable piece of real estate. East Germany is the most industrialized of the Communist countries and their leading exporter of machine goods. Furthermore, the twenty-odd Russian divisions garrisoned in East Germany not only sustain the unpopular Ulbricht regime but keep Poland and Czechoslovakia in a military vise. The Russians could scarcely agree to the NATO proposals for reunification unless they first decide to surrender their dominant position in Eastern Europe. The NATO demand that a reunified Germany be free to determine its own alliance policy is, of course, even less realistic than the demand for free elections.

The Soviet counterdemands are that West Germany be demilitarized, neutralized, "democratized," and joined to East Germany in a confederation; in this confederation the puppet rulers of 17 million East Germans would have the same voice as the elected representatives of 58 million West Germans. Acceptance of these terms would leave the Federal Republic defenseless. The West would be as foolish to accept them as the Russians would be if they agreed to the NATO proposals. Both sides, of course, would modify their demands during serious negotiations, but it is still very difficult to see any basis for agreement on reunification. The West could hardly give up its demand for free elections at some predetermined stage, while the Russians simply could not afford to risk them now, or in the foreseeable future.

West German leaders have always conceded that the Kremlin is unlikely to agree to reunification except as part of a global settlement in which Russia could be granted compensation elsewhere. Adenauer has pinned his hopes not only on building up a position in the West of overwhelming strength, but on developments in the East that would greatly weaken Russia. In particular, he expects that the pressure of the mounting Chinese population upon Siberia will eventually drive the Russians to invoke Western help. This, he believes, will be the appropriate moment to discuss reunification.[1] It is true that worry about China is one reason why the Russians are now more restrained in Europe; if the rift widens, they may become even more amenable to reason. It is difficult, however, to envisage the Russians ever being prepared to pay for German assistance, or forbearance, by surrendering East Germany. Rather than pay such a price, they would surely be prepared to employ their overwhelming nuclear superiority to repel an invasion from China.

As far ahead as one can see, there is little possibility of an agreement to reunite Germany. On the other hand, it would be unwise to assume that the present situation will remain static. The German Problem has already altered in character since 1945, and further changes are probable. As World War II drew to a close, it was widely believed that world peace would depend upon the continued collaboration of the wartime allies, most notably the Russians and Americans. It was assumed that Germany would make this collaboration easier by providing the allies with a continuing threat, and a common task. The need to de-Nazify the Germans, and to keep them under firm control, was expected to provide a unifying bond between Russia and the leading Western powers. The extraordinary regime established for Berlin illustrates the degree to which it was

---

[1] Adenauer, in his final appearance as Chairman of the Christian Democratic Union, startled his hearers by proclaiming that Russia had become a peaceful nation, at least in Europe. His party, however, did not seem to agree. See "Surprise in Bonn: Adenauer Considers Moscow Peace-Loving," *Die Welt* (*The World;* Hamburg), March 22, 1966.

assumed that the wartime allies could and would collaborate in sitting on the "Hun."

These illusions were short-lived. The Germans let us down! They turned out to be far more thoroughly defeated and docile than had been expected. They failed to provide a threat sufficiently credible to maintain the unity of the major allies. Instead, Germany became the principal bone of contention. The Russians and the Western powers accused each other of trying to grab the whole country. They incorporated their occupation zones into their respective alliance systems, and engaged in the competitive rearmament of the Germans under their control. Berlin, carved into four sectors to facilitate four-power collaboration, became the focus of several of the most frightening of Cold War confrontations. Even the crisis of October, 1962, which was touched off by the erection of missile bases on Cuba, had its roots in the Russian campaign to force changes in the rules regulating the partition of Berlin and Germany.

Since the Cuba crisis, and the erection a year earlier of the Berlin Wall, the German Problem has become more stable. Few in the West now accuse the Russians of planning to seize West Berlin, still less the whole of Germany. The consolidation of the *status quo* appears to be the goal of the Kremlin, at least as far as Europe is concerned. For their part, the Americans have clearly abandoned any thought they may have had of employing force to roll back the Iron Curtain; even the Russians seem to be convinced that their principal Cold War antagonists now share their interest in stabilizing Central Europe; their only worry is that the Germans will start trouble and drag their American allies along.

We have entered a new phase in which it is conceivable that the superpowers will be brought together by the nuclear standoff, the rise of China, and the threat inherent in the unresolved German Problem. There is one crucial difference, however, between 1945 and 1966: The Germans are back on their feet. No longer can they be treated as mere objects of politics. The 58 million West Germans, with our assistance, have created the most powerful state in Western Europe. East Germany, with but 17 million people, is the second most important industrial power among the Communist countries. Both the Americans and the Russians, moreover, have made the defense of their sectors of Germany the center of gravity for their entire alliance systems, and both have made promises to their German clients that would be highly embarrassing, perhaps dangerous, to ignore. They cannot simply put the clock back a generation and start again. In any European settlement, German interests and German sensibilities cannot be left out of account.

One might be tempted to leave aside the intractable German Problem and concentrate upon more promising measures of *détente*. Unfortunately, the official West German position has generally been to oppose any such measures as threats to vital German interests and a breach of the commitments made to Germany by the NATO allies. From being a unifying factor, and then a bone of contention, Germany has emerged as a stumbling block in the way of *rapprochement* between the superpowers. Why is this so?

When the West Germans were persuaded reluctantly to rearm, the NATO allies promised to make German reunification a basic goal and to reject any general settlement with the Russians that did not provide for its attainment. Without this promise, Adenauer could never have persuaded the German parliament to support rearmament. In retrospect, it is at least arguable that German rearmament, and the NATO commitment to reunification, were both misguided. They are now important facts, however, that cannot be wished away. The Germans, with considerable cause, believe that they have honored their pledges to the alliance, and that they are entitled to expect their allies to keep faith with them. Most of them fear that if the superpowers manage to patch up all their other important differences, they will then have less inducement than at present to negotiate reunification. They fear that the German Problem would simply be forgotten by everyone, except the Germans. It has been official German policy, therefore, to resist even minor steps towards *détente* unless they entail some tangible progress towards solving the German Problem. Bonn often acts as if Germany had a vested interest in perpetuating the Cold War, and appears to substantiate the Communist propaganda portraying Germany as an unreformed *revanchist* power.

Many of the specific proposals for agreement between the superpowers, moreover, entail a further degree of recognition for the East German puppet state and, at least formally, would imply a firmer acceptance of the partition of Germany. Most of the proposals for arms control, for example, or new arrangements for Berlin, fall into this category, and are resisted by Bonn because they appear retrogressive with respect to the achievement of German unity.

No one likes to have the legitimacy of one's offspring challenged; understandably it is an important goal of Soviet policy to win recognition for its puppet state in East Germany, the German Democratic Republic (G.D.R.). The Kremlin tries to incorporate into new agreements clauses which would upgrade the political respectability of both the G.D.R. and its government situated in Pankow. Bonn feels bound to resist. The result is one of the most tedious and sterile struggles in the history of diplomacy.

An important consideration often overlooked is that the West Germans are more vulnerable to Russian pressure than the other West Europeans, and much more skeptical about Russian intentions. The precariousness of West Berlin's situation is obvious, and the Germans cannot be entirely oblivious to the steady barrage of hostile propaganda directed against them by Moscow. Their longing to reattain national unity, combined with their fear of Communist encroachment, has produced a paradox: The Germans are the Europeans who are the most hostile to the *status quo,* and, at the same time, the most apprehensive of change. A certain schizophrenia in their policies is hardly surprising. Whenever in doubt, however, the contemporary Germans have tended to be cautious and to cling to the *status quo.*

No nation, of course, should be permitted to block a genuine *rapprochement* between the superpowers. Too much is at stake for the entire human race. Circumstances could arise in which a Russo-American deal over the heads of their German allies would be justified. We must recognize, however, that any such deal would not be without grave risk; it could easily re-create a disillusioned Germany that would again disrupt the peace of Europe.

I am suggesting that the Germans might again cause trouble, but not because the Germans themselves are especially troublesome. As individuals they tend no more to be saints or sinners than any other people. Collectively they bear responsibility, it is true, for the most repugnant chapter in human history; on the other hand, nations can learn from history, and, whatever their faults, few observers accuse the Germans of being devoid of intelligence. The crimes committed by Germany under the Nazi regime, and the subsequent degradation and suffering experienced by most Germans, have probably left them less prone than most other nations to favor nationalistic policies disruptive of peace and order.

The German postwar record is certainly reassuring. Although relatively inexperienced in democratic government, the Germans have succeeded better at it during the past eighteen years than any other major power. The German achievements in reconstruction, economic growth, and the integration of about 11 million refugees are widely recognized. Equally impressive have been the political stability of West Germany, the attention paid to individual liberties, and the vigorous freedom of the German press, radio, and television. Most Germans are critical of the meager results of their foreign policy, but it is by no means clear that any alternative policy could have gained reunification in freedom; and it is certainly no small achievement that Germany should have recovered a position of strength and respect so soon after launching and losing the most vicious war in history. West German foreign policy, moreover, has not been disfigured by such errors in judgment as those that culminated in Suez, the Bay of Pigs, or Vietnam.

The attitude of the West German voter has been one of cautious realism. *"Keine Experimente"*—no experiments—has proved to be the most effective slogan, while the radical parties of the Right and Left have faded into insignificance. A Gallup Poll conducted in 1964 in eight Western countries showed that only the Swiss were more contented than the West Germans; a whopping 86 per cent of the Germans expressing an opinion said that they were, on the whole, satisfied with the position of their country in the world.[2]

It would be an error, of course, to conclude from this that the Germans are indifferent to the division of their nation, or prepared to be passive in international affairs, regardless of what other nations do—or fail to do. While the Cold War was intense, and the threat of Russian aggression appeared to be significant, the Germans naturally gave security priority over reunification, and

[2] See the report of the Canadian Institute of Public Opinion in the *Montreal Star,* March 7, 1964. The corresponding percentage for Canada was 72; for the United States, 49; and for Britain, 42.

they were tolerant of the failure of their allies to do anything but pay lip service to the goal of German unity. This situation is changing, and German priorities with it. In addition to the partial *détente,* and the resolution of Germany's most pressing internal problems, men are now coming to power who are not inhibited by a sense of personal responsibility for the Nazi crimes. They are demanding more realistic policies to gain the liberation of their brethren in East Germany.[3]

The Germans do not say precisely what they would do if their allies broke their commitments and concluded a deal with the Kremlin that appeared to sanctify the partition of Germany. They themselves probably do not know. On the other hand, they do not discourage predictions that the results would be unpalatable to all concerned. They are compelled to live down their past and earn a reputation for reliability and gentleness; otherwise no one would take a chance on permitting 75 million Germans to form a single state. At the same time, they must get across the message that they cannot be betrayed with impunity; they must convince the powers that it is unsafe to leave the Germans disunited and discontented; otherwise, they fear, no one will make the necessary effort to end the enforced partition of their nation. More than most countries, Germany needs to project the image of being "nice but not too nice"—restrained, but likely to fly off the handle if provoked or betrayed.

What, in fact, are the ways in which the Germans might react to the abandonment—express or strongly implied—of reunification as a major goal of Western policy? Would they leave NATO and seek alliance with the Soviet Union? Would they revert to an opportunistic policy of playing the powers off against one another? Or would they knuckle under without any shift of alignment?

A Russo-German alliance would be neither the likeliest possibility, nor the most alarming. The Germans are the most anti-Communist and anti-Russian of the West Europeans. Even if disappointed in the West, or more desperate to attain reunification than they now appear to be, they are highly unlikely to enter into arrangements which might leave them subservient to the Kremlin. Nor is it cer-

[3] See Richard Lowenthal, "The Germans Feel Like Germans Again," *The New York Times Magazine,* March 6, 1966.

tain that the Russians would welcome a bid by Germany to join
the Warsaw Pact. They are having problems with 20 million Romanians. How would they digest 75 million Germans? In the very
unlikely event that the Russians and Germans did join forces, the
result would not necessarily be an intolerable increase in the military threat to the West; the nuclear standoff, and the Sino-Soviet
rift, would probably continue to preserve a tolerably stable balance
of power. A Russo-German military alliance would certainly be
regarded as a serious setback for the West. On the other hand, a
substantial degree of *rapprochement* between Moscow and Bonn,
especially if it followed an accommodation between Moscow and
Washington, might well be the surest means to promote stability
in the world's most critical area. It is more to be encouraged than
feared.

More probable, and also more disturbing, would be the adoption
by Bonn of an independent, nationalistic policy. Disillusioned with
allies, the Germans might well conclude they had no alternative
but to rely entirely on their own wit and muscle. Because of their
exposed position, and the need to protect West Berlin, they would
undoubtedly conclude that an independent nuclear deterrent had
become essential. Although their purpose in building up strong,
independent forces might be strictly defensive, Germany's neighbors—to the West as well as the East—would be understandably
alarmed. The Communist powers might even feel compelled to take
pre-emptive measures.

If the West Germans acquired independent control over strong
military forces, would they again stand idly by during a popular
uprising in East Germany? Or would they be tempted to mix in
if Russia became militarily entangled anywhere within the Communist camp? They would probably seek to stir up trouble behind
the Iron Curtain, especially if they were in a position to employ
nuclear blackmail. The scope for miscalculation would increase if
the trend toward polycentrism continues, and any fighting between
Germans and Slavs would be difficult to contain. It is by no means
certain, of course, that the West Germans would employ force to
change the *status quo* in Eastern Europe even if the temptation
was great, but the possibility that they might would be in itself
unsettling. Clearly it is in everyone's interest that the West Germans

remain firmly anchored in their present alliance system and continue to foreswear independent control over nuclear weapons.

Indeed, the continuation of NATO—or something very like it—is now just about as important to Eastern Europe as it is to the West. The need for NATO as a means to deter Communist aggression has not entirely vanished; if it were completely broken up, Soviet military ambitions in Europe just might revive. It is more certain that, with the rearmament of Germany, the need for NATO as a control mechanism has greatly increased. West Germany is the only power to have committed all its regular forces to an integrated NATO command. They will remain there, and be incapable of independent action, just so long as the Germans have confidence in the preparedness of their allies to defend the vital interests of Germany. If the Germans lose that confidence, it will be difficult indeed to persuade them not to beef up their forces, establish full national control over them, and develop their own nuclear deterrent. This would be contrary to the obligations undertaken by Germany when she joined NATO, but no nation can be bound by treaties when it feels that its survival is seriously threatened.

One must have every sympathy with the Russian and French hostility to the acquisition by Germany of nuclear power. On the other hand, if the Russians really want to prevent this development, they should give up their Cold War tactics of trying to sow dissension and distrust within NATO; they could also do more to make the partition of Germany tolerable to the Germans and to ease their worries about West Berlin.

The policies of President de Gaulle are even harder to comprehend. In seeking to loosen the NATO ties, and to destroy German faith in the American deterrent, he clearly hopes that the Germans will seek shelter under the French nuclear umbrella. If the Germans lose faith in the Americans, however, it is unlikely that they will choose to rely on the *force de frappe,* even if it comes to be a more credible deterrent than now seems possible. Disillusioned with allies, they would almost certainly decide that they must work their own way into the nuclear club. Bonn's interest in the MLF[4]

4 The MLF (multilateral nuclear force) was proposed by Washington in 1961 as a means of giving the European allies a share in the management of the nuclear deterrent. It was to consist of surface vessels carrying Polaris missiles and

can be understood only in the light of the growing uncertainty about the future of NATO, and the German desire to entangle the Americans ever more inextricably in the defense of Europe. Bonn's nuclear aspirations are not unrelated to the French and British examples, but they have even more to do with the French campaign to destroy the credibility of NATO and the American deterrent. In reawakening German nationalism, and whetting the German appetite for nuclear independence, De Gaulle is playing a dangerous game.[5]

We need not rule out the possibility that the West Germans would elect to remain in NATO even if it clearly abandoned reunification as a condition for a general settlement with Russia. After a period of bitter recrimination, and "agonizing reappraisal," they might still conclude that their interests would not be served by a major shift in alignment. They know that they have a great deal to lose, and they are far from optimistic about the prospects for reunification. Nor are they under any illusion about the enthusiasm of their allies for the restoration of the unity of the German Reich. If the West appeared to write off its demand for reunification, German pride would suffer a good deal more than German expectations.

This is not to say, however, that the German reaction would be calm and sensible. Peoples who feel betrayed do not necessarily react rationally. They do not always adopt courses that are in their own best interests or those of their neighbors. The Western allies would be wise, therefore, as well as honorable, to take seriously their commitments to help the Germans realize their legitimate national aspirations.

Thus far the argument leads to a melancholy conclusion; although German reunification is improbable, the NATO allies are committed to making it a condition of *détente* with the Kremlin; there would be grave risks in disregarding that commitment; Bonn

---

manned by mixed crews from three or more NATO allies. Bonn was the only European capital to display any enthusiasm for the proposal.

[5] For the troubled German reaction to De Gaulle's withdrawal from NATO's integrated military structure, see Max Frankel, "Germans Nervous Over Crisis in NATO Affairs," *The New York Times,* March 31, 1966.

opposes measures of *détente* that fail to advance the cause of reunification; as a result, the West is left with little scope for fruitful negotiation with the Soviet Union. Fortunately this is not the whole picture. German attitudes are changing in a manner that should make it feasible to negotiate *détente* without sending Germany off the rails, politically speaking.

In the first place, the Germans want to regain the full confidence and respect of the world community. They know they still have some distance to go and are decidely uncomfortable whenever accused of blocking progress toward a more peaceful world. For this reason they accepted the 1963 test-ban agreement even though it appeared to them to worsen the German Problem by providing for the accession of East Germany. Similarly, although Germany has an excellent case for an increased share in nuclear deterrence, German opinion has not sustained the Erhard Cabinet's demand that the MLF be kept afloat. The Germans are generally prepared to yield to foreign opinion even when apprehensive that their national aspirations will suffer.

Another hopeful factor is the growing realism in Germany concerning the best means to tackle the German Problem. The men rising to power in Bonn are far less disposed to cling to positions that may be magnificent in law but are certainly devoid of political substance. They appreciate that a superpower, armed with the full range of nuclear weapons, is unlikely to be frightened into making such tremendous concessions as the abandonment of East Germany. They realize that there is virtually no prospect of reunification during a period of Cold War; that reunification can only be the product of *détente*—not the precondition.[6] Reunification, if it ever comes, will follow long years of relaxed tension, during which the other Europeans gradually lose their fear of consolidated German power. More than anything else, the German Problem needs to become a bore.

Easier to conceive in the foreseeable future, and essentially more important, are further measures that diminish the cruel significance of the Iron Curtain without upsetting the European balance of

[6] ". . . the increased concentration on the question of national unity has tended not to revive the aggressive nationalism of the past but rather to force a realistic reexamination of nationalist shibboleths." Lowenthal, *op. cit.*

power. Such measures facilitate human contact and mitigate the Stalinist conditions that still prevail in East Germany. They take some of the explosiveness out of the German Problem and, by reducing the discrepancies between the living conditions in the two Germanys, increase the possibility that the two might again become one. Even the dismantling of the Berlin Wall is improbable while hundreds of thousands of disgruntled East Germans are poised to seize the first opportunity to flee westward.

A diminishing minority in Germany still clings to disengagement as the most promising solution to the German Problem. They are confident that if all the foreign divisions left German soil, the two German states would merge instantaneously—like two blobs of quicksilver. They might well be right. Unfortunately, the resultant situation would probably be less stable than the present. As Henry Kissinger observes in his latest book,[7] it has been Germany's tragedy throughout much of history to be either too weak or too strong for the stability of Europe; if, after disengagement, Germany were to be kept weak, she would again become a power vacuum in the heart of Europe and a standing invitation to other powers to interfere; if permitted to be strong enough to defend herself on all sides, she would again loom as a menace to her neighbors. Foreign forces in Germany are the product—not the cause—of tension; they will disengage promptly enough when the German Problem eases, and all the countries in the neighborhood acquire confidence in the permanence of their borders. In the meantime, the prospects of stability, even *détente,* are enhanced by the presence of foreign divisions in Germany and the firm anchoring of Germany's own forces in the two alliance systems.

Another theory, that reunification can be advanced by means of *rapprochement* with the countries of Eastern Europe, is currently more popular in Germany. Foreign Minister Schroeder has wide support in his campaign to extend trade and cultural relations in this area. Related to this campaign is the growing willingness of prominent Germans to say out loud what they have been whispering for years about the Oder-Neisse frontier with Poland. Most Germans know, of course, that a minimum requirement for reunification is

[7] Henry A. Kissinger, *The Troubled Partnership* (New York: McGraw-Hill Book Co., 1965), pp. 65–66.

the unambiguous acceptance of their present borders. One excuse
for the politicians' lack of public candor on this point has been the
fear of losing a substantial number of votes among the 11 million
expellees and refugees in West Germany. The electoral risk in being
honest appears to be diminishing and could probably be rendered
tolerable by a tacit agreement between the three parties in the
Bundestag not to make an issue of the border question. It should
not even be necessary to form an all-party coalition for the purpose.

The second main argument for official reticence is the proposition that, since Germany has so few bargaining counters, she cannot
afford to surrender her legal claims to a quarter of her former territory without a tangible *quid pro quo*. Gradually the realization
is spreading, however, that the Russians, who hold the key to reunification, are unlikely to pay very much for a German pledge to
accept the Oder-Neisse border. Indeed, they may prefer to perpetu-
ate the present doubts about this border since they serve admirably
to keep the Poles and Czechs nervous about Germany and dependent for military support upon Moscow. In any case, recent statements by German church leaders, and even a Bonn Cabinet
minister, suggest that Germany may be moving toward the painful
but necessary acceptance of the Oder-Neisse border.[8] This would
not only remove the principal barrier to reconciliation in the East
but would improve Germany's reputation in the West for realism
and reliability.

Another fading impediment to better relations is the Hallstein
Doctrine—the principle in West German diplomacy that calls for
the rejection of formal relations with any country, except Russia,
that recognizes East Germany. It is not difficult to understand the
repugnance that Germans feel for Walter Ulbricht and his puppet
regime. These men were imposed, and are maintained, by Russian
power in its crudest form. But for the Wall, thousands of their subjects would still be running away. Germans have cause to feel
insulted whenever the credentials of the Pankow puppets are treated
as if they were comparable to those of the freely elected government
in Bonn.

[8] Herr Gradl, Federal Minister for Refugees, said in several speeches early
in 1966 that a settlement in the East would entail territorial sacrifices. See, e.g.,
The Economist, March 12, 1966, p. 989.

Many Germans are nonetheless coming to consider the Hallstein Doctrine too heavy a burden for German diplomacy, especially in seeking *rapprochement* with the East. Even though Ulbricht appears to be no more respected in the East than in the West, it is unrealistic to expect the East European governments to break with another Communist regime, and defy Moscow, in order to oblige the West Germans. An increasing number of Germans, therefore, advocate the scrapping of the Hallstein Doctrine, at least in dealings with Eastern Europe.

The West German campaign to improve relations in this area, much as it is to be welcomed, is based in part upon a new fallacy. This is the belief that the G.D.R. might become so isolated in the East that the Kremlin would decide to cut its losses by abandoning its East German puppet state; it is even hoped by some that conditions in the G.D.R. might deteriorate so much that there would be a second, more successful, uprising, and that the Russians would not interfere. The worse the conditions in the G.D.R., it is reasoned, the better the prospects for reunification. This general line finds support in the recent writings of such otherwise sensible commentators as Kissinger and Brzezinski,[9] but it is profoundly mistaken. Indeed, the opposite is closer to the truth: The *better* the conditions in the G.D.R., the *easier* it will be to solve the German Problem.

We are living in a period of coexistence made necessary by the balance of terror. Under these circumstances, there is no point in adopting policies that rely for success upon the humiliation of a superpower. In Vietnam we can see the lengths the Americans are prepared to go rather than abandon an insignificant ally to which they have pledged support. The Russians would find it many times as difficult to write off the G.D.R. and its puppet regime. In a matter of such importance to the prestige and power of the Soviet Union, the influence of its former satellites is not likely to be great.[10] Nor is there much reason to expect that, in the event of a

---

[9] Kissinger, *op. cit.*, pp. 211–18; Zbigniew K. Brzezinski, *Alternative to Partition* (New York: McGraw-Hill Book Co., 1965), pp. 99–101.

[10] This is not to say that the governments of these countries might not prevail upon Moscow to modify certain conditions in the G.D.R., perhaps even to replace Ulbricht with a less embarrassing East German Communist.

second uprising in the G.D.R., the Soviet tanks would fail to perform their function. Any deterioration in the conditions in East Germany would simply increase the discrepancy with the West, and reduce still further the prospect for removing, or eroding, the barriers that divide the nation.

In tackling the German Problem, the relations between the two German states are of much greater significance than the relations that each of them maintain with the countries of Eastern Europe. Moscow may hold the key, but Pankow cannot be circumvented. Many Germans are urging the expansion of the technical operation that has long existed between Bonn and Pankow, especially in such fields as trade, law enforcement, and transportation. New agreements have in fact been concluded between West Berlin and Pankow to permit West Berliners to visit relatives in the East during specified holiday periods. Less publicized have been the recent deals between Bonn and Pankow for the purchase of the freedom of more than 2,000 East German political prisoners. The West Germans complain that the Pankow regime seeks to exploit each and every negotiation to upgrade its political respectability, and they have turned down East German requests for large-scale credits. In principle, Bonn favors increased collaboration in the interest of more tolerable living conditions for the East Germans; increased collaboration, however, is difficult to attain while the West Germans are obsessed by the fear that the recognition of the East German regime would eliminate all prospects for reunification.

This apprehension is not well founded. Nationalism is too potent a force to be bottled up forever by diplomatic or constitutional formalities. Moreover, the essential first step in transcending the division of Germany may well prove to be the frank recognition of that division.

Recognition of the G.D.R. would grant increased security of tenure to the ruling elite in that unhappy territory. Although in itself distasteful, this step could be the means of unleashing latent German patriotism in the G.D.R. to yield something like the national Communism of Poland or Yugoslavia. By refusing to recognize the G.D.R., the West, in effect, has served notice that it intends, if it can, to destroy the ruling elite in Pankow. This leaves that elite no alternative but to cling to Moscow. As Germans, they are less likely to be Russophile than the Poles or Yugoslavs; in practice, Ulbricht and his colleagues are proving to be the most docile of Russian puppets. The habit of subservience to Moscow may be indelibly ingrained upon the character of Ulbricht, but this is less likely to be true of the bulk of the technicians and officials whose support is vital to his regime.[11] If accepted by the West as the *de facto* rulers of East Germany, they might well become less dependent upon Moscow, and more willing to cultivate relations with the West Germans to the maximum extent consistent with the preservation of at least the semblance of Communist society in the G.D.R.

A change in the G.D.R. to political conditions approaching those that prevail in Poland would be conceivable, and a considerable gain. East German national Communism might be more easily sustained because of the G.D.R.'s contiguity to a thriving Western state with which it shares a language, culture, traditions of unity, trading interests, and transportation systems. The greater strength of the West German economy, and the magnetism of the European Community, could well be exploited to obtain further concessions designed to liberalize conditions in East Germany and facilitate human contact across the Iron Curtain. We need have no fear about which German state would exercise the greater pull on the other.

It would be extravagant to predict that the gradual lifting of the diplomatic curtain, and a great increase in collaboration between the two Germanys, would ever blossom into the full, formal restoration of the German Reich. If the *rapprochement* seemed to proceed too far or too fast for the comfort of the Russians, they could call a halt—at the price, of course, of considerable damage to the new image that the Kremlin is trying to project. The Russian temptation to apply the brakes might be lessened if the *rapprochement* proceeded gradually. A substantial *rapprochement* could occur without the necessity of basic changes in the economic and military align-

[11] This suggestion is contested by some Germans and difficult to establish. It appears to have been lent some substance, however, by the demonstrative suicide of Dr. Erich Apel, the chief economic planner in the G.D.R., on December 3, 1965, the day that a new economic agreement with the Soviet Union was signed. See "The Death of the Technocrat," *Die Zeit* (*The Times;* Hamburg), December 14, 1965.

ment of either state, or the acute embarrassment of their respective "Big Brothers." The G.D.R. could remain within the Soviet economic system and the Warsaw Pact; the Federal Republic could keep its association with NATO and the West European Community. The unsettling specter of an unanchored, dissatisfied Germany would not arise.

Even if this *rapprochement* stopped a long way short of fulfilling German aspirations, it could at least help to mitigate the human suffering caused by the enforced division of Germany. By reducing tensions, and the discrepancies between the conditions in the two Germanys, it would also improve the long-term prospects for restoring German unity. At very worst, it could hardly be a less promising approach to reunification than the course that has been steered by the Bonn government for nearly two decades.[12]

The Germans who advocate small steps toward a Bonn-Pankow *rapprochement* generally do so on strictly humanitarian grounds, and in spite of the risk of improving the political status of the G.D.R.; most of them would reject arguments in favor of recognition as heresy. Nevertheless, it is encouraging that West Germans are now less inclined to be shocked by fresh ideas on the German Problem.[13] They are scrapping the rigidities and clichés that were appropriate only in the waging of Cold War and are receptive to

[12] For a fuller discussion of this problem, see Lyon, "The Case for the Recognition of the G.D.R.," in *International Journal*, Vol. XV, No. 4 (Autumn, 1960).

[13] See "Thoughts about Germany," *Die Zeit*, March 15, 1966, for a report suggesting that the German public is more realistic about the German Problem than its political leaders. "The Dream of a 'Great Left,'" in *Die Zeit*, March 8, 1966, is an account of the current thinking of the important segment of the German Social Democrats that advocates small steps toward collaboration with the G.D.R. In "Conditions of Reunification," *Die Zeit*, March 1, 1966, a Christian Democratic Deputy set forth realistic views after a trip through the G.D.R. On March 1, 1966, three West German television networks carried a remarkable program showing how reunification might come about as the result of a confederation with the G.D.R., acceptance of the Oder-Neisse border, and an exchange of security guarantees; its author was Rüdiger Altmann, a respected free-lance journalist; see "No Permanent Way Through the Wall," *The Economist*, March 12, 1966; also in March, 1966, the West German Social Democrats, with the concurrence of the other parties, entered into a cautious dialogue with the East German Socialist Unity Party. See "A Dialogue Among Germans," *Die Zeit*, March 29, 1966.

more imaginative and flexible proposals. If, as I urge, the NATO allies keep their commitments to Germany, they are not necessarily condemning themselves to diplomatic sterility. The aspirations, susceptibilities, and judgments of the Germans should be sympathetically taken into account in the formulation of alliance policies vital to German national interests. This may slow the course of negotiation, but the results will be more reliable. In particular, although German interests would be served if the West accepted the existence of two German states, it would be a mistake for the NATO allies to recognize the G.D.R. before Bonn is prepared to do so.

Rapprochement between the Federal Republic and the G.D.R. is unlikely to yield a complete solution to the German Problem. Unlike problems in geometry or algebra, political problems rarely lend themselves to tidy solutions. The best that can realistically be hoped for is a gradual easing of the German Problem—the creation of a new situation which, while still distressingly untidy and unsatisfactory, will be easier for the contending parties (especially the Germans) to live with.

If the powers involved in the German Problem can identify their true interests, if they make due allowance for the interests, susceptibilities, and fears of the other powers, if memories and ideological considerations are not permitted to dominate, and if events in other continents—notably Asia—fail to destroy the growing community of interest between the two superpowers, the German situation can be gradually defused. These are formidable "ifs." Nevertheless, current trends warrant cautious optimism that the German Problem can be reduced to manageable proportions.

7. France's Foreign Policy

JEAN ETHIER-BLAIS

THE FRENCH POSITION with regard to Eastern Europe and the Communist world rests on certain broad principles and notions of a geographical or historical nature. The first of these, and the most important in the eyes of the makers of French foreign policy, including especially General de Gaulle, is the conception of Europe and of the role it is destined to play in the evolution of mankind. Today, General de Gaulle is a staunch partisan of a dynamic form of European neutralism, but this has not always been so. When in the early 1950's *Le Monde,* prodded by the philosophical reasoning of Etienne Gilson, initiated discussions about the pros and cons of European neutralism, General de Gaulle, then head of the RPF (Rassemblement du peuple français) rejected the idea outright on the grounds that Europe could never prosper except with strong American military and economic help and guidance. De Gaulle has indeed come a great way from this original period, when he could have been described as a NATO fundamentalist. The views of the French concerning ideological evolution have been conditioned by their thinking about the nature and life of Europe itself. Two aspects of Europe are worthy of particular attention in French thinking today: first of all its unpredictability, and secondly its visionary instinct and universal mission in world affairs.

What, then, is Europe? According to Paul Valéry's celebrated formula, Europe is but the most advanced geographical point of Asia. The territorial smallness of Europe is a recurrent theme in present French pronouncements. However, this smallness is counterbalanced by the extent of Europe's historical past and by the force of its intellectual dynamism, so that it represents not only the cradle of civilization but also a mosaic of creative units in all fields that is in a state of constant evolution. This state of flux has taken on a new meaning in recent years, and Europe, having been as it were in progressive making since 1945, constitutes an unpredictable element in world politics.

When General de Gaulle, who is of course the foremost exponent of his own foreign policy, interprets the world as it now stands, he begins with the following premise: Three great blocs, easily categorized, rule our universe—the United States, the Soviet Union, and China. These three blocs have individual, and sometimes conflicting ideologies; they pursue aims which they claim are different. In addition, it has become apparent over the years that they will not shy away from using traditional methods to foster their particular interests. And these interests in each case can be boiled down to some measure of desire for world domination. It is also apparent from General de Gaulle's speeches and writings that there is in his mind a quality of static consistency necessarily associated with the very nature of a bloc, so that once one is familiar with the aims and methods of one of the blocs, it is not impossible to surmise how its foreign policies will be conducted in a given area. One of the basic assumptions of French foreign policy today is the existence among great powers of natural zones of interest; in this context, it is logical to think that China would not allow large segments of the Far East to fall within the American orbit of influence; and if China does allow this to happen, it would be a temporary solution to a long-range problem, a solution imputable only to the present weakness of China. In the same manner, it is inconceivable that, if it is in a position to retain control, the United States will let South America leave the American continental zone of influence. From this, two conclusions can be drawn: first, that

French foreign policy is based on the notion that national self-interest still transcends ideology, and therefore that ideological factors can be treated in foreign affairs as instruments of particular policies; and secondly, that by their very nature, blocs are predictable entities.

Europe is of a different composition and this is why French policy makers always revert to it as the center of origin of contemporary history. Europe today is groping through a kind of semidarkness where interests are temporarily set aside in an effort to achieve unity. This means that at this stage no single country can speak for Europe. It is very significant, in this regard, that when General de Gaulle speaks of, and sometimes for, Europe, he does so in the context of a Europe of the future, which does not yet exist but which he hopes will exist. This process of change has naturally given rise to a variety of ideas about the shape of Europe's future, including (a) the Europe which the United States has been trying to foster since the end of the last war, with Germany as its base; this Europe rests economically on a face-lifting of traditional capitalism and, politically, on a strict adherence to the principles of NATO; (b) the Europe of the technocrats, with its vision of mechanistic prosperity; Europe in this case serving as an example to the world of material (and eventually political) success achieved through ingenious organizational methods; (c) finally, there is the Europe of General de Gaulle which could extend "from the Atlantic to the Urals," a new entity serving as a bridge of peace between conflicting ideologies.

The immediate aim of French foreign policy in Europe is to adapt (a) and (b) to the particular needs of (c). An essential difference between (a) and (b) on the one hand and (c) on the other is that the two first conceptions of Europe stand outside any dynamic relationship to the Soviet Union and the Balkans, the French solution alone encompassing the whole of the traditional European culture. The nuance is an important one not only in flexibility and room for maneuver which it implies, but also in a global context. No single conception of Europe has yet been generally accepted as valid. This unpredictability with regard to the future can be construed as an asset in the present state of world affairs to the extent that Europe can act as a source of equilibrium between the existing blocs, in spite of the fact that Western Europe is globally on the side of the United States in the present situation. General de Gaulle, who is the leader of such fractional and independent thinking as there is in Europe, has made that very clear himself. The extent of his freedom of maneuver in international affairs can serve as an example of what can be achieved through practical thought by a smaller nation when great powers are in a state of ideological immobility.

The first effect of the particular situation created by the uncertainty in European affairs is that the Soviet Union and the United States are forced periodically to reassess both the plausibility and the formulation of their foreign policies. The second effect is that the Gaullist example is extending to Eastern Europe. Already in 1964, the Romanian Government sent its first official delegation to the West—to France. De Gaulle's policy has served to emphasize the global aspects of European political practice of which the French are very much aware. Both the Soviet Union and the United States, secure in their ideological thinking, have been following nationalist and expansionist policies. Their two basic traits have been, on the one hand, ideological immobility and, on the other, nationalist dynamism. The Soviet Union has been forced to allow its satellites some measure of ideological experimentation, but any venture into "irredentism" or the pursuit of national economic policies has been viewed with alarm. The United States has been content with sound economic progress under the NATO umbrella as long as they have held its handle. At the same time, there has been a definite tendency in, for example, Poland, France, and Romania, to dispense with rigid ideology and to revert to traditional diplomatic means. Partial political realignments seem to be becoming the rule.

This in a general way is the conception of Europe upon which present French foreign policy rests—a continent in the making which, while it is transforming itself along lines which are suited to its own interests, can serve as an element of equilibrium in the definition of global policy. It is through analyzing the process of (a) decolonization and (b) European unification that the French views with regard to the Communist bloc can best be described.

Decolonization has brought out one trait of French diplomatic methods that is of great interest: supremacy of pragmatism over ideology. The French had already recognized during the last war that Africa would be the center of decolonization. The difference between their attitudes in Africa and Indochina is significant in this regard and General de Gaulle, who was one of the prime movers of the Indochina war and therefore the epitomy of the colonizer, became in Africa as of 1958 the epitomy of the decolonizer. Already in his famous Brazzaville speech during the war, De Gaulle had accepted the principle of eventual African decolonization and some measure of its implementation. But it was only in 1958, when he resumed power in France, that he applied this principle fully in practice. In this connection, it is interesting to note that the implementation by the French of the principle of decolonization coincided with the militant emergence of China, coupled with the realization that the Chinese considered Africa as a suitable terrain for the propagation of their doctrinaire views.

There is a direct link based on thrust and counterthrust between Chinese and French policy in Africa, Chinese policy acting as a sort of continental incentive to which the French replied by the furtherance of African decolonization. This relationship became evident during the settlement of the Algerian conflict, which posed more far-reaching problems to France than the decolonization of the rest of Africa. The links between the provisional government of the Algerian Republic (G.P.R.A.) and Chinese officials in Peking are well known, and it is in Algeria that the fusion of pragmatism with ideology on the French side can best be witnessed. There would seem to be a law in French thinking with regard to the relationship between Communism and decolonization that would read something like this: the rate of decolonization should be in direct proportion to the dynamism of Communist influence in the area concerned. The important element in this "law" is that decolonization should precede any undue extension of Communist (and in the case of Africa, Chinese) influence.

At the same time that this law is at work, another one, which De Gaulle, like his predecessors, calls *"grandeur"* or *"mission civilisatrice de la France,"* blazes forth. Some historians and several journalists have tried to reduce the word *"grandeur"* to a mere Gaullist propaganda device; in reality, it corresponds to a clear-cut form of pragmatism deriving from the belief that it is important for any country or area to benefit from some sort of French influence, and that it is generally better for a country, especially if it is under-developed, to come under French influence than under any other.

Although decolonization is important in itself, it is particularly so in Africa, because it throws some light on the relations of France with aggressive Communist countries, in this case, China. African decolonization could in the long run only mean a decrease of Chinese influence in Africa, and we are in fact witnessing today a weakening of ties between China and the republics of Africa. This decrease of Chinese influence on the African continent cul-minated in the recognition of China by France. In a sense it could be argued that French official recognition of China was the last blow, because it meant that General de Gaulle and his govern-ment could acknowledge, through the exchange of diplomatic mis-sions, the immense influence of China in world affairs precisely be-cause they had tested its limits within the French zone of influence. Thus, the decolonization process is closely linked with the world prestige of China. It was accomplished to a certain extent because of the emergence of Chinese influence in Africa; it helped to de-stroy the immediate impact of this emergence and French recogni-tion of the Chinese regime followed upon Chinese decline. In Africa in 1958, the French found China arriving on the stage; through the efficiency and farsightedness of their decolonization, they brought China back to its point of departure.

General de Gaulle tried to apply the same principle to South America in 1965, another zone of Chinese influence in the forma-tive stage. Here this principle met with the gigantic and immobile force of a counterprinciple.

Decolonization was and is an outward-looking European policy; unification, on the contrary, is inward-looking. Since the inception of the Coal and Steel Community under the Schumann-Adenauer aegis, two main traits of European unification have become ap-parent. In the first place, unification, from a political viewpoint, was conceived as a solidification of economic interests with a view eventually to countering the political ambitions of the Soviet Union, and secondly therefore, from an economic viewpoint, with a view to enhancing the cause of traditional business interests in Europe. Today, European unification in the Western sense has become the intellectual *"chasse-gardée"* of the European bourgeoisie. The policies furthered both at Brussels and Strasbourg impinge both on East-West relations and on the position France is slowly adopting between the two blocs in the following ways: (a) France and the Soviet Union share a similar preoccupation about the future of Germany and especially about German reunification. The French Government has virtually recognized the validity of the Oder-Neisse line. On the other hand, Germany, under American guidance, has quickly recovered her predominant position in Europe and has therefore, in spite of whatever pious appearances may be maintained, resumed a position of strength which the Soviet Union and France do not relish; (b) The possibility of an American-German *de facto* alliance which would be tantamount to a condominium in Europe cannot be ignored, especially in view of nuclear implications; (c) The looming preponderance of Western Germany is not made more palatable by the fact that the European Common Market means in effect the acceptance in Europe of an economic doctrine that serves best the interests of Germany. A direct consequence of this is an ideological hardening of the Soviet Union and its allies, who are forced to compensate for the losses consequent upon the relaxation of their impracticable economic methods. As a result, Western and Eastern Europe continue to evolve along divergent lines and unification is postponed; (d) The French view appears to be that unification should transcend economic doctrines and especially that European unification (which ought to include Eastern Europe) should not be sacrificed to the demands of political and economic ideologies; (e) Nevertheless an internal evolution of Europe that will necessarily overcome doctrinal rigidity is under way. This is a fundamental cultural fact which, in the French view, is of paramount importance because all other European developments will stem from it in the long run.

The French believe that the whole of Europe will never be unified unless some measure of flexibility is introduced into the economic system which is at the basis of the present attempts to unify Western Europe. The ultimate aim is, of course, that Western Europe should be able to meet Eastern Europe half way. A great deal of change has been witnessed in the Soviet Union and Eastern Europe in recent years, and it is assumed that this evolutionary process is not yet over. Western Europe should not therefore harden its position unnecessarily within an orthodox capitalist framework. This flexibility in approach might permit liberalization measures in Eastern Europe to obtain for a long enough period to permit real progress toward East-West unification. French foreign policy with regard to Europe conceived as a whole (and it is in this framework that De Gaulle's formula about Europe extending from the Atlantic to the Urals takes its proper meaning) is based on the assumption that, things being as they are, risks must be taken in order to ensure that peace is eventually achieved on the European continent.

What is the position of France and what are its aims in the present conflict between the Soviet Union and China? It should first be noted that General de Gaulle predicted this conflict, not because this prediction is indicative of his clairvoyance, but because it means that the possibility of such a rift, as well as its repercussions, had been present in official French thinking for some time before it occurred. In the first place, with regard to the Soviet Union, the French aim appears to be a diminution among underdeveloped countries of Soviet influence by helping to transform the image of the Soviet Union into that of a Western nation. The more the Soviet Union appears to be engulfed by and part of the Western world, the more therefore it is considered as a "have" country by the "have nots." China is the best instrument for bringing about this change of image, because it stands only to gain from the Soviet Union's partial demise, thus killing two birds with one stone, for the image of a prosperous and bourgeois Soviet Union implies, especially in the eyes of underdeveloped countries, an *objective rapprochement* between the Soviet Union and Europe. Any such objective *rapprochement* will eventually carry with it some measure of liberalization within the Soviet Union itself. Measures of liberalization have as a direct consequence a better understanding of Western problems in the Soviet Union, and better understanding in turn reinforces the desire for a *rapprochement*. It is through a process of this type that the Soviet Union will be made aware of its dual capacity as a member of the world Communist movement on the one hand and of Europe on the other.

The French Government is apparently prepared to go a long way to impress this concept upon the Soviet Union. Other countries in Eastern Europe have realized the far-reaching significance of this Gaullist policy. As early as August, 1964, Mr. Maurer, the Romanian Prime Minister, was visiting France; on the eve of his visit, General de Gaulle held a press conference in which he said that the Soviet Union was "the last and greatest of all imperialist powers." A remark of this kind, at such a time, was pregnant with meaning and was certainly not lost, as events have since shown, on the Romanian rulers. It meant especially that the Soviet Union would, at some point, have to accept becoming part of a larger political and economic entity, one not based on ideology or developing according to ideology; that the rule of Soviet imperialism was over in Europe but that the Soviet Union nevertheless was, and would remain, part of Europe. It is toward this eventual absorption of the Soviet Union by Europe that General de Gaulle's thinking is proceeding. By using the expression "to the Urals," he clearly indicates that there is a part (but only a part) of the Soviet Union that belongs to Europe. A divisive policy with regard to the Soviet Union is at work. Viewed from the outside (Washington in particular), General de Gaulle's thinking appears nefarious; it must also appear so to the Soviet Union, which is called upon to become the leader of a unified greater Europe at the expense of some sort of world leadership.

There is no doubt whatsoever that the French Government, even when it is pressing with the greatest vigor for greater French autonomy, considers the United States as the leader of the West. General de Gaulle himself has made that clear. It is likely that for a long time to come this U.S. position of supremacy will endure. What the French Government is trying to achieve at this stage is some sort of prototype relationship within a given alliance between a supreme power and one not so supreme. The two main features of such an alliance are: (a) inevitable economic interference on the part of the preponderant country, and (b) reduction to the minimum of military and political intervention. What is retained is the permanence of the present Western economic regime; what is reintroduced by French thinking is the classic notion of effective national sovereignty. This is undoubtedly a very difficult and precarious balance to want to achieve, since national sovereignty responds in an automatic fashion to economic pressures. In this context, national sovereignty will eventually have to be exercised in full, with the implication that economic interference should bow before national sovereignty. Therefore, national sovereignty is the ultimate aim from the French viewpoint. It is noteworthy that this "old-fashioned" view appears to be shared by East European countries, especially Poland, Romania, and Albania, countries which in recent years have enjoyed a favored treatment on the part of the French. There are here the makings of a subterranean alliance between France and the Balkans, an alliance in depth, at the level of a conception of history. It is based on a recent past, directed against Germany, on a strong tradition of cultural relations, and a desire on both sides for a diminution of foreign influence in Europe. In this connection, the recent French decision to withdraw from the integrated NATO military structure has been understandably well received in Eastern Europe, where NATO symbolizes the avowed desire of the United States to deal harshly with Communist governments.

Thus France, on the whole, has a conception of Eastern Europe, and of Eastern Europe's possible political and economic development, which is somewhat different from that of her allies. Is it perhaps because General de Gaulle has taken a more historical and a less ideological view of Europe's evolution since the war? One thing is certain: The French think that, generally speaking, the range of political, economic, and military interests in the world today is the same as that which existed before the war. The basic traits of humanity have not changed. The only thing that has changed are the "imperialist" countries themselves. Before the war, they were England and France; since the war, they have become the Soviet Union, the United States, and China. In short, the French believe that all strong and dynamic countries are, by their very nature, bound to evolve into imperialist powers. What matters therefore is not to try and transform an imperialist country into a nonimperialist one, or an ideology into an ethereal discussion. Imperialism and ideological faith are facts of present-day political life. What should be attempted by countries not affiliated in depth with blocs is to bring imperialist nations and ideological blocs to move forward by creating zones of interests. A dual process is involved in this form of action; at the same time that an evolutionary step is achieved in one direction, it changes the conditions of reaction in the other. This interplay is of the essence in world politics. It is evident that, if one takes French national interest into account, this thinking is rewarding and based on historical reasoning; there is a long tradition of intimate relations between France and the Balkans. Also, De Gaulle believes that the Communist doctrine carries within itself the seeds of its own destruction. His policy is built upon this confidence about the past and the future. If Communism were eternal, the French attitude would be irrelevant. It is because most people feel that, in spite of transitory imperialistic triumphs, the French views about the evolution of the world are rooted in reality, that General de Gaulle is fought with such bitterness by some and exalted with such fervor by others.

8. Communist China's Foreign Policy Toward the West

FRANZ MICHAEL

By THEIR WORDS and actions, the Chinese Communists have made it amply clear that the main purpose of their foreign policy is to advance the Communist world revolution and play a major part in directing it. This purpose, which has been constantly reiterated in official and unofficial statements and proclamations, was very forcefully expressed only recently in a major policy statement by the Chinese Communist military leader, member of the Politburo, and Defense Minister, Lin Piao, published in the official journal *Hung Ch'i* (*Red Flag*) on September 2, 1965, under the title "Long Live the Victory of the Peoples' War." It was a statement that hailed the world-wide use of "wars of national liberation" to conquer "imperialism" and establish Communism and that committed China to the support of this policy.

The strategy of wars of liberation, which is now promoted by Communist China on a world-wide scale, is the very same that was applied by the Communists in China itself. This strategy, based on Communist exploitation of revolutionary potentials in the under-developed world for the advance of Communist world revolution, has been one of the two major Communist strategies which were once evolved by Lenin himself and which, in combination, make up the Communist program for world conquest. The relationship of these two strategies is at the heart of the conflict between Moscow and Peking, which in itself has had its impact on Chinese Communist foreign policy toward the West.

The two Communist strategies are "proletarian revolution," which was to occur in the industrialized West, and which, in the Communist view, was accomplished in Russia, and "national-liberation movements" sponsored, promoted, and exploited by the Communists, which were to lead to the Communist victory in the developing countries of Asia, Africa, and the "New World," and thus to undermine world capitalism in this "weakest link" of its world position.

"Proletarian revolution" was, of course, the original concept of Communism as taught by Karl Marx, who believed in the inevita-bility of a breakdown of what he regarded as the capitalist system of exploitation, under which the gap between an ever-smaller number of capitalists and the ever-larger exploited group of the proletariat would finally lead to a collapse of capitalist domination and to the takeover of power by the proletariat under its dictator-ship over state and society. When the Communist takeover suc-ceeded in Russia, Lenin and his Communist friends still expected the Communist revolution to occur immediately in the indus-trialized heart of Europe. It was to be only a matter of weeks or months until soviets controlled by the workers and peasants would be established in Germany and in other European countries to join the Russian Revolution in what was to be the beginning of the world proletarian revolution. The *Räterepublik* in Munich and Bela Kun's Soviet Government in Hungary were to be part of such a proletarian revolution spreading throughout Europe, a revolution that was to lead to a combined Communist union of Soviet Socialist republics, of which the U.S.S.R. at Moscow was only the beginning.

The first damper to the concept of Communist internationalism in the Western world came with the Treaty of Brest-Litovsk in 1918, which forced the Russian Bolsheviks into accepting a more traditional state concept for their own dictatorship. But the dream of proletarian revolution throughout Europe remained strong and its immediate fulfillment was not doubted until the Communist disappointments with events in Germany in 1922 and 1923 demonstrated that proletarian revolution outside the Soviet Union was not imminent.

Then another opportunity of Communist advance became apparent to Lenin, who desperately sought to broaden the revolution, which, Lenin believed, if limited to Russia alone, would be threatened. This second opportunity Lenin saw in the revolutionary tensions and potentials in Asia, as demonstrated at the time by the revolutionary ardor of Asian representatives invited by the Soviet Union to participate in the congresses of the Comintern and such special meetings as the Congress of the Toilers of the East held at Baku. The exploitation of this revolutionary potential for Communist purposes was to be justified by Lenin's theory of imperialism, which applied the Marxian concept of world history to the world scene, and of the inevitability of Socialist victory. Imperialism was for Lenin the last stage of monopoly capitalism, which had moved from the exploitation of its own proletariat to that of colonial countries. Under this concept of colonial rule, it was possible for the Communists to regard all discontent in the colonies—or in what the Communists described as quasi-colonies—as anticapitalist revolutions which the Communists could support and eventually take over.

The possibility of thus shifting the world revolution of the proletariat to Asia was made possible by Lenin's concept of a disciplined Communist party of revolutionaries claiming to be "the vanguard of the proletariat" and the executor of its will, as interpreted by the prophets of the alleged science of dialectic materialism. Communist parties could represent the spirit of the proletariat on a world-wide scale even in countries where no proletariat existed. It is this concept of sharing in the world role and of the imminence of the alleged proletarian revolution which permitted Communist parties to represent the doctrine and apply the strategy in countries like China and other predominantly agricultural regions of the world. Establishing branches of this world party anywhere where revolutionary tensions of any sort made Communist revolutionary work profitable fitted well into Lenin's concept of a world Communist party. Thus Lenin's vanguard theory provided the organizational basis for Communist revolutionary activities in the same way as his theory of imperialism provided the justification of the exploitation of revolutionary tensions and discontent for Communist purposes.

There were two elements of this revolutionary potential in the nonindustrial countries. On the one hand, there was a new Western-educated elite that, concentrated in the cities, turned to Western forms of economic and social life. This proportionately small elite had grown up in the concepts of the Western world of the national state and was opposed to whatever political or economic control the Western countries had established in the age of colonialism. The nationalist, anticolonial aspirations of this Western-oriented upper group could be linked in Communist doctrinal interpretation to the battle against monopoly capitalism. In Communist doctrinal terms, these nationalists represented an early stage of indigenous capitalism, nationalist in character, and, in Communist terminology, progressive. At this stage, this nationalist bourgeoisie would be an ally of the Communists in the fight against what they called Western imperialism. The Communists could, therefore, in these countries support nationalist movements which they regarded as a necessary part of a development that would lead from this capitalist interval to the inevitable socialist conclusion. The Communists' support of these "nationalist capitalists" was, therefore, temporary and would lead to eventual Communist takeover and liquidation of the former ally.

The second revolutionary element to be used for Communist purposes was the peasant, who made up the vast majority of the population of the agricultural countries that had become the target of Communist advance. Peasant discontent had been used by Lenin in the Bolshevik revolution when he had, much to the surprise of his socialist colleagues, taken over the program of the nonsocialist opposition to give the peasants the land they asked for. This, too, was a temporary concession, to be countermanded later by collectivization. But this Communist future was distant and was not emphasized in the Communist proclamations of the time, and neither the "nationalist capitalists" nor the peasants realized when they accepted the Communists that this acceptance would lead to their own eventual physical or social liquidation.

The strategy of using nationalist aspirations and agrarian discontent for Communist purposes was not altogether new. Marx and Engels had recommended the use of these two elements of revolutionary ferment for Communist purposes. The discontent of the French peasants and the nationalism in Poland and Ireland had seemed to the fathers of Communist doctrine factors that could well be manipulated for Communist purposes. But Lenin used these two factors as the major elements of strategy in another part of the world. There, nationalism and peasant discontent had to be the dominant elements in a revolution—in which the Communists claimed to be allies—that was only eventually to lead to a socialist stage and in which the role of the Communists as heralds of the future was even more fictitious than it had been under the claim of the proletarian revolution in the West. Yet it provided them with an effective explanation for a Communist role in a non-Western revolution that was anything but Marxian in its aspirations but was ideally suited for infiltration and Communist takeover.

The two elements of this Communist strategy were, however, at times difficult to coordinate. Communist cooperation with the nationalist urban elite might be endangered by a Communist call for agrarian revolution, and it was a problem for Communist strategy in China as it is a problem for Chinese Communist policy in the Afro-Asian world today to correlate and time properly the two elements in order to prevent a conflict that might endanger the Communist strategy as a whole. The history of Communism in China is a major example of this problem. In the first stage of Communist strategy, the Communists were to cooperate under nationalist leadership in a nationalist revolution led by Sun Yat-sen and his successors. As long as there was success in this stage of cooperation, the second element, that of agrarian revolution, had to be played down. There was no disagreement among Communists on this postponement of the peasant policy, but there was disagreement as to the timing of the shift from one policy to the other. It is sometimes not realized how close the Communists came to an actual takeover of the nationalist revolution in China in 1927. But when the Communist strategy was defeated in what became a major debacle for them, and when the power struggle was over in Moscow and Stalin emerged the victor, Communist policy in China shifted to agrarian revolution.

It cannot be stressed enough that this shift was not a Chinese Communist departure from the Moscow line—let alone an invention by Mao Tse-tung who, at that time, was not yet the leading figure in the Chinese Communist organization. The directives for the shift of strategy clearly came from Moscow and from Stalin. These directives were spelled out in February, 1928, at the Ninth Plenum of the Central Committee of the Comintern, and in June of that year, at the Sixth Congress of the Chinese Communist Party, held in Moscow under the thumb of Stalin, they were accepted as Chinese Communist Party policy. They contained three major points: agrarian revolution, rural soviets, and guerrilla warfare. These basic ingredients of what is the communist strategy today as emphasized by the Chinese Communists are, therefore, not a Chinese invention but part of the general strategy of warfare as conceived by Lenin and directed by Stalin in his time. It is of utmost importance to remember that this major aspect of Communist China's foreign policy toward the West is Communist and not a Chinese peculiarity.

In the late 1920's and in the 1930's, this strategy was attempted in China, but it was not successful. Communism was losing and the National government was clearly gaining the upper hand when the Japanese attack on China that later merged with World War II destroyed the basis of Nationalist strength and gave the Communists their chance.

For the evaluation of this strategy, which today is stressed by the Chinese Communists, it is important to remember that in China as elsewhere, Communist guerrilla warfare has only been successful where it has had access to outside aid. It was in Manchuria that, after World War II, the outcome of the Chinese Civil War was decided. And it was there that the Chinese Communists were given the opportunity by the Soviets to move in first after the Japanese surrender and to obtain the equipment taken by the Soviets from the Japanese armies, which was then used by the Chinese Communists to move on from the stage of guerrilla fighting to that of regular warfare.

After their victory, the Chinese Communists became the model for success of this Communist strategy, which was now to become the strategy of "wars of national liberation." As the Bolsheviks had become the model of a "proletarian revolution" leading to a "socialist" system, the Chinese Communists were the example of a successful takeover through a liberation war that would lead to a presocialist system—a "peoples' republic" in which the fiction of a joint revolution based on an alliance of the Communists with non-Communist revolutionary groups was maintained. China thus joined the group of peoples' republics which were based on a fictitious united front—which in practice, of course, was under complete Communist control.

Communist strategy in China thus fell within the framework of the over-all Communist line, and the role that China was to play in world Communism was in keeping with Lenin and Stalin's concept of strategy and was in itself no cause for any conflict, certainly not any Communist "heresy." In 1956, when the conflict leading to the alienation of Peking from Moscow began, it was therefore not caused by any basic ideological reasons that would take Chinese Communist foreign policy out of the framework of Communist doctrine and action. There was then not only agreement on the strategy of national-liberation movements and on China's role in promoting them, but the Chinese Communists also fully supported the Soviet line with regard to strategy toward the West. When, after Stalin's death, Soviet policy began to shift from one of threat and bluster to "peaceful coexistence," the Chinese Communists gave their full backing to this strategy, once used before by Stalin in the 1930's in order to gain the support of the West against the threat of Hitler. At that time, the "imperialist" powers became the Western "democracies," the Soviet control over the movement was loosened, and the Comintern was played down and eventually abolished in 1943. After the war, Stalin established the Cominform, and the Communist parties in Eastern Europe openly took power. Now, after Stalin's death, "peaceful coexistence" was reintroduced. The Chinese Communists not only followed the line but were even the first to apply it. In their agreement with India they formulated the five principles of peaceful coexistence, which were, in turn, incorporated in the Ten Points of the Bandung Conference of 1955. And when Khrushchev, in 1956, first brought up peaceful coexistence as the basic principle of Soviet policy, he referred to the Sino-Indian agreement and the Bandung Conference as proof that peaceful coexistence was "one of the cornerstones of the foreign policy of the Chinese Republic."

If the Soviet and Chinese Communists both accepted a strategy of peaceful coexistence having as its aim the avoidance of hydrogen war, both also stressed the limitations of such peaceful coexistence. As each has indicated, "peaceful coexistence" was not meant to exclude the use of violence in a revolution or in "wars of national liberation." For the Soviets, according to a statement issued by the CPSU in 1963: "The peaceful coexistence of states with different social systems presupposes an unremitting ideological, political, and economic struggle of the working people *inside* the capitalist system, including armed struggle when the peoples find that necessary, and the steady advance of the national-liberation movement among the peoples of colonial and dependent countries." And Khrushchev had distinguished between world wars that would lead to a hydrogen catastrophe and thus had to be avoided, local wars that could escalate into world wars and were, therefore, dangerous, on the one hand, and "wars of national liberation," which were "just" wars and which were "inevitable" and which the Communists had to support, on the other. The Chinese Communists' concept is very similar, and to both the Soviets and the Chinese Communists peaceful coexistence means only that wars, world wars that is, are not necessary. But they are still possible, since, in Communist terms, imperialism might provoke them. In this case, as the Soviets have it: "It stands to reason, of course, that if the imperialist madmen unleash a war, the peoples will sweep capitalism away and bury it." And the Chinese declared that should the imperialists start the war, this would result in "the very speedy destruction of these monsters encircled by the peoples of the world." And in this context, Mao Tse-tung made his oft-quoted statement that "on the ruins of the destroyed imperialism, a beautiful future will be built."

There is thus no conflict between the ideological views expressed by the Soviets and Chinese Communists. Yet in the mutual vituperations that characterize the political estrangement between Moscow and Peking, both sides have hurled at each other accusations in which such an ideological disagreement was proclaimed. In the verbal battle that sharpened after the Twenty-second Soviet Party Congress in 1961, the Soviets accused the Chinese of being "warmongers," out to engulf the world in a catastrophic hydrogen war, while the Chinese Communists in their turn accused the Soviets of being "peacemongers," of having abandoned proletarian revolution and "wars of national liberation" in favor of a conspiracy to divide the rule of the world with the imperialist United States. In checking the statements as well as the actions of the two protagonists in the inter-Communist power struggle, we find that both accusations are patently wrong, being based on statements that are taken out of context. The Soviets have not abandoned world revolution or "wars of national liberation," and the Chinese have not propagated hydrogen war.

The reason for the distortions of each other's views is only too obvious. Authority in Communist terms is sanctioned by the claim of the leadership to possess the right understanding and application of the allegedly scientific proof of Marxism-Leninism. All opposition is therefore to be accused of ideological deviation, whether the case can be truly made or not. Within any one party, the power struggle can be organizationally resolved in the highest councils of the Party—the Central Committee and the Politburo—while in the bloc and movement no such body exists. Since the dissolution of the Comintern and the Cominform, the only institutional structure of the movement is the inter-Party meeting, which has become itself a battleground for the conflict. In the absence of a central organization, the Communist parties must use ideological accusations as the main forum for their battle for leadership. In the inner Party battles such accusations were usually revealed when the battle was over and when the winner could accuse his defeated opponent, rightly or wrongly, of the deviationism that would disqualify him from leadership. In the amorphous state of the bloc and movement, the ideological battle has to be fought in the open. But the accusations of warmongering and peacemongering must not mislead us into disregarding the true stand taken by either side with regard to Communist world strategy.

If there is no basic ideological conflict between Moscow and Peking on the major strategies of Communist advance, there nonetheless is, in the statements as well as in the actions of each, a difference of emphasis and priority of policy which can easily be understood in terms of the special role which the two parties have assumed in the Communist movement.

The Soviets, themselves the representatives of a Bolshevik revolution and still in the leading position for the over-all policy of Communism, have to balance their propagation of Strategy Two and Strategy One. Their support of wars of national liberation must be attuned to their greater concern for the strategy of peaceful coexistence. And they have to weigh the advantages of Communist-directed warfare in the Afro-Asian world against their attempts to strengthen Communist advance in the industrial world of the West by the new image that enables Communist parties to appear as indigenous movements and gain new possibilities for impact on public opinion and—at least so they hope—participation in government.

The Chinese Communists stress the strategy of wars of liberation, which has been their own success story and for which they claim the experience that they are eager to share, with the Communist parties in the Afro-Asian and the American world. The statement of Lin Piao has been but the latest reassertion of this strategy. His only shift from the line originated by Lenin and promulgated by Stalin and Mao Tse-tung has been the claim of the priority for this Strategy Two, of wars of liberation, over Strategy One. The decisive sentence of Lin Piao's formulation is the one in which he declares: "Since World War II, the proletarian revolutionary movement has for various reasons been temporarily held back in the North American and West European capitalist countries, while the peoples' revolutionary movement in Asia, Africa, and Latin America has been growing vigorously."

Lin Piao claims that through this strategy of national-liberation movements the industrial states of the world will be engulfed by the Communist advance in the Afro-Asian and American countries as the cities were engulfed by the rural revolution in the wars of national liberation. If there is, therefore, any argument between the Chinese Communists and the Soviets on Communist strategy, it is only on the question of priority between the two strategies in the over-all advance. In this argument the Chinese have then become the champions of wars of national liberation. To them Vietnam is to provide the proof that this kind of war is the strategy most likely to succeed. They have already started similar movements in other countries of Asia, Africa, and the New World, which are most likely to lead to further advance if the events in Vietnam prove to be successful for the Communists.

But elsewhere this Communist strategy for which the Chinese Communists have become the main spokesmen has not gone so well. The attempt at a violent coup in Indonesia backfired, and as of now the Chinese Communists seem to have lost their position there. Their attempt to dominate the Afro-Asian Solidarity Organization to the exclusion of their Soviet Communist opponent forced them in the fall of 1965 to cancel the Algerian Conference, and the entire Afro-Asian policy and its organization have been gravely weakened. As main protagonists of this strategy, the Chinese Communists have had to bear the odium of the defeat. In some cases, as in Ghana and in other countries of Africa, the reaction against Communist or pro-Communist politics has led to an over-all setback for the Communists, Soviet as well as Chinese. In other cases, as in the conflict between India and Pakistan or in the Americas, the Chinese loss became the gain of the more cautious, more sophisticated, and shrewdly calculated Soviet strategy. When Castro in Cuba turned against Peking, the Communist conspiracy and infiltration policy continued and was propagated by the inter-Party meeting held in Havana without the Chinese—a clear indication that the strategy of national-liberation movements and wars is not, after all, a Chinese Communist prerogative.

The Chinese Communists have thus come out second best in the critical points of conflict the world over during the last year [1965]. As of now that has not affected their assertion that wars of liberation are Strategy One and that militancy has to remain the password of Communist policy today. As long as "the East wind prevails over the West wind," as Mao proclaimed in 1957, this trend is likely to remain. But if, in Vietnam and elsewhere, the Chinese Communists should detect a shifting of the wind, they could very well themselves shift back to a strategy of nonviolent means of advance, even under the leadership of Mao Tse-tung, though perhaps with greater ease after Mao's demise.

Such a shift could come independently of a reconciliation between Moscow and Peking, but it would, of course, be more likely connected with the healing of the rift caused by the power struggle. Such reconciliation is entirely possible, especially after Mao's disappearance from the scene. The Soviets have apparently left the door open for such a re-establishment of cooperation, when, after the fall of Khrushchev, they ceased to answer the Chinese accusations in kind. The Chinese claim, first expressed in October, 1963, that Khrushchev and his successors in the Soviet Party had lost their vanguard role because of their revisionism, and that the mantle of Marxist-Leninist leadership had fallen on Chinese shoulders has been the most extreme challenge to Moscow. But even this charge could be dropped once Mao is gone.

In the meantime we have to remember that neither for the Soviets nor for the Chinese "peaceful coexistence" has to conflict with "wars of national liberation." And we might go further. Peaceful coexistence does not only have to apply to the "proletarian revolution." If the United States finds the answer to the strategy of wars of liberation, there is no reason for the Communists not to shift to nonviolent means of "national-liberation movements." Today, both the Soviets and the Chinese Communists have spoken of the inevitability and justice of "liberation wars." It is for us to defeat the Communist strategy of that warfare and to force our Communist antagonists to shift to the weapons of nonviolent battle under this strategy as well.

To bring about such a change we have to demonstrate to the Communists that their present military aggressiveness is not successful. This is not a matter of the friendly persuasion of a group of political psychopaths who suffer from the hangover of nineteenth-century humiliations of Imperial China. The Communists of today are no more paranoid nationalists suffering from "isolation" from the civilized world than they were once agrarian reformers. They are entirely rational within the framework of their doctrine. They can also understand defeat, but have no reason today to give up a strategy that, so they believe, will lead us to abandon the battle.

Communist Chinese policy toward us at the moment stresses the militant aspects of the strategy of wars of national liberation. This strategy is based on capturing leadership of the rural and, when the time is ripe, the urban communities in the country under attack. It is a strategy that plays with emotional, psychological, and economic factors, but it is also a strategy that uses one major tool of control that is not described in the textbooks on guerrilla warfare coming out of Peking: the strategy of terror. Under this form of warfare, terror is a well-calculated means of destroying the existing leadership of the communities. The assassination of tens of thousands of local leaders, of the teachers, the monks, the village heads, and all those who oppose Communist rule, and of the families of these victims, has the double purpose of removing the existing leadership and of terrorizing the population into acceptance of the Communist cadres. It is a strategy that has to be carried out by local Communist organizations, albeit with outside support.

Our answer to this strategy must be more than military. No defeat of Vietcong soldiers will remove the Communist advance unless the military action can be followed up by safeguarding the local leadership against the threat posed by its Communist opposition. No election makes any sense unless this has been done. The enemy is not so much the Vietcong soldier as the Communist organization, the National Liberation Front, acting under direction from Hanoi. Any indication that we are willing to compromise with this enemy will weaken the willingness of the anti-Communist forces to fight and strengthen the Communists in their conviction that their strategy is paying off.

As important as protection is as an answer to the strategy of terror in guerrilla warfare, it can be only part of the answer to the Communist strategy of "national-liberation movements." The Communist advance is much broader. Protection can only provide a framework that has to be used for constructive effort. The Communists have been exploiting a revolutionary transformation that is taking place in the developing countries. There is a true discontent of the agrarian population, which has been so much neglected by the urban Western-thinking minority. There is a true nationalism, which is, in the main, a combination of traditional beliefs and values with modern concepts of national life. To bridge the gap between city and countryside, to create an institutional framework of the true national revolution, which the Communists are only exploiting, is the real task for the countries of Asia that are the objects of this Communist attack led today by Communist China. Modernization within the cultural framework of the people concerned, the bridging of the gap between town and countryside, the reintegration of society, these are the tasks of a true revolution. Communist policy has been attempting to exploit this revolution for its ends. It is for us to understand this revolution and to capture and support it.

9. The Conflict in the Far East*

WILLIAM E. BAUER

THE MILITARY career of Viscount Garnet Wolseley, who, on his retirement in 1900 was British Commander in Chief, encompassed almost every major British campaign of the latter half of the nineteenth century. He saw action in the Second Burmese War, the Crimean War, the Indian Mutiny, the 1860 campaign against China, the Ashanti, Zulu and Egyptian campaigns, and the Riel rebellion. At the turn of the century, having had ample opportunity to test and ponder the mettle of a wide variety of opponents, Wolseley singled out the Chinese as "the coming rulers of the world," who needed only their own Peter the Great or Napoleon to lead them to this goal.

Wolseley did not envisage that the Chinese would reach their objective unopposed. At the "great battle of Armageddon" which

* Any views expressed in this chapter are those of the author. They should not be interpreted as reflecting the official opinion or policy of the Government of Canada.

he saw in the world's future, they would be confronted by the people of the United States of America.

The concept of confrontation was part of Wolseley's trade, if not of his vocabulary. He could recognize the vigor, resilience, and self-assurance of the ancient Chinese race, and the unlimited vitality and evangelistic brashness of the young United States, which had already established itself next door to China, in the Philippines. For him, these two Pacific powers were natural antagonists.

One might look upon developments in Asia in the 1960's as evidence of Wolseley's prescience, to see in the clash of arms in Vietnam, as many Western observers do, the preliminary stages of a chain of events leading to the Armageddon that Wolseley foresaw. But to a generation of policy-makers accustomed to living under the immanent shadow of a nuclear holocaust, whose efforts have been turned to finding ways in which "natural" antagonists could develop techniques of accommodation, prophecies of doom are not only irrelevant but dangerous, if they induce—as they could have in Europe between 1948 and 1960, and as they may yet in Asia in the 1960's—a paralysis of policy leaving unchecked those forces that could lead ineluctably to the final confrontation which foreign policy is supposed to avert.

The conflict in the Far East, involving as it does global as well as local issues and requiring decisions which are not only complex but often unpalatable and fraught with risk and uncertainty, could very well lead to such a paralysis of Western policy. The Western allies, who were united and determined in 1949, and whose unity in NATO helped persuade the Soviet Union to adopt certain minimum standards of international behavior in the pursuit of its objectives, are clearly divided in their assessment of events in the Far East and their choice of policies to meet them. Collective security under American leadership, combined with massive economic assistance, is recognized by most NATO governments to have been the salvation of Western Europe in the postwar period. Most of the same governments, however, show little confidence in collective-security arrangements, or even in United States military involvement, as an instrument of policy in Asia. The basis of this attitude (or, it could be argued, the effect and justification of it) is an interpretation of the conflict in the Far East very different from their interpretations of the European situation in the postwar years. More extreme observers have adopted as the basic premise of their position the judgment that U.S. military involvement in the Far East, and in Vietnam in particular, is politically misguided and even morally indefensible. In the field of East-West relations in the 1960's, this is beyond any doubt the fundamental question; the answer to it and, more important still, the policies flowing from that answer, will have as great an impact on the course of the world as did policies in similar situations immediately before and after World War II.

The issues of the 1960's in Asia, to be placed in their proper perspective, must be traced back to the Korean war. Until 1950, when North Korea marched across the 38th parallel, U.S. policy in Asia was developing into one of disengagement. Throughout the disintegration of the Nationalist cause in China, the United States used every method short of military force to achieve a political settlement; when the situation on the mainland became irretrievable in 1948, the use of American forces to defend Formosa was also ruled out. As Secretary of State Marshall explained it, "direct armed intervention in the internal affairs of China runs counter to traditional American policy toward China."[1] President Truman, on January 5, 1950, stated that the United States had "no desire to obtain special rights or privileges or to establish military bases on Formosa at this time." Furthermore, "the United States will not pursue a course which will lead to involvement in the civil conflict in China."[2] Policy aside, the U.S. Government recognized that there was no assurance that armed intervention could change the outcome in China. Furthermore, the American public was busy beating swords into ploughshares. It had acceded to the U.S. commitment in Europe, and when the time came, it would be induced to support the U.S. action against aggression in Korea; a leap into China on behalf of one party in a civil war probably would not have been tolerated so readily.

[1] Department of State, *United States Relations with China* (Washington, D.C.: Government Printing Office, 1949), p. 280.
[2] *Department of State Bulletin,* January 16, 1950, p. 79. Quoted in Tang Tsou, *America's Failure in China, 1941–50* (Chicago: University of Chicago Press, 1963), p. 531.

At the beginning of 1950, therefore, the U.S. Government, despite strong Congressional opposition, had decided not to intervene in the Chinese civil war and not to take any action to defend Formosa. It had also made it clear that the American line of defense in the Pacific, which stretched from the Aleutians through Okinawa to the Philippines, did not include either Formosa or Korea. U.S. troops had been withdrawn from South Korea in 1949, despite signs of Communist subversion and guerrilla activity, and the fears expressed by the South Korean Government that a U.S. withdrawal would be the signal for a North Korean attack. There were clear indications that the United States was disinclined to commit troops to any part of the Asian mainland,[3] that it considered military guarantees in the Far East and Southeast Asia as "hardly suitable or necessary within the realm of practical relationship,"[4] and that it had discarded the possibility of any Asian collective security treaty backed, like NATO, by U.S. military power.[5] Although the U.S. Government viewed the emergence of a Communist China with apprehension, and saw it as a manifestation of the same Soviet imperialism it was confronting in Europe, it hoped that "ultimately the profound civilization and democratic individualism of China will reassert themselves and she will throw off the foreign yoke."[6] In the meantime, however, it was made clear that any attempt by the Communist regime to engage in aggression against China's neighbors would confront the United States and other members of the United Nations with a situation "violative of the principles of the United Nations Charter and threatening international peace and security."[7] This formula, drawn from Chapter 7 of the Charter, should have been interpreted by Communist China and the Soviet Union as a clear warning that the United States might not only invoke Security Council action against aggression in Asia, but also exercise "the inherent right of individual or collective self-defense" sanctioned by Article 51. They chose to ignore the warning, just as they were later to ignore the identical warning given

---

[3] Alexander L. George, "American Policy-making and the North Korea Aggression," *World Politics*, January, 1955, p. 224.

[4] Dean Acheson, in *Department of State Bulletin*, January 23, 1950, p. 115.

[5] Tang Tsou, *op. cit.*, p. 506.

[6] *United States Relations with China*, p. xvi.

[7] *Ibid.*, p. xvii.

by the United States at the conclusion of the 1954 Geneva Conference on Indochina.

It is impossible to determine with any certainty the considerations that entered into the Communist decision to attack South Korea. It is generally accepted, however, that the primary responsibility lay with the Soviet Union; certainly, an initiative of this magnitude could not have been taken by a satellite regime like North Korea without, at the very least, the encouragement of Moscow and the assurance that Soviet support would be available. To Stalin, the move must have seemed consistent with the situation existing at the time. The Zhdanov "two-camp" line, although in full swing since late 1947, had produced few results. The Berlin Blockade had failed, and the formation of NATO, backed by the U.S. nuclear deterrent, had made it clear that any further Soviet adventures in Europe could be unacceptably expensive. A Communist-sponsored youth conference held in Calcutta in February, 1948, had been followed by a series of uprisings in South and Southeast Asia, directed mainly against newly independent governments; they had all been unsuccessful, although those in Burma, Malaya, and the Philippines were still dragging on. If, as seemed evident, the Zhdanov doctrine and Communist morale in Asia needed a boost, Korea must have appeared to Moscow as the best, or even the only, available theater for a quick and spectacular Communist victory. The Southern regime was weak both militarily and politically, and was already trying to cope with infiltration and subversion from the North. The United States had withdrawn its troops, and Moscow was aware that Korea lay outside the U.S. defense perimeter in the Pacific. Finally, it is tempting to speculate in retrospect about Stalin's possible calculations concerning the effect of the move on Communist China, whose unexpectedly sudden emergence he undoubtedly found unsettling: Quick success would have strengthened Soviet control of the Pyongyang regime and preempted any move by Communist China to replace Moscow; failure, which by definition could occur only if the United States entered the war, would bring the United States back to China's doorstep and thus provide a continuing restraint on the Peking regime.

In any event, the Chinese Communists, flushed with success, undoubtedly acquiesced in the Korean venture. Their later intervention against U.N. forces probably was prompted not only by their desire to block the establishment of U.S. forces on the Yalu, but also by the opportunity it presented them to reduce the likelihood that Soviet influence in Korea might gain permanent roots. By any normal standards of foreign policy, however, the Korean war did not serve to advance China's long-term interests. As pointed out above, the United States, on the eve of the Korean war, was showing a strong aversion to any major involvement in Asia. A more subtle attack on the Seoul Government by means of stepped-up infiltration and subversion stood a good chance of succeeding without provoking American intervention. The long-term benefits to the Peking regime of American passivity and noninvolvement could have been substantial: Formosa probably would have remained unprotected; the French cause in Indochina might have appeared less deserving of support by Washington, which was not interested in propping up colonial regimes; the new governments of Asia might have been more open to Communist persuasion and penetration and, without the accelerated conclusion of a security pact with the United States, Japan's future role would have been open to question.

The Communist powers lost their gamble. The U.N. Security Council reacted decisively, and the United States took the first steps to provide military assistance to South Korea. Events were moving so swiftly that the U.S. decision to intervene must have been in the nature of a reflex action. There was time enough, however, to realize the great risk of defeat that existed for the sparse ground forces that could be committed, and to assess the implications of a decision not to oppose aggression. The risk was taken, and aggression was met. "A return to the rule of force in international affairs," President Truman pointed out in a White House statement issued on June 27, 1950, "would have far-reaching effects. The United States will continue to uphold the rule of law." Not unexpectedly, the Soviet Union accused the United States of "outright acts of aggression," "open intervention in Korea's domestic affairs," and "armed intervention in Korea." The United States, U.S.S.R. Deputy Foreign Minister Gromyko said in Moscow on July 4, intended "to deprive Korea of her national independence, to prevent the formation of a united, democratic Korean State, and forcibly to establish in Korea an antipopular regime that would allow the ruling circles of the United States to convert the country into their colony and use Korean territory as a military and strategic spring-board in the Far East." Although this line was to have greater success later in the Korean war and again during the Vietnam war of the 1960's, it did not convince many nations outside the Communist bloc in 1950. At a press conference in New Delhi on July 7, Prime Minister Nehru, for example, pointed out that "when North Korea launched an invasion against South Korea it became evident from all the information available that this was a large-scale and well-planned invasion. . . . In the delicate and precarious balance existing in the world, any such invasion was fraught with the most dangerous possibilities. If aggression was allowed to succeed, the entire structure of the United Nations would have inevitably collapsed and a large-scale war resulted."

The invasion precipitated not only U.N. intervention, but also a series of American moves that were to shape developments in Asia to China's disadvantage for years to come: the Seventh Fleet moved to neutralize the Formosa Straits; American bases in the Philippines were reinforced; military assistance to the French in Indochina was stepped up, and a security pact and peace treaty were concluded with Japan. More important still, perhaps, was the effect of the Korean war on the American attitude to the Chinese Communist regime. Disappointment at the Communist success and suspicion of Peking's intentions mounted. Open Communist aggression in Asia prompted the United States to turn to the same policy of military containment that had been adopted to meet a similar threat in Europe—in other words, to accept the necessity for U.S. military involvement in Asia for an indeterminate period. But in the case of Korea, strategic considerations were less influential than in Europe. They existed, but were probably balanced by the unpopularity among the public of a war in "a faraway country among people of whom they knew nothing" on behalf of a doubtful regime. The deciding factor was the act of aggression which, if successful, would have led to others. By refusing to repeat the mistakes of the 1930's, by meeting the challenge to the rule of law, the United States entered upon a policy that, once adopted, would be difficult to discard.

There is no need to assume, however, that Peking in 1950 overlooked the possibility that unfavorable developments might flow
from the attack on South Korea, or that its appraisal of these made
it reluctant to see the project undertaken. The Chinese regime was
part of the world Communist movement headed by the Soviet
Union, and was prepared at that time to follow Moscow's lead. It
was, moreover, wholeheartedly behind the current Marxist-Leninist
strategy in world affairs. Mao had made clear in 1949, when success
was within his grasp and dissimulation about CCP views on international relations was no longer tactically necessary, that he considered the United States to be the last major imperialist power—it
wanted "to enslave the entire world" and it had "aided Chiang
Kai-shek with arms to slaughter several millions of Chinese."[8] In
the same statement, he made it clear that the Chinese Communist
regime adhered to the two-camp doctrine: "To sit on the fence is
impossible; a third road does not exist." Liu Shao-chi, in November, 1949, had also made it clear that "imperialism" was the
main target and that it was to be opposed by armed struggle—
"the main form of struggle for the national liberation struggles of
many colonies and semicolonies."[9] Thus, whatever course of action
a cool appraisal of China's long-term interests might have dictated,
Communist doctrine and strategy probably was the deciding factor
in the Korean equations. With experience, Communist regimes can
develop Marxist-Leninist doctrine to further what they judge to
be their national objectives; occasionally, however, the doctrine
overrides and undermines national interests, especially if the regime
concerned is not adept and powerful enough to produce the tactical
shift needed to meet the requirements of a new situation. This was
the case with Communist China in 1950. The Peking regime was
firmly tied to the Moscow line; even if it had had conscious reservations—and there is no evidence that this was the case—its utter
reliance on Soviet support during its formative period made a
divergence of policy impossible.

By mid-1951, it had become apparent to Moscow and Peking

[8] Mao Tse-tung, "On the People's Democratic Dictatorship," July 1, 1949, in
Selected Works of Mao Tse-tung (Peking: Foreign Languages Press, 1961), IV, 414.
[9] Liu Shao-chi, Statement at Asian and Australasian Trade Union Conference,
Peking, November 16, 1949, New China News Agency, November 23, 1949.

that they could not achieve their military objectives in Korea and that further escalation of the war would involve a serious risk of large-scale U.S. retaliation. Following a Soviet initiative, cease-fire talks began in Korea. The Communist negotiators showed no interest in reaching agreement, but it soon became apparent that Peking and Moscow, having failed to defeat the U.N. forces militarily, were attempting to achieve their objective by other means. As one writer observes, "the point of this move seems to have been to improve the Russian position in the peace campaign which was then launched by all organs of Communist propaganda designed to exploit war-weariness, fear of a new world war, and anti-Americanism in Asia."[10] The campaign to brand the U.N. action as a cloak for U.S. aggression was fairly successful, particularly in Asia. Even in Western countries, public opinion was affected by the concentrated propaganda disseminated by the Communist bloc following the November, 1950, Warsaw "Peace Congress," which, in the first point of its manifesto, had called for the termination of the Korean war, the withdrawal of all foreign troops from Korea, and "the peaceful settlement of the Korean question with the participation of the Korean people." Not surprisingly, this proposal was coupled with a demand for "the cessation of the intervention of American troops on Formosa and of the hostilities against the republic of Vietnam, which are also fraught with the danger of world war."[11]

After two years of stalemate, a rough *status quo ante* was accepted by both sides in the armistice agreement signed on July 27, 1953. The sudden Communist desire to reach an agreement probably was motivated by the policy changes necessitated by the abandonment by Stalin, at the Nineteenth Congress of the CPSU, of the Zhdanov "two-camp" doctrine, and the adoption by Moscow and Peking of a completely new approach to foreign policy. In Asia, the Soviet Union and China (and, of course, the local Communist parties) abandoned their policy of military insurrection against the newly independent countries. Peace and understanding were the new watchwords, and both China and the Soviet Union devoted par-

[10] J. H. Brimmell, *Communism in South East Asia* (London and New York: Oxford University Press, 1959), p. 277.

[11] *Keesing's Contemporary Archives*, VIII, 11220.

ticular attention to India, Burma, and Indonesia, in an attempt to drive a wedge between the West and the nonaligned Asian states. The new diplomacy of "peaceful coexistence" was skillfully pressed by China at the 1954 Geneva Conference on Indochina, at the 1955 Bandung Conference, and during a series of meetings with key Asian statesmen. While making clear its desire for a "relaxation of tension," China emphasized the "aggressive" nature of U.S. policy in Asia and of the South East Asia Treaty Organization, which had been formed in 1954, at U.S. initiative, as a means of providing collective security guarantees to the smaller Asian countries on China's periphery.

By 1954, U.S. policy toward Communist China was hardening into "a cold war waged under the leadership of the United States, with constant threat of attack against Red China, led by Formosa and other Far Eastern groups and militarily supported by the United States."[12] While the French will to continue the fighting in Indochina was rapidly draining away, Secretary of State Dulles enunciated the doctrine of massive retaliation and suggested the possibility of U.S. intervention in Vietnam. At the same time, the U.S. position in Asia was declining. It was being undermined to some extent by the increasingly militant anti-Chinese posture of the United States—a posture which contrasted unfavorably with the benign peaceful coexistence line emanating from Peking, and which raised in Asian minds the specter of a major war. In addition, China, as an Asian power, was able to create in many minds an image of the United States as a non-Asian power which was not only committing aggression against China by occupying Taiwan, but also increasing tension in Asia by sponsoring SEATO. The credibility of this approach was strengthened to a significant extent by the actions of the United States itself. From 1950, it had become heavily committed to the support of France in Indochina as part of its policy of opposing the extension of Communist control in Asia; many Asian states, however, inter-

---

[12] Summary by Congressman Coudert of off-the-record remarks by the U.S. Assistant Secretary of State for Far Eastern Affairs, Walter S. Robertson. *Department of State, Justice and Commerce Appropriations for 1955,* Hearings before the House Committee on Appropriations, 83d Cong., 2d sess., p. 125. Quoted in Oliver E. Clubb, *The United States and the Sino-Soviet Bloc in Southeast Asia* (Washington, D.C.: The Brookings Institution, 1962), p. 55.

preted American policy in Indochina only as support for one of the last vestiges of European colonialism. SEATO itself, as a Western-dominated alliance, was inevitably an object of suspicion for newly independent states. These factors, combined with the racial appeal of China's "Asia for the Asians" line and the recognition by China's neighbors that the good will of their powerful neighbor was more important to them than that of the United States, led to the increasing isolation of the United States and its Asian allies.

It was in this unfavorable climate that the United States found itself reluctantly drawn into the Geneva Conference on Indochina, which took up its work late in April, 1954, following a decision of the Berlin Conference of February, 1954. Washington was reluctant to see Communist China achieve de facto "Big Five" status and was apprehensive about a negotiated settlement which would move the frontier of Communism into Southeast Asia. Any alternative to negotiation, however, was blocked by the unwillingness of France to continue the war, and the refusal of Britain to support an escalation of hostilities. The war was over for France even before the fall of Dien Bien Phu in May, 1954. The French public and government were strongly affected by the casualty figures of what seemed to be an interminable war (although in 1952, for example, four nationalist Vietnamese soldiers were falling to Vietminh action for every Frenchman). It was hard, after all, in an era of decolonization, to maintain a war which, while bringing independence to the Associated States, looked very much like a defense of purely French interests. The British had their own reasons for desiring a settlement. Foreign Secretary Eden, thinking about the situation in Malaya, wanted "an effective barrier as far to the north of that country as possible,"[13] and early in 1954 had begun to look upon some form of participation as the key to a lasting settlement. In any event, Eden considered that "the longer negotiation was delayed, the more difficult the situation would become for the French."[14]

The Soviet Union, which, as was the case in Korea, was the first to indicate that negotiations would be possible, was still pursuing

13 Sir Anthony Eden, *Full Circle* (London: Cassell & Co.; Boston: Houghton-Mifflin Co., 1960), p. 87.
14 *Ibid.*, p. 87.

its peace offensive. It has also been plausibly suggested that the Soviet desire to accommodate the French on Indochina negotiations arose, in part at least, from Molotov's awareness that "the prospect of such a conference would be sufficient to deter the French National Assembly from ratifying the EDC Treaty."[15] Communist China, too, was still pursuing the peaceful coexistence line, and besides, being completely dependent on the Soviet Union for supplies, was in no position to support the Vietminh adequately if the United States were to enter the war.[16] Although there is reason to believe that the Vietminh authorities were not in complete agreement with Moscow and Peking about the desirability of a negotiated settlement, they undoubtedly were reassured by their allies that domination of all of Indochina would come more quickly and cheaply by agreement than by continued fighting.

For the Associated States, whose independence had been extracted in painful stages from France, and who participated in the Geneva Conference as sovereign states, the requirements of the major powers were to prove overwhelming. Cambodia, and, to a lesser extent, Laos, stubbornly opposed partition of their countries and unreasonable restraints on their future defense policies; the major participants were primarily concerned with Vietnam, and in the rush to meet the July 20 deadline set by Mendès-France, were prepared to make some concessions on these lesser issues. The uncompromising position of the State of Vietnam, however, had to be ignored by France and Britain if a settlement was to be reached with the Communist side. At the time, this probably seemed like a necessary course of action.

The 1954 settlement, insofar as it concerned Vietnam, rested on two documents—a cease-fire agreement, and the Final Declaration of the conference. The cease-fire agreement, signed on behalf of the High Command of the French Union Forces and the Commander in Chief of the People's Army of Vietnam (PAVN), was essentially a military truce agreement providing for the disengagement of Franco-Vietnamese and PAVN forces; within periods of up to 300

---

[15] Donald Lancaster, *The Emancipation of French Indochina* (London and New York: Oxford University Press, 1961), p. 252.

[16] Victor Bator, *Vietnam: A Diplomatic Tragedy* (Dobbs Ferry, N.Y.: Oceana Publications, 1965), p. 129.

days, depending on the area involved, Franco-Vietnamese forces were to withdraw to the zone south of the 17th parallel and PAVN forces to the zone north of it. The administration of territory controlled by one party at the time of the cease-fire, and in the zone assigned to the other party, was to be turned over to the zonal authorities following the transfer of troops. A 5-kilometer demilitarized zone was to be established on either side of the demarcation line dividing north from south. The importation of fresh arms and munitions was prohibited, as was the introduction of "troop reinforcements and additional military personnel." The agreement also prohibited reprisals or discrimination against persons or organizations "on account of their activities during the hostilities" and required the parties to "guarantee their democratic liberties." In addition, civilians in one zone were to be permitted and helped to move to the other if they wished. An International Commission, consisting of representatives of India, Canada, and Poland, was to supervise the implementation by the parties of the provisions of the Cease-fire Agreement.

The Final Declaration, in eight of its thirteen paragraphs, simply took note of, recognized the purposes of, or expressed convictions about, various provisions of the cease-fire agreements for Vietnam, Laos, and Cambodia. In two paragraphs it emphasized the undertakings of the parties in Vietnam concerning freedom of movement and freedom from reprisals. Paragraph 12 stated that each member of the Geneva Conference undertook to respect the sovereignty, independence, unity, and territorial integrity of Vietnam, Laos, and Cambodia. Paragraph 13 provided for consultation among members of the Conference, "to study such measures as may prove necessary to ensure that the agreements on the cessation of hostilities in Cambodia, Laos, and Viet-Nam are respected." Paragraph 7, the key to the settlement and later developments, stated,

The Conference declares that, so far as Viet-Nam is concerned, the settlement of political problems, effected on the basis of respect for the principles of independence, unity and territorial integrity, shall permit the Viet-Namese people to enjoy the fundamental freedoms, guaranteed by democratic institutions established as a result of free general elections by secret ballot. In order to ensure that sufficient progress in the restoration of peace has been made and that all the necessary conditions obtain for free expression of the national will, general elections shall be held in July 1956, under the supervision of an international commission composed of representatives of the Member States of the International Supervisory Commission, referred to in the agreement on the cessation of hostilities. Consultations will be held on this subject between the competent representative authorities of the two zones from 20 July 1955 onwards.

It is impossible to interpret with any certainty the obscure circularity of the first two sentences. The general intent of the drafters, however, was that general elections were to be held in both zones of Vietnam in July, 1956, and that consultations leading to these elections were to be started between the authorities in the two zones on July 20, 1955. In 1956, the Foreign Secretary of the United Kingdom and the Foreign Minister of the United Kingdom and the Foreign Minister of the U.S.S.R., in their capacities as co-chairmen of the 1954 Conference, referred to "the preparation and holding of free, nationwide elections . . . with a view to the re-establishment of the national unity of Vietnam";[17] this interpretation must be considered authoritative.

Many of the misconceptions about the present situation in Vietnam arise from the misunderstanding surrounding this crucial paragraph of the Final Declaration. The Declaration emerged from the Geneva Conference at its closing session. It was an unsigned document in the form of a final act summing up the various cease-fire agreements and unilateral declarations. It was neither a treaty nor an agreement. As one authority describes it, "the Final Declaration is not a document *binding the participants towards each other. . . .* As the 'members of the Conference' had not signed this declaration, even if its dispositions did 'commit' them, it is merely a collection, in merged form, of unilateral pronouncements without mutuality and inter-connection."[18] Furthermore, only seven of the nine governments represented at the Conference contributed or subscribed to the Declaration. The delegation of the State of Vietnam had, as

---

[17] Message of May 8, 1956, from the co-chairmen to the two governments in Vietnam, para. 2, *Documents Relating to the British Involvement in the Indo-China Conflict, 1945–1965* (London: Her Majesty's Stationery Office, Cmnd. 2834, December, 1965), p. 73.

[18] Bator, *op. cit.*, pp. 142–43.

early as May 12, and consistently throughout the Conference,[19] opposed any partition, *de facto* or *de jure,* of Vietnamese territory, demanding free elections under U.N. auspices.[20] It had maintained this position throughout the negotiations and protested "the fact that the French High Command has arrogated, without the preliminary agreement of the State of Vietnam, the right to fix the date of the future elections."[21] Consistent with this position, the State of Vietnam explicitly dissociated itself from the terms of the Final Declaration.

The United States also made a separate declaration, taking note of the various cease-fire agreements and of all paragraphs of the Final Declaration except the one providing for consultations among members of the Conference. Like the State of Vietnam, it supported unity achieved "through free elections, supervised by the United Nations to ensure that they are conducted fairly." The United States declared that, in accordance with Article 2(4) of the U.N. Charter, it would refrain from the threat or the use of force to disturb the cease-fire agreements and the Declaration. It also made it clear, however, that it would view any renewal of aggression in violation of the agreements "with grave concern and as seriously threatening international peace and security." As in 1950, this was a clear indication that the United States was placing Vietnam within the framework of Chapter 7 of the U.N. Charter, and a warning that it would contemplate "the exercise of the inherent right of individual or collective self-defense" sanctioned by Article 51.

As of July 21, 1954, therefore, the authorities of the Democratic Republic of Vietnam (soon to become "North Vietnam," following the regroupment of opposing forces into the newly created northern and southern zones of the country) were legally bound by the terms of the cease-fire agreement they had signed with the French. The State of Vietnam (to be identified as "South Vietnam") although it had not been a party to the cease-fire agreement, had given a

---

[19] See statements by the representatives of the State of Vietnam in *Conférence de Genève sur l'Indochine, Procès-verbaux* (Paris: Ministère des Affaires Etrangères, 1955), pp. 59–64, 143–44, 157–58, 162–63, 187–90, 237–46, 377, 383, 385.

[20] *Documents Relating to the British Involvement . . . ,* pp. 72–73.

[21] Declaration of Tran Van Do, Delegate of the State of Vietnam, quoted in *Minutes of Proceedings and Evidence,* No. 1, Standing Committee on External Affairs, House of Commons of Canada (June 9–10, 1965), p. 94.

unilateral guarantee not to use force to resist the implementation of its cease-fire provisions. Although no member of the Conference was legally bound by the Final Declaration, the DRVN had formally accepted its provisions. The State of Vietnam, on the other hand, had specifically dissociated itself from the terms of the Declaration, and particularly from the election provisions.

It is difficult to understand how the Communist side at Geneva could have assumed that French agreement to the elections paragraph of the Final Declaration would be enough to ensure its implementation. The government of the State of Vietnam, both before and after Diem became Premier on July 7, 1954, had made its position eminently clear. Furthermore, it was a sovereign state, which, since 1950, had been recognized by thirty-five countries. All participants at the Geneva Conference had accepted the State of Vietnam as a full member of the conference. France, in a unilateral declaration, had formally undertaken to "proceed from the principle of respect for the independence and sovereignty of . . . Vietnam." Admittedly, France still exercised command over the nationalist Vietnamese armed forces, which had been delegated to it by the Vietnamese Government, and it seemed probable that any government in power in Saigon would be politically and economically dependent on France. But possibly both the French and the Communist side had been deceived—the former by wishful thinking, and the latter by their own propaganda concerning "colonial puppets." Neither recognized that Diem was a determined nationalist who intended to exercise in full, over the territory left to him, the sovereignty and independence extracted from Paris under a series of agreements extending back to 1949. Neither expected him to survive the political and economic chaos confronting him.

The consummation of the 1954 settlement, and the complete realization of the DRVN's objectives, therefore, depended on the implementation of the election provision, which South Vietnam had rejected and had made clear it would not implement. The future peace of Vietnam depended upon the observance of the cease-fire agreement, which North Vietnam had signed, but soon made clear it would not observe. Today, when South Vietnam and the United States on the one hand, and North Vietnam and its allies on the other, call for a return to "the Geneva agreements," the appeal is essentially to two mutually exclusive myths. For South Vietnam, "the Geneva agreements" mean the cease-fire agreement, which forbade intervention by the North in the affairs of the South. For Hanoi, they mean the Final Declaration, which envisaged elections that the North, with its larger population and its controlled and regimented electorate, would win.

It is clear from the early reports of the International Commission for Supervision and Control that those military provisions of the cease-fire agreement that the parties found advantageous to observe were implemented. The French had negotiated the agreement in order to make their military withdrawal from Vietnam possible; it was not surprising, therefore, that they ensured that they evacuated their own and Vietnamese nationalist troops under their command from their regroupment areas in the northern zone. The DRVN, however, looked upon the agreement as a temporary obstacle on the path to their minimum ultimate objective—control over the whole of Vietnam; it very soon became evident that it had no intention of implementing those provisions that would have involved relinquishing, for an indeterminate period, military and political control of large areas of what had become South Vietnam. The Hanoi authorities were to violate most of the provisions of the 1954 settlement; however, their decision to maintain in being in South Vietnam the entire apparatus they had built up since 1946 to prosecute their war against the French and the non-Communist Vietnamese authorities was the violation which, more than any other, led directly to the second Vietnam war.

Hanoi's intentions were announced in general terms as early as July, 1954, in a statement by the Lao Dong (Workers') Party:

Naturally, at a time when our troops and our administrative authority are being withdrawn towards the North, the Party members and co-patriots in Nam Bo [South Vietnam] will continue to remain in the zones on the other side. The war-mongering elements seek to sabotage the armistice and re-establish a state of war. Our compatriots and our members must continue to wage a hard struggle.

The Party must struggle; its cadres must remain with the people educating them, unmasking all activities of war-mongers, maintaining the influence of the Party and the government with the people, and winning the respect of the masses for President Ho Chi Minh.[22]

In December, 1954, Joseph Alsop paid a visit to what he described as "the southern base" of the Vietminh in the Mekong Delta area. He saw Vietminh troops and talked to Vietminh officials. The "strong, self-contained Viet Minh state, with a loyal population of nearly two million, a powerful regular army, a complete civil administration, and all the other normal apparatus of established government authority" had, according to Alsop, been "officially dismantled" in accordance with "the terms of the Geneva treaty." On the other hand, the underground had been left behind; according to Alsop, "the Communists' appeal and power of organization that were proved in the delta are still the keys to the battle for Indo-China, which still goes on beneath the impenetrable surface of Indo-Chinese village life."[23]

Bernard Fall, writing in 1955, stated:

Ho Chi Minh's "Democratic Republic of Vietnam" has already taken over the Red River Delta (with the exception of the Haiphong perimeter, which is to be transferred on May 19, 1955) without in fact relinquishing much of the effective control it previously held over large pockets of territory south of the 17th parallel. Thus the southern government of President Ngo Dinh Diem effectively controls less territory today than any Vietnamese government since 1948. In fact, long pacified provinces in South Vietnam are again subject to strong Viet Minh infiltration, and in some districts the population openly has recourse to Viet Minh tribunals or administrative officials, whose chances of enforcing a decision are far better than those of local South Vietnamese Government authorities.

. . . The DRVN's control has . . . increased in the Southern areas which it is supposed to have evacuated. True, most of the Viet Minh pockets south of the 17th parallel were officially evacuated by Viet Minh administrative officials and regular troops, but these operations may be considered something of a "smoke-screen." French intelligence and press reports show that in many cases, the Viet Minh did not remove its most important personnel, but shipped out its inexperienced levies for politi-

[22] Standing Committee on External Affairs, *op. cit.*, p. 19.
[23] Joseph Alsop, "A Man in a Mirror," *The New Yorker*, June 25, 1955, pp. 35–58.

cal indoctrination and military training in the North, while the hard core of *Chu-luc* (army regulars) and *Can-bo* (party cadres) have remained behind with their weapons stored in well-hidden caches.[24]

Other observers have drawn attention to Hanoi's strategy. Robert Shaplen states that in 1954, "some fifty thousand troops and twenty thousand Vietminh sympathizers went north, but as they withdrew from areas they had controlled, it soon became evident that they had left behind a strong network of cadres."[25] By the end of 1958, according to Shaplen, "the Communists had begun to smuggle in armed guerrillas from the north. These were southerners who had gone north in 1954 and been retrained as the vanguard of the new revolutionary army to 'liberate' South Vietnam; they now joined the stay-behinds who for four years had been organizing militant village cells and were engaging in widespread terrorism."[26]

This terrorism may have been widespread, but it was not indiscriminate. By concentrating on village chiefs, police, teachers, and security officials, the Communists during this early period achieved what Bernard Fall considered to be their objective—"gradual 'insulation' of the central authorities from direct contact with the grass roots, serious interference with accurate reporting about the state of the population to the central authorities."[27] In addition, threats of execution and other forms of coercion, combined with the distribution of the land of absentee landlords and lower taxes, ensured cooperation from the villagers. The hard-core areas controlled by the Communists for years prior to the cease-fire were, by these methods, held and extended. Control was exercised by the Lao Dong Party, the headquarters of which was, of course, in North Vietnam.

24 Bernard B. Fall, "Indochina since Geneva," *Pacific Affairs*, March, 1955, pp. 4, 15.

25 Robert Shaplen, *The Lost Revolution* (New York: Harper & Row, 1965), p. 114.

26 *Ibid.*, p. 140. See also Brian Crozier, *South-East Asia in Turmoil* (Baltimore: Penguin Books, 1965), p. 136; Denis Warner, *The Last Confucian* (New York: Macmillan Co., 1965), pp. 142–53; Anne M. Jonas and George K. Tanham, "Laos: A Phase in Cyclic Regional Revolution," in Franklin M. Osanka (ed.), *Modern Guerrilla Warfare* (New York: Free Press of Glencoe, 1963), p. 284.

27 Fall, "South Vietnam's Internal Problems," *Pacific Affairs*, September, 1958, p. 257.

The International Commission, beginning in 1955, was kept informed of these developments by the South Vietnamese authorities through an increasing number of complaints submitted to it. However, it took years before the Commission took any action. In the meantime, however, it diligently dealt with complaints from the Hanoi authorities that the South Vietnamese government was violating the rights guaranteed by Article 14(c) of the cease-fire agreement to what Hanoi and the Commission called "former resistance members." As Bernard Fall pointed out in 1958, the areas of major Communist activity (assassinations, raids, and subversive cells) were the areas to which most 14(c) complaints referred. Furthermore, the complaints were "sufficiently precise in their details to have been based upon information given to the Communist North Vietnamese authorities by Viet Minh agents who have remained behind in the South after the armistice or who have been infiltrated into the area since."[28] According to Fall, the inescapable conclusion was that coordination existed between the rebels and the North Vietnamese Government. It also seems evident that North Vietnam was using the International Commission and complaints concerning Article 14(c) to impose restraints on the limited efforts of Saigon to counter the terrorist activities of Hanoi's agents.

After more than five years of consideration, and an examination of South Vietnamese complaints going back to 1955, the Commission reported to the co-chairmen of the Geneva Conference on June 2, 1962, that North Vietnam had, in violation of Articles 10, 19, 24, and 27 of the 1954 cease-fire agreement, sent "armed and unarmed personnel, arms, munitions, and other supplies" into South Vietnam "with the object of supporting, organizing and carrying out hostile activities, including armed attacks," directed against the armed forces and administration of South Vietnam. Furthermore, the People's Army of Vietnam had allowed "the Zone in the North to be used for inciting, encouraging and supporting hostile activities in the Zone in the South, aimed at the overthrow of the Administration in the South."[29]

[28] *Ibid.*, p. 255.

[29] International Commission for Supervision and Control in Vietnam, *Special Report to the Co-Chairmen of the Geneva Conference on Indo-China,* Saigon, June 2, 1962 (London: Her Majesty's Stationery Office, Cmnd. 1755, June, 1962), p. 7.

By 1959, North Vietnam had completed in the South the first stage of Mao Tse-tung's general theory of revolutionary war. Large areas had been organized and indoctrinated, and maximum results had been achieved by the relatively limited forces available for terrorist and sabotage operations. The second stage, involving an increase in conventional small-scale engagements mounted from the secure base areas built up in the South, required not only stepped-up reinforcements from the North but also a broader political organization in the South. While the necessary troops and political cadres were being provided (about 10,000 in 1959 and 1960), the Lao Dong Party made preparations for the creation of a "national democratic front" in the South. On September 5, 1960, at the Third Congress of the Party, Le Duan, First Secretary of the Central Committee, stated:

> In the South we have to make every effort to achieve a broad national unity embracing all the national and democratic forces, all forces opposed to the U.S. imperialists and Ngo Dinh Diem. . . . We must . . . help create further conditions for the rallying of all patriotic forces opposed to the U.S.–Diem régime in the South into a broad national united front with the worker-peasant alliance as its basis, and ensure the victory of the revolutionary struggle in the South.[30]

On September 10, 1960, the Congress dutifully passed a resolution implementing Le Duan's proposal, and on December 20, 1960, the establishment of the South Vietnam National Front for Liberation was announced. The standard pattern for Communist revolutionary organization was completed with the "creation," a year later, of the Vietnam People's Revolutionary Party—the "Marxist-Leninist Party" which Le Duan had stated should assume the leadership of the Liberation Front, and which was an extension of the Lao Dong Party.

The nature of the Liberation Front and its armed forces was clearly established by the Legal Committee of the International Commission in 1962, which stated that their "aim and function . . . are to organize and to carry out under the leadership of the Viet-

---

[30] Le Duan, Political Report of the Central Committee of the Lao Dong Party. Quoted in *Studies on Viet Nam,* Information Handbook No. 1 of 1965 (Canberra: Department of External Affairs, August, 1965), p. 14.

nam Lao Dong Party, hostile activities against the Armed Forces and the Administration of the South by violent means aimed at the overthrow of the Administration of the South."[31]

Thus, during the period from 1954 to 1960, the Democratic Republic of Vietnam not only failed to withdraw all its forces from the southern zone and to turn over to the Saigon authorities the administration of the areas controlled by the Vietminh during the war against the French, but it also maintained and built up its campaign in the South by means of infiltration. These activities were in direct contravention of the cease-fire agreement the DRVN had negotiated and signed in 1954. They also constituted aggression, for despite the various arguments that have been made to establish a qualitative difference, the attack against South Vietnam differed only in technique from the invasion of South Korea in 1950. These arguments are worth examining, however, since they indicate the extent to which the basic issues can become obscured if a conventional military attack of the Korean type is avoided by an aggressor. The most persistent arguments are the following.

South Vietnam, by refusing to participate in nationwide elections, provoked Hanoi into seeking unification by other means. As has been pointed out above, the Saigon Government not only was not bound by a Final Declaration of doubtful legal force, but had also made it clear that it would not participate in the type of elections envisaged by the big powers at Geneva. President Diem, on July 16, 1955, expressed his support for unification through free elections. He nevertheless was skeptical about the possibility of "fulfilling the conditions of free elections in the North," where, he said, "terrorism and totalitarian methods" reigned. The Hanoi regime in October, 1956, made it clear that this skepticism had been well-founded. In his report to the Central Committee of the Lao Dong Party in October, 1956, General Giap criticized the "land-reform" program carried out in the period 1953–55. "We executed too many honest people," he said. "We attacked on too large a front and, seeing enemies everywhere, resorted to terror, which became far too widespread. . . . Torture came to be regarded as a

[31] International Commission for Supervision and Control in Vietnam, *Special Report to the Co-Chairmen of the Geneva Conference on Indo-China,* Saigon, February 13, 1965 (London, Her Majesty's Stationery Office, March, 1965), p. 13.

normal practice during Party organization."[32] Bernard Fall has estimated that close to 50,000 North Vietnamese were executed, and that at least twice as many were sent to forced-labor camps.[33] A well-informed French author, who left Hanoi in 1959, states that "this indescribable butchery resulted in 100,000 deaths."[34] A Vietnamese who had been a member of the Vietminh, and who had attended "land-reform" trials, estimates that about 5 per cent of the population perished.[35] Serious unrest and revolt in the North during 1956 forced the regime to abandon the excesses of the land-reform campaign, but political conditions remained unchanged. In 1960, for example, 99.85 per cent of the eligible voters, in the first DRVN elections since 1946, cast their ballots for candidates of the Lao Dong Party. Thus, even if one ignores the chaotic security conditions and the imperfections of democratic institutions in South Vietnam, it is evident that free elections would have been impossible in the North. Diem's position thus was correct in fact as well as in law. In addition, it represented no change from the State of Vietnam's position at Geneva and should not have surprised the Hanoi regime. Obviously, the growing possibility that a viable regime might emerge in the South must have disappointed the DRVN authorities; by normal standards of international behavior, however, disappointment is not sufficient justification for the violation of agreements and aggression.

The majority of the Communists (the Vietminh, Vietcong, National Liberation Front) in South Vietnam are natives of the South. Their efforts to overthrow the Saigon regime, therefore, represent a form of civil war, not aggression. This argument overlooks the fact that North Vietnam and South Vietnam did not exist in their present geographical form before the creation of the demarcation line in 1954. Until partition, two political entities—the DRVN and the State of Vietnam—claimed sovereignty over all of Vietnam.

[32] *Nhan Dan* (Official Organ of DRVN Lao Dong Party), No. 970 (October 31, 1956).

[33] Fall, *The Two Viet-Nams* (rev. ed.; New York: Frederick A. Praeger; London: Pall Mall Press, 1964), pp. 155–56.

[34] Gérard Tongas, *J'ai vécu dans l'enfer communiste du Nord Viet-Nam et j'ai choisi la liberté* (Paris: Débresse, 1960), p. 222.

[35] Hoang Van Chi, *From Colonialism to Communism: A Case History of North Vietnam* (New York: Frederick A. Praeger; London: Pall Mall Press, 1964), p. 166.

Thousands of "Northerners," natives of the area north of the 17th parallel, paid allegiance to the government of the State of Vietnam, while thousands of "Southerners" were loyal to the Communist DRVN; the cease-fire agreement was designed to separate armed forces and administrations on the basis of political loyalties, not regional affiliations. Thus, the "Northerners" who were loyal to the State of Vietnam were withdrawn from areas such as Hanoi and the Red River Delta north of the demarcation line to the zone south of it, which, as "South Vietnam," was to be administered by Saigon. The DRVN thus was enabled to establish a zone of homogeneous political affiliation. As has been pointed out, however, the DRVN did not withdraw from the southern zone all the troops and political cadres who, although "Southern" in regional origin, were Communist and "Northern" in political loyalty, and under the direction of the North Vietnamese authorities. Division of the country under the cease-fire agreement was geographical, but regroupment was political, and it was the failure of the DRVN to implement the regroupment of all the "Southerners" under its political and military direction, and to turn the areas under their control over to the Saigon authorities, which led to the second Vietnam war.

It must also be recognized that, since about 1961, as Hanoi's pool of reindoctrinated and trained "Southerners" who did regroup in the North in 1954 dried up, an increasingly higher proportion of "geographical" Northerners has been infiltrated into the South.

North Vietnam was justified in taking action to counter the efforts of the United States to build up in the South, in violation of the 1954 settlement, military forces and bases that represented a threat to the Hanoi regime. North Vietnam's direct intervention against the Saigon Government began in 1954, and entered a new stage in 1959 when, according to U.S. estimates, "at least 1,800 men, and possibly 2,700 more," moved into the South.[36] Throughout this period, the entire continuing U.S. military presence consisted of the 342-member MAAG training and advisory group that had been in operation in 1954. In 1960, the International Commission agreed to an increase of MAAG to 685—a total which was less than the

[36] Department of State, *Aggression from the North* (Washington, D.C.: Department of State Publication 7839, February, 1965), p. 3.

combined French and American membership at the time of the cease-fire.[37] Later increases of U.S. military strength, which, unlike that of 1960, were not consistent with the provisions of the 1954 cease-fire agreement, were in direct response to greatly increased infiltration of North Vietnamese troops. (It is also often overlooked that the military balance existing in 1954 had been drastically altered in Hanoi's favor by the withdrawal, at the request of the Saigon Government, of the French Union Forces, which had evacuated South Vietnam by early 1956.)

The guerrilla war in the South, led by the broadly supported Liberation Front, represented a response to the dictatorial regime of Ngo Dinh Diem. North Vietnam has simply lent support to what is essentially an indigenous movement of protest. The increasingly authoritarian methods of the Diem regime led to opposition and, eventually, to the coup that destroyed Diem and Nhu. Diem never found the combination of authoritarianism and efficient ruthlessness that enabled the Hanoi regime to remain in power despite serious discontent. Neither he nor the governments which succeeded him were able to establish channels through which the groping forces of nationalism and social discontent could flow freely and constructively. Like so many Asian states at the dawn of independence, South Vietnam lacked the traditions and institutions of responsible party politics. Unlike Burma, Pakistan, Indonesia, and Cambodia, for example, it has been unable to resort to the alternatives that, while authoritarian in nature, have been able to promote unity and a sense of purpose. On the other hand, although the Liberation Front has obtained some willing adherents, the forces of political opposition have not to any significant extent, aligned themselves with it. The Cao Dai and Hoa Hao sects, the Catholics, the organized Buddhists, and political parties such as Dai Viet, have all operated within the non-Communist, non-Liberation Front environment. Thich Tri Quang, who led the Buddhist agitation that overthrew Diem in 1963, made clear in March, 1966, his view that the "government of national union" demanded by South Vietnamese Buddhists should not include Vietcong political figures.

---

[37] International Commission for Supervision and Control in Vietnam, *Eleventh Interim Report*, Saigon, September 18, 1961 (London: Her Majesty's Stationery Office; Cmnd. 1551, November, 1961), p. 18.

Calling such an idea "silly," he explained that the concept was of a union of "nationalist" elements, which in Vietnamese political language meant anti-Communist.[38]

As crisis succeeds crisis in Saigon, it becomes increasingly evident that the war being conducted by Hanoi behind the façade of the Liberation Front has as one of its major tactical objectives the prevention of the emergence of a unified government representing the inchoate nationalism which exists in South Vietnam. Hanoi, since 1954, has devoted its efforts to destroying not only the Diem Government but every regime that has followed it. No Saigon government not controlled by the NLF, and thus by the People's Revolutionary Party and Hanoi, can be relied upon to bring about unification on Hanoi's terms. The DRVN's demand that the internal affairs of South Vietnam be settled "in accordance with the program of the National Liberation Front" and its contention that the NLF is "the sole genuine representative of the South Vietnamese people" are, therefore, indispensable components of its strategy.

For the vast majority of South Vietnamese, and particularly for the political elite, the need is to find a reasonably stable coalition of forces capable of representing all major segments of the political, religious, and economic spectrums and responding to the demands for social and economic justice. Few developing countries have been successful in achieving such a coalition even in a peaceful environment; South Vietnam, entering the second decade of a war for survival against a disciplined and ruthless neighbor, and groping its way through the vicissitudes of what one observer has termed "the real revolution,"[39] faces even bleaker prospects. As the military pressure from the North mounted in 1962 and 1963, it became painfully obvious that the Saigon regime was no more able to withstand the assault than had been South Korea in 1950. It was at this stage that the United States began to alter its commitment quantitatively. In 1965, with the employment of combat troops, a qualitative change was made. By 1966, it had become apparent that the United States, with more than 200,000 troops in Vietnam, had once more,

---

[38] Charles Mohr, "Buddhist Assails 'Rotten' Ky Rule," *The New York Times*, March 16, 1966.

[39] George A. Carver, Jr., "The Real Revolution in South Vietnam," *Foreign Affairs*, XLIII, No. 3 (April, 1965), 387–408.

in response to aggression, become involved in a ground war on the Asian mainland.

Many see in the Vietnam war a reflection of the deeper conflict between Communist China and the United States. This conflict obviously does exist and does impinge on events in Vietnam. However, any valid interpretation of the situation in the Far East must differentiate between the relations of Communist China with, on the one hand, the United States and other countries of the Western world, and on the other, the developing countries and, in particular, its Asian neighbors. The two sets of relations, because they have common factors, are not discrete. Nevertheless, attempts to assess events in Vietnam, for example, primarily in terms of U.S.–China relations can lead to a blurring of the fundamental issue at stake in Vietnam, i.e., whether international violence, in the guise of "liberation wars," can be permitted to threaten world order and the security of individual states. Similarly, any tendency, particularly on the part of the United States, to allow events in Vietnam to play a determining role in developing policies toward China itself may, by perpetuating a situation in which only one side is subject to the entanglements and restraints flowing from full membership in the international community, lead to an unending series of Vietnams in which an increasingly effective Communist challenge is met by an inevitably weaker response.

The foreign policy objectives of Communist China fall into three broad categories. In the field of conventional foreign policy, it wishes to expand its power and influence; in this respect, the Communist regime is continuing the traditional pattern of strong, centralized Chinese governments and, indeed, of all major powers. Within the ideological context, China is attempting to promote the spread of Communism throughout the world, and primarily in the developing countries of Asia and Africa. Finally, in order to achieve these mutually related objectives, the Peking regime must wrest from Moscow the leadership of the world Communist movement (along with the concomitant ability to determine its tactics and strategy), and destroy the ability of the United States to block its expansion. The "war of national liberation" has been chosen as the instrument of Chinese policy in part because it is consistent with the politico-military experience of China's leaders. In addition, the technique is well adapted to the needs of a major power that does not possess the immense diplomatic, economic, and military resources which can be utilized by the United States and the Soviet Union in the pursuit of national goals by more conventional methods. Finally, the wider dangers implicit in a permanently unstable world are less inhibiting to a rogue regime that considers itself beleaguered and deprived within the existing framework.

One of the most systematic and authoritative of the recent expositions of the Chinese Communist approach to international relations was contained in an article by Lin Piao, CPR Minister of National Defense, commemorating the twentieth anniversary of the defeat of Japan.[40]

Mao's theory of people's wars, according to Lin, is "in accord with the objective laws of such wars" and is "invincible." From the lessons of the Chinese civil war came Mao's thesis that "political power grows out of the barrel of a gun": "the seizure of power by armed force, the settlement of the issue by war, is the central task and the highest form of revolution." This principle applies to all countries, and in the "oppressed" countries (i.e., all those that are not Communist or "imperialist") the people should rise up against "the imperialists and their lackeys." These wars of liberation will have their ups and downs, but they will inevitably triumph. All reactionaries are "paper tigers" and the masses are always on the side of the revolution.

Once they have launched their wars of liberation, the revolutionaries should base their strategy on the countryside and the peasants, then go on to encircle the cities. On a global scale, revolution in the "countryside"—Asia, Africa, and Latin America—will eventually lead to the encirclement of the "cities of the world"—North America and Western Europe—and to the success of revolution throughout the world. In the favorable conditions existing in the world, "people's wars," if widespread enough, can pin down the

[40] Lin Piao, "Long Live the Victory of the People's War," *Jen-min Jih-pao* (*People's Daily;* Peking), September 3, 1965. See also speech by Lo Jui-ching, Chief of the General Staff of the PLA, "The People Defeated Japanese Fascism and They Can Certainly Defeat U.S. Imperialism," broadcast by Peking home service, September 3, 1965. BBC *Summary of World Broadcasts: Part 3—The Far East,* September 6, 1965, pp. A3/1–A3/12.

leader of the imperialists, the United States, and "destroy it piece by piece." Nuclear weapons and modern technology are useless against revolutionary wars.

Vietnam, according to Lin, is the most convincing example of a "people's war." The Americans there are "in danger of being swamped," and when the inevitable defeat takes place, "the people in other parts of the world will see still more clearly that U.S. imperialism can be defeated, and that what the Vietnamese people can do, they can do too. . . . All revolutionary people will learn to wage people's war against U.S. imperialism and its lackeys."

The Soviet Union is wrong in its "general line of 'peaceful coexistence, peaceful transition and peaceful competition.'" War brings destruction, sacrifice, and suffering, but "the sacrifice of a small number of people in revolutionary wars is repaid by security for whole nations, whole countries, and even the whole of mankind; temporary suffering is repaid by lasting, or even perpetual, peace and happiness. War can temper the people and push history forward. In this sense, war is a great school." China has supported and is supporting revolutionary wars, and, promises Lin, will provide still more support as it grows in strength. The people in a country must be "awakened, mobilized, organized, and armed" before they can carry out their revolution; but although their role cannot be replaced from outside, China provides support and aid. The revolutionary peoples of the world, through people's wars, "will wipe off the earth once and for all the common enemy of all the peoples, U.S. imperialism and its lackeys." The Vietnam war is "the focus of the struggle of the people of the world against U.S. aggression."

It could be argued, of course, that this blueprint of world revolution does not accurately reflect either Chinese intentions or the actual pattern of China's foreign policy. This is a comforting thought, but not a tenable one. First of all, although the article was by Lin Piao, the approach and the ideas originate with Mao and are consistent with the main lines of his thought during at least the past two decades. Furthermore, the article reflects the policies consistently enunciated by the leading officials and organs of the Peking regime. Finally, convincing evidence exists of Peking's attempts to implement the policy wherever it considers conditions look promising. Its efforts in Africa have not, so far, been very successful. The clear impression left by the Tricontinental Solidarity Conference held in Havana in January, 1966, was that the major burden of subversion in Latin America would be borne by the U.S.S.R. and Cuba. In Asia, however, and particularly on the mainland, China is in a position to maintain constant pressure against independent regimes by fomenting "wars of national liberation" and in keeping with the traditional Chinese desire to "use barbarians to deal with barbarians" by training and supporting the indigenous leaders of these wars. The approach to countries dependent on the United States tends to be different from that followed in the case of those with pro-Peking or neutralist leanings; the difference, however, appears to be mainly tactical. In Indonesia, the PKI received strong support from China and there is evidence to suggest that Peking was implicated in the abortive coup attempt of October 1, 1965,[41] the main objective of which was to destroy the power of the army—the PKI's main adversary. The Burmese Communist Party, which is Peking-oriented, remains in a state of insurgency, despite the neutralist policy of the Ne Win regime and its evident desire to avoid any provocation of China; in addition, there is reason to believe that Peking, by establishing "autonomous" minority zones across the Burmese border, and infiltrating Burmese minority groups such as the Kachins and the Karens,[42] is laying the groundwork for a "liberation struggle" at a later date. Prince Sihanouk of Cambodia, who has courted Peking and Hanoi assiduously, announced in February, 1966, that his security police had captured a number of documents belonging to the Pracheachon (the Cambodian Communist Party), indicating that "their authors aim at nothing but overthrowing the legal existence of a national regime . . . and initiating a civil war."[43]

Countries like Malaysia and Thailand, which maintain friendly relations with the United States, receive the same treatment. In their cases, however, China acknowledges its own involvement by encouraging the creation of "liberation fronts" with headquarters

[41] See, e.g., Denis Warner, "Indonesia's Communists: Down But Not Out," *The Reporter*, November 18, 1965, pp. 23–26.

[42] A. Doak Barnett, *Communist China and Asia: A Challenge to American Policy* (New York: Vintage Books, 1960), p. 321.

[43] Statement by Prince Sihanouk, February 20, 1966. Pnom Penh radio in French, February 22, 1966.

in Peking, by providing broadcasting, organizational, financial, and military support, and by throwing the weight of its own policies and propaganda behind these insurrectionary movements. Laos and South Vietnam are special cases: North Vietnam's Lao Dong Party is the direct descendent of the *Indochinese* Communist Party, and the subordinate positions of the Neo Lao Hak Xat in Laos and the People's Revolutionary Party in South Vietnam reflect Hanoi's determination to establish its hegemony over all the Indochina states. The motives of North Vietnam's leaders are nationalist and economic as well as Communist; the Peking regime, however, presumably counts on being able to maintain adequate political control for an indefinite period.

The fate of the 1962 Declaration on the Neutrality of Laos, in which the world's major powers and all countries bordering on Laos agreed to respect that country's neutrality and territorial integrity, raises further serious doubts about the willingness of Communist China and North Vietnam to be satisfied with neutrality as a policy for their neighbors, or to observe treaties designed to guarantee such a status.

In 1961, as hostilities in Laos threatened to plunge the United States into direct military confrontation with North Vietnam, supported by both the Soviet Union and China, President Kennedy enunciated American support for a negotiated settlement making possible in Laos "a truly neutral government, not a cold war pawn." However, while the United States favored "a prompt end of hostilities and prompt negotiation," it also demanded "a cessation of the present armed attacks by externally supported Communists."[44] Implicit in this stand, and in American participation in the negotiations leading to a settlement in Laos, was the decision not to commit U.S. forces to a ground war in Laos in support of a right-wing, pro-U.S. regime. More far-reaching in significance, however, was the decision to work actively for the neutralization of Laos and to accept as the basis of that neutralization the concept of a *troika* coalition government with the "neutralist" party of Prince Souvanna Phouma as its foundation. Throughout negotiations, and in the implementation of the settlement, the United States showed a

[44] *Public Papers of the Presidents, 1961* (Washington, D.C.: Government Printing Office, 1962), p. 214.

determination to give the concept of neutrality every opportunity to work. In accordance with the terms of the settlement, all MAAG personnel were withdrawn from Laos under the surveillance of the International Commission for Supervision and Control. As one writer has observed, "This strict compliance with the Geneva Protocol must have dumfounded the North Vietnamese. The American behavior was inexplicable, if not downright unimperialist."[45] North Vietnam, it soon became clear, did not intend to reciprocate. Of an estimated 10,000 North Vietnamese military personnel in Laos at the time of the settlement,[46] only 40 "technicians" were checked out in accordance with the protocol. Evidence obtained by the International Commission, furthermore, established that North Vietnamese troops continued to enter Laos. (In its Message No. 35 of September 15, 1965, to the co-chairmen of the Geneva Conference, the Commission, on the basis of its interrogation of prisoners captured during 1964, reported that North Vietnamese regulars had entered Laos in units of from 50 to about 650 soldiers and had fought on Laotian territory against Laotian government forces.) The Neo Lao Hak Xat, by maintaining and extending its military and political control over a large part of Laos, by direct attack against General Kong Le's neutralist forces, and by withdrawing from the coalition government, ensured a parallel breakdown of the internal settlement. In retrospect, it is impossible to avoid the conclusion that North Vietnam had no intention of observing the 1962 Laotian settlement, which it considered primarily as an instrument for guaranteeing its complete freedom to build up the Communist-held areas of Laos as a channel and base of operations for a stepped-up flow of its troops into South Vietnam. The insistence of the Communist side, during the Geneva negotiations, on restrictive terms of reference for the International Commission was a corollary of that objective.

As long as Communist China's policy maintains its present course, the "war of national liberation," it seems clear, will represent a constant threat to the countries of Southeast Asia, irrespective of their relationships with the United States. Although the

---

[45] Arthur J. Dommen, *Conflict in Laos: The Politics of Neutralization* (New York: Frederick A. Praeger, 1964), p. 239.

[46] *Ibid.*, p. 238.

Chinese Communists did not invent the concept, they have developed it into an effective instrument of foreign policy well adapted to China's resources. China and North Vietnam possess, within the areas controlled by them, adequate reserves of indoctrinated minority races—Thai, Lao, Kachin, Karen, Shan, Kha—which can be used to infiltrate neighboring states. In addition, large colonies of overseas Chinese exist as latent bridgeheads in these same countries; Thailand, with substantial numbers of Vietnamese and Lao as well, is triply vulnerable. Clandestine preparations for this form of aggression, in countries with little national consciousness, poor communications, inadequate internal security forces, and serious economic and social problems, can reach a dangerous level before the need for countermeasures is recognized. Once open insurrection is initiated, the rebels, trained in techniques developed in China and Vietnam over the past thirty years, have a major tactical advantage over government forces, since both the political and military techniques of antiguerrilla warfare are at a comparatively rudimentary stage.

The Maoist theory of guerrilla warfare is escalatory in nature, and the countermeasures adopted by a government will reflect this. The first stage, which involves the establishment of a political basis for insurrection, the indoctrination and organization of small groups of "liberation forces" and limited terrorist operations (i.e., the type of operations carried on in Thailand under the aegis of the Peking-based "Thailand Patriotic Front") can normally be countered by the government concerned. Land reform, adequate employment opportunities, a more equitable sharing of available wealth, responsive and, where feasible, representative government—these are some of the ingredients able to arm a population against the economic and ideological blandishments of Communism. The techniques of blackmail and terrorism, however, can be thwarted only by effective security measures and the extension of government authority into every village. For most of the countries of Asia, the simultaneous pursuit of all these objectives, because it involves a financial and technological burden beyond their own resources, requires outside assistance. As the second and third stages of guerrilla warfare are initiated, the government under attack faces the additional burden involved in fighting widespread military engagements and in meeting the large-scale incursion of regular and irregular forces from outside its borders; at this point, the military resources of the government may not be adequate, and its survival may depend on the commitment by its allies of sufficient combat forces to redress the military balance. This was the case in Korea in 1950 and in South Vietnam in 1965.

The war in Vietnam in the 1960's is in a very real sense a continuation of the Korean war. However, although its essential characteristic is identical—U.S. support of an Asian state against Communist aggression—the circumstances surrounding the war are very different. The problems of Indochina have never been dealt with in a U.N. context, and the allies of South Vietnam, unlike those of South Korea in 1950, do not have behind them the moral authority which formal support by the world organization can convey. In this war, the victim of aggression has fewer allies than did South Korea; most of the countries that contributed troops to the U.N. Command in Korea have shown a distinct lack of enthusiasm for sharing the military burden in Vietnam. Public opinion in all Western countries is deeply divided on the issues involved. And surrounding public discussions of the war and of the U.S. involvement in it is a haze of misconceptions and irrelevancies. The fact that the war has become an obscurantist's dream is in large part due to the superb techniques of indirect aggression, encompassed by the concept of the "liberation war," which have been brought into play by the Communist side to replace the frontal assault used in Korea, and the skill and finesse with which the Communist bloc has perfected the propaganda line, developed during the Korean war, accusing the United States of aggression against Asia. The Vietnam question is, in addition, easily linked with appeals to pacifism, anti-Americanism, and the widespread fear of any situation that might carry the risk of a major war. To a certain extent, moreover, U.S. policy in Vietnam is being judged in the 1960's as an extension and reflection of the attitude of intransigent hostility toward Communist China that formed the basis of its policy in Asia during the 1950's. This interpretation, however, overlooks the evolution of U.S. policy which has been taking place and which has been reflected by continuing American support of Laotian neutrality; the benign tolerance with

which Washington has viewed pro-China policies of Cambodia
that have at times noticeably annoyed even Moscow; repeated
American assurances that the United States has no designs against
the regimes in Peking and Hanoi; and the maintenance in Warsaw
of a regular, if unproductive, diplomatic dialogue with China
despite an unending stream of abuse from Peking. The objectives
of U.S. policy in Vietnam are consistent with this pattern. They
are, as described by President Johnson in their simplest terms,
"the independence of South Vietnam and its freedom from attack
. . . that the people of South Vietnam be allowed to guide their
own country in their own way."[47] There are, of course, broader
considerations. Failure to support South Vietnam effectively would
undermine, for allies and adversaries alike, the credibility of the
U.S. commitment to come to the assistance of countries that are
attacked. A successful "war of national liberation" in South Vietnam would encourage further use of this instrument of aggression.
Abandonment in Vietnam, as much as in Korea or Berlin, of the
principle of the inviolability of existing *de facto* and *de jure*
borders between Communist and non-Communist regimes could
destroy the tacit balance that has been painfully established since
1948. Finally, the United States looks upon the war in Vietnam as
"part of a wider pattern of aggressive purposes";[48] its involvement
therefore represents an attempt to prevent the extension by unacceptable means of Communist China's control over the independent countries of Asia.

The limited objectives of the United States in Vietnam are overshadowed by the wider implications of a war whose paradoxes
make its outcome increasingly more difficult to predict. It seems
evident, for example, that the war places additional strains on
relations between Washington and Moscow. As long as Moscow
gives first priority to its competition with Peking for leadership of
the world Communist movement, it will continue to be forced
into wholehearted support of North Vietnam and thus, ironically,
into involuntary adherence in practice to the particular theory of
liberation wars that forms the basis of its dispute with China.

[47] President Lyndon B. Johnson, speech at Johns Hopkins University, Baltimore, Md., April 7, 1965; reported in *The New York Times,* April 8, 1965.
[48] *Ibid.*

North Vietnam, by its aggression against the South, has brought about the establishment of major United States military bases on the Asian mainland—the prevention of which was one of the fundamental objectives of Communist Chinese foreign policy. The Hanoi authorities, drawing on Maoist guerrilla strategy and their own experience in the war against the French, protest their willingness to wage a protracted war; however, although the theory was appropriate, or even inevitable, in wars waged by inferior forces against established regimes, it may seem increasingly costly to an established government.

Early in 1966, there were indications that a reassessment of policy might be possible in Hanoi and Peking. An authoritative article published in the theoretical journal of the North Vietnamese Lao Dong Party early in February admitted that "many difficulties and complexities" would inevitably be encountered during the war. Although an "absolute majority" of cadres and Party members "have a steadfast stand and views," a number "still fear sacrifices and hardships, shrink from difficulties, and lack an exemplary vanguard spirit in production and combat." All cadres and Party members have to be educated "to enable them clearly to understand the situation, their duties, and the new revolutionary requirements so that they can shape a correct view of the balance of power between the enemy and us, of opportunities and difficulties, *and of the possible changes in the situation*" (italics added).[49]

Communist China's foreign policy suffered enough setbacks during 1965 and early 1966 to lead to some tempering of the determined optimism which had been the hallmark of the Peking regime's pronouncements. An article in *Jen-min Jih-pao*,[50] while still contending that "the East wind prevails over the West wind" in the existing international situation, went on to admit:

This does not mean that there are no twists and turns in this excellent situation. The imperialists, colonialists, and neocolonialists headed by

[49] Le Duc Tho, "Let Us Change the Trend and Step Up the Party Building Task. . ." *Hoc Tap* (*Studies;* Hanoi), February, 1966.

[50] "About Twists and Turns and Progress," *Jen-min Jih-pao*, March 7, 1966. See also "The Great Upheaval Is an Excellent Thing," *Jen-min Jih-pao*, March 1, 1966.

the United States, and their flunkies, are making frantic counterattacks; the modern revisionists who act as accomplices of the imperialists and reactionaries are disrupting revolution; in some lands, revolutionary struggles have temporarily suffered reverses and in others the political situation has taken an adverse turn.

"Twists and turns" in the revolutionary path, the article explained, are inevitable; occasionally, "the leadership of revolution itself may make a mistake of one kind or another." Correct strategy and tactics must be worked out "to preserve in revolution"; true Marxist-Leninists do not sink "into passivity and despair."

It is probable that both Peking and Hanoi are beginning to recognize that the countries of Asia, although weak and vulnerable and divided, do not represent targets of opportunity so long as they can call upon the United States, and so long as the United States is committed to its role as a third force prepared to redress the military balance. If so, it is not inconceivable that the Asian Communists will re-examine their announced policy of unlimited revolution in Southeast Asia and revert to the "peaceful coexistence" line pursued so effectively for a short period in the 1950's. Because of the ideological dispute with the Soviet Union, such a shift would be fraught with difficulties. Furthermore, there are no grounds for expecting Peking to abandon its objectives; a change in policy at this stage would in all likelihood be only tactical. The cynicism with which North Vietnam and its allies have violated the 1954 settlement, and, with even less justification, the 1962 Laos agreements, raises serious questions about the viability of any new settlement along traditional, "Geneva" lines. Nevertheless, despite the obvious difficulties and risks, a break in Communist China's policy could unfreeze the existing situation and open up a new series of opportunities for encouraging the abandonment by Communist China and its allies of war and revolution as preferred instruments in their attempts to extend their influence.

10. The Conflict in Vietnam

RICHARD LOWENTHAL

In Vietnam, the United States is now involved in a full-scale war on the mainland of Asia. President Johnson's Administration had not planned to fight this kind of war; it has drifted into it under the pressure of events, that is, of the unforeseen consequences of earlier American policies in the area. Yet having come to the parting of the ways, the present American leaders have deliberately set a new course in world affairs and developed a doctrine for its justification: They have not only increased their stake in Vietnam, but have assumed a wider, long-term commitment to maintain a military presence in continental Southeast Asia as part of their policy for containing Communist China. It is this crucial decision that is now shaping the American response to the new international constellation created by the Sino-Soviet conflict, shifting the center of gravity of American foreign policy and changing its methods—with possibly fateful consequences for every part of the world.

In trying to analyze the causes and effects of this major change in the official American outlook, we shall first seek to distinguish between the origins of the U.S. involvement in Vietnam and the new concepts that have led President Johnson and his advisers to persist in this involvement and extend it, and then examine the validity of the latter.

Leaving the fringe groups of right-wing extremists and fellow-travelers aside, there have long been three main positions in the American discussion on Cold War strategy. On one side, a school most effectively represented by Walter Lippmann has considered that the United States should limit its commitments to the defense of areas of direct importance to its own security. On the other hand, a tendency expressed most clearly in the practice of the late John Foster Dulles has been to seek military alliances with anti-Communist governments everywhere, regardless of whether the governments were popular and stable or whether the people felt threatened by Communist attack. In the middle, the concept followed—with occasional deviations—under Presidents Truman and Kennedy has been to accept the world-wide nature of the conflict with the Communist powers and to seek to compete with them everywhere for political influence, but to give military backing only to politically viable governments that requested it against a genuine threat. My own opinion has always been that both the "cut commitments" school of Lippmann and the pactomania of Dulles looked at the problem in too exclusively military terms, underestimating the ideological and political nature of the conflict:[1] that the former, if applied, would have led to unnecessary retreats, while the latter did lead to unnecessary defeats for the United States, as weak allied governments crumbled in Iraq and Laos; and that the "middle course" of a world-wide political struggle with military backing where there was a sound popular basis corresponded best to the realities of the situation.

The decision taken by the United States in 1954 not to sign the Geneva agreement that ended the Indochina war, and subsequently to back the South Vietnamese government of Ngo Dinh Diem in refusing the all-Vietnamese elections proposed in that agreement, like the parallel U.S. initiative in creating the SEATO pact, were, of course, conspicuous examples of the Dulles policy. At the time, Vietnam appeared as a uniquely unfavorable terrain for a political struggle against Communism. It was then—and has remained to

[1] Cf. Lowenthal, "The Balance and the Mission," *Encounter*, August, 1961.

this day—the only country in the world whose people had won freedom from colonial rule under Communist leadership. Ho Chi Minh's Communists and their front were the only major organized political force in the country; in the South the existence of several private armies, ranging from armed sects to armed gangs, seemed to augur ill for Diem's chances of building up a viable state.

Yet as it turned out (and as a handful of American experts predicted at the time) Diem had a chance. He was a nationalist of known integrity who had not collaborated with the defeated colonial power, and the private armies quickly surrendered to his authority once their French backers had withdrawn. He succeeded at first in creating a peaceful and orderly, if authoritarian, state, and a large influx of refugees from the Communist North (many of them Diem's Catholic co-religionists) testified to its comparative attraction. It was this initial success of the Southern regime, combined with the moral impression created by the flight of hundreds of thousands, that caused many Western observers who had been critical of the U.S. attitude at Geneva now to endorse the American backing for the South. In the United States, it was henceforth accepted by the middle-of-the-roaders as well as by the supporters of Dulles and became a bipartisan policy.

As the years went by, however, the weaknesses of Diem and his regime became increasingly apparent. Conceiving of government in terms of a benevolent autocracy, he alienated the modern-minded intellectuals; he could not create a substantial political force in his support and would not tolerate one in opposition. He understood the need for agrarian reform, but not for popular participation in carrying it out: It had to be an orderly, bureaucratic operation—yet there were not enough administrators of the independence and integrity needed to enforce it against the landowners. As suppressed criticism turned into conspiracies, Diem came to rely increasingly on the political police, headed by his brother Nhu, and to distrust all critical advice. This deterioration of the regime accelerated as the Communists, sensing the chance offered by the regime's increasing isolation, resumed their guerrilla activities.

There can be no doubt that the decision to restart the civil war was taken by Hanoi; but it was carried out in the first place by Communists who had always remained in the South, biding their time.

Supplies and returning cadres from the North certainly helped, particularly after the road through Laos had been opened. But more decisive for their success was the active support of part of the peasantry and the lack of equally active support for the government in many areas. Six years after the creation of independent South Vietnam, the Communists were still the only solidly organized political force in the country. That was the measure of Diem's failure.

By that time, the Kennedy Administration had come in. It realized that things were going badly in Vietnam, but also that—in contrast to Laos—there was still much determined opposition to the Communists, and that the army was really fighting the Vietcong. It concluded that aid should be stepped up and reforms be pressed on Diem at the same time. When Diem became increasingly stubborn, he was finally warned that he risked losing American support. It was at this moment that a military coup—not the first that had been attempted—overthrew him, and that Diem and Nhu were killed. Despite the shock at the murder, the change of leadership was welcomed not only in the United States, but by Western democratic opinion generally in the hope that now the way would be open for a more broadly based regime. "No Nhus is good news," wrote the *Economist*. Yet within a short time, the instability of the new regime with its intense personal rivalries revealed the truth: Diem's fall had further weakened what limited political legitimacy the government of South Vietnam possessed.

By 1964, the civil war in Vietnam had been politically lost by the opponents of the Communists—as clearly as the civil war on the Chinese mainland had been lost when President Truman decided that further aid for Chiang Kai-shek's forces had become useless. There was no indigenous force left strong enough to stabilize the situation, let alone beat the Vietcong. Hanoi, now under predominant Chinese influence, was stepping up its support for the Vietcong in the expectation of imminent military victory. To President Johnson fell the bitter choice between accepting political defeat while trying to limit and disguise it by negotiation, or ordering large-scale American military intervention in the hope of thus reversing the political verdict of the civil war. It is hardly surprising that he hesitated until the American elections had given him Presidential authority in his own right. When, in February, 1965, he first authorized the bombing of North Vietnam (in conditions other than direct retaliation for specific North Vietnamese attacks on U.S. forces), his action appeared to many critics as an impulsive improvisation. In fact, the opening of graduated hostilities against North Vietnam turned out to be the first act of a fully considered new policy of direct, large-scale military intervention.

It has taken time for the full implications and the real motives of this decision to become clear. The frequent complaint of American critics that the Administration is misinforming the people does not, on the whole, have a basis in the reporting of actual events in Vietnam, which by now is reasonably truthful. It is due to the widespread feeling that the political *aims* of American intervention have been obscured rather than clarified by a flood of contradictory official statements. To sort out the substance from the verbiage, it is best to start by considering the one alternative to direct intervention that was still open to Johnson at the time.

As I have suggested, that alternative would have been to seek negotiation on the implied basis of accepting political defeat in Vietnam. This would have meant a conference in which the "National Liberation Front of South Vietnam," the political arm of the Vietcong, would be represented as an official partner, while representation of the Saigon Government would have to be insisted on at the same time; the procedural problems involved are familiar from the Laos conference in 1962. The outcome would at best be a coalition government including the Communists—again as in Laos, but probably in proportions more favorable to them. American and North Vietnamese troops would then have to be withdrawn, which in the case of the latter would be difficult to check, whatever control arrangements could be agreed on. Within a limited time after the end of the fighting, this government would then hold elections, presumably followed by a plebiscite on unification with the North; and, given the outcome of the fighting and the power relations resulting from it, it seems safe to expect that unification would be approved. In short, the Communist aim of a single Communist Vietnam would be achieved; however, it would be achieved not by military victory, but as a result of formally democratic procedures, with a delay that might permit saving the active opponents of the

Communists from their revenge, and in a framework that would reduce the dependence of a Communist Vietnam on China and might even take the form of an international agreement on its military neutrality. This, on the whole, seems to have been the kind of solution General de Gaulle had in mind when he first called for an international conference on Vietnam—except that his manner of proposing it seemed to suggest that it could be achieved without American consent.

President Johnson's refusal to envisage this kind of solution is not based on a substantially different estimate of the present relation of forces inside South Vietnam. Its motives are to be found in a new concept of the importance of Vietnam in the wider conflict between the United States and Communist China. The Administration believes, first, that acceptance of political defeat would constitute a surrender to indirect (and increasingly direct) military aggression against "the independent nation of South Vietnam," conducted by Hanoi and masterminded by Communist China; second, that such a surrender would undermine confidence in American protection and encourage similar indirect Chinese aggression throughout Southeast Asia, leading to its conversion into an uncontested Chinese power sphere, with incalculable repercussions on India and Japan; third, that such a surrender is not necessary, because the United States has the military strength to hold on indefinitely at least to a coastal strip of South Vietnam while inflicting severe damage on the North, thus proving to both Peking and its neighbors that "indirect aggression" by civil war is no more successful than open aggression of the Korean type and that the United States will stand by its Asian commitments at any cost. The primary purpose of the American direct intervention, then, is no longer to "help the Vietnamese people to help themselves," even though the President never tires of repeating this. It is to ensure the containment of Chinese Communist expansion throughout Southeast Asia by the long-term commitment of American military force—in whatever quantity and for whatever duration may be needed to achieve the aim.

It is for the sake of this commitment, adopted without advance consultation with America's European allies and not explained to the American people until many months later, that the Johnson

Administration has decided to take on the main burden of the war in Vietnam. It is on the basis of this concept that it has opened graduated hostilities against North Vietnam without either a previous appeal to the United Nations or a constitutional declaration of war. I believe that this concept is based on a false analysis of the conditions for successful guerrilla warfare and of the nature of the danger threatening from Communist China, on a misjudgment of the priorities of American national interest and of the limits of American military power, and on a failure to appreciate the moral basis of Western strength in the contest with Communist dictatorship, and that, unless this policy is corrected in time, it may do incalculable harm to the cohesion of the Western alliance, to the world position of the United States, and even to its internal stability.

The evidence is conclusive that "indirect aggression" from Hanoi —orders and cadres, slogans and supplies—has played a substantial part in the Vietcong campaign; it is not convincing that its role has been decisive for the Vietcong's success. A guerrilla uprising is a political war, and its outcome depends on a combination of political and military factors. The Communist guerrillas in Malaya could not have been put down without tough fighting, but neither could they have been defeated if Malaya had not become independent or if the bulk of its Chinese population had felt sufficiently disaffected to support them in the long run. The Hukbalahaps owed their ultimate defeat not to the geographical isolation of the Philippines, but to their political isolation by Magsaysay's reforms. By contrast, the Chinese Communists did not owe their success against the Japanese and their final victory over the Kuomintang to Soviet aid, but to the popular hatred for the former and to the political disintegration of the latter. The decisive cause of the Vietcong's success in South Vietnam has not been the aid from the North, but the absence of an alternative, of any other cohesively organized and popularly based political force: In guerrilla warfare, you cannot beat something with nothing.

The importance of this question lies not in fixing the blame, but in the light thrown by past experience on the future chances of the Chinese to start "wars of liberation" in other neighboring countries by "pushing a button"—by starting, say, a subversive radio station near the frontier and sending in some trained agents. The anxiety of the Thailand Government about the beginnings of Chinese-sponsored guerrilla action among the tribes of the northeast is said to have been an important factor in the U.S. Administration's decision to "stop the rot" by direct military intervention. Would not success in South Vietnam encourage the multiplication of such activities? Yet in 1948–50, when the Communists were winning a much greater victory in China itself, the "push-button" strategy was tried by them in South India, Burma, Malaya, Indonesia, and the Philippines, and failed everywhere. Only Ho Chi Minh's rising against the French, which had started earlier, for serious indigenous causes and with a broad popular basis, was successful in the end. Once more, it was this leadership in a genuine anticolonial uprising that enabled the Vietnamese Communists to gain their unique strength. No comparable force exists in any neighboring country. "Indirect aggression" depends for its success on the political weakness of the attacked regime; it cannot be carried out according to plan in one country after another.

The idea that a Communist success in Vietnam would automatically start a series of similar takeover bids throughout Southeast Asia until "all the dominoes had fallen" ("If we don't fight in Vietnam we may have to fight in Hawaii") thus must be regarded as an artificial nightmare. Yet it contains one important element of truth: American withdrawal from Vietnam, in whatever face-saving conditions might be negotiated, would certainly lead some of the Asian members of SEATO to reconsider the usefulness of the American alliance. Pakistan is friendly with Peking even now, and Thailand would probably think a switch to neutrality more useful for her internal stability than American bases might prove to her defense. The U.S. Administration is therefore right in believing that a negotiated withdrawal from Vietnam might be the beginning of the end of the American military presence in continental Southeast Asia (though not in Korea, Japan, Formosa, or the Philippines). Two questions then arise: How indispensable is this presence for the containment of Chinese Communist expansion, and how important is that containment for the world role of the United States?

It is true that Communist China is a militant revolutionary power, committed to the expansion of its area of domination both by Communist ideology and by nationalist tradition—and where neighboring countries with American bases are concerned, for obvious strategic reasons as well. It is also true that Peking is steadily probing these latter countries for the chances of "indirect aggression" by revolutionary guerrilla warfare. But observation of Peking's actual strength and behavior does not suggest that it would attempt, in its present phase of development, to take over neutral neighboring states by open and direct aggression. Even the 1962 attack on India was a limited operation aimed to intimidate and humiliate the chief rival in the region, not to achieve domination over him. The reason is obvious: In its difficult early stage of industrialization, Communist China needs international tension but not major war. Hence if the neighboring states are free of American bases and do not show a degree of instability that invites a bid for Communist revolution, Peking seems likely to respect their neutrality for the next period. This is not meant to impute an improbable modesty and love of peace to the Chinese Communists, but merely to suggest that their actions will be based on a more realistic estimate of their strength than their talk.

A neutral Southeast Asia, then, would not be a bastion for the military containment of China, but neither would it simply become a Chinese power sphere, provided that Western interest in maintaining the economic and political viability of these countries continued, and that the major non-Communist nations of Asia, India, and Japan would be encouraged to play their natural role in assuring the cohesion of the region and balancing Chinese influence. Indeed, a maximum investment in the development and security of neutral India would probably make a far more effective contribution to the containment of Chinese expansion in the present period than any number of American alliances with weak governments whose people hanker for neutrality. As China gets stronger and more threatening, the need for such alliances may one day come to be really felt by these peoples; but for the time being, the encouragement of neutrality and regional cohesion appears as the most effective "strategy of denial" at a limited cost.

Limiting the cost is important, because Southeast Asia is, after all, neither an area of vital importance to American security nor of crucial weight in the world balance of power; and American military strength, however great, is not unlimited and must be allocated between different regions of the world in some proportion to the importance of the objectives at stake. If the U.S. Administration insists on maintaining a military presence on the mainland of Asia now, it may succeed only at the price of being drawn into more conflicts of the Vietnamese type. For it is American presence rather than American withdrawal that is likely to expose weak Southeast Asian governments to Chinese-stimulated guerrilla uprisings, and to provide Communist propaganda among the suffering peoples of the region with the slogan that peace depends on expelling the Western imperialists. As the United States is drawn deeper into the mire, Communist China will be able to cause a mounting drain on American blood and treasure by a comparatively limited and indirect expenditure of its own strength; and America's freedom of action in other parts of the world will be correspondingly diminished.

This brings me to the wider risks of the present policy. In contrast to many of its American critics, I do not see among these risks the likelihood of open Chinese intervention and eventual nuclear escalation. Peking is anxious not to provoke the destruction of its embryonic nuclear establishment by American bombs, and the Soviet Union, while embarrassed ideologically by its comparative inaction in the face of the bombing of a Communist state, is profiting practically from the American involvement in Asia and wisely concentrating on objectives nearer home. Nor do I fear that anything short of a full-scale American attack on China could effectively bring the two main Communist powers together again. The basic fact is that the Sino-Soviet rift has given the West for the first time the chance to choose its priorities in dealing with its two major opponents. The tragedy, from a world-wide point of view, is that instead of a common rational choice reached in consultation among the Western powers, the Americans have drifted into a unilateral choice under the pressure of events in Vietnam.

For it is impossible that this American commitment on the mainland of Asia could be maintained for any length of time without diminishing the American concern about balancing Soviet strength in Europe. The economic and military resources of the United States may well be sufficient for the dual task; the psychological and mental resources are not. Even now, the American public is beginning to think of Communist China as the one irreconcilable enemy, and of the Soviet Union as a potential ally to be wooed by concessions if necessary; and the Administration, while naturally more aware of the unresolved issues in dispute with the Soviets, is driven by its preoccupation with Vietnam to look on the conflict with China as urgent and immediate, and on that with Russia as dormant and requiring no action at the present moment.

Yet this is a fallacy. For while the Chinese Communists' policy toward the United States is militant and irreconcilable, their power, despite those nuclear explosions, will remain limited so long as they have not solved their problem of industrialization; and the region immediately threatened by them is also of limited importance in the world balance of power. Conversely, while the Soviet Union is undergoing an evolution that may make possible a genuine solution of her conflicts with the West within a foreseeable time, it is a true world power, facing the United States in the most important single contested region, the powerhouse called Europe. The undermining of West European confidence in the American alliance could easily lead to a crucial shift in the world balance of power here. If the United States concentrated now on achieving a stable European settlement with Russia instead of the present inherently unstable one, they could face any future Chinese challenge from a position of unassailable strength. If they now fritter away their energies on China's periphery, they may suffer an irretrievable loss in Europe without achieving a decision in Asia.

When the Johnson Administration was confronted with its crucial decision, the local situation in Vietnam was desperate, but the general world situation was extremely favorable to the United States. Since the Cuban missile crisis, its place as the world's greatest military power was uncontested. The Sino-Soviet conflict had destroyed all effective coordination of policy between the two principal Communist powers, and the United States was free to choose its priorities in dealing with them. Yet they seem not to have chosen in the light of a careful review of the importance of the issues involved, but to have reacted to the pressure at their point of greatest weakness; and the manner of their choice is proving as harmful as the matter.

They have refused to recognize the fact that even the greatest military power must in certain conditions accept political defeats—a fact recognized by Truman in China, by Eisenhower in Iraq, and by Kennedy in Laos—and committed themselves to the attempt to reverse a political defeat by military force. As a result, withdrawal now would be regarded not merely as a political, but also as a military defeat of the United States, with correspondingly graver and truly unacceptable consequences. Even if military action succeeds in bringing about a negotiated compromise, that compromise will divide the American people because it cannot truly secure the "independence of South Vietnam," proclaimed as the purpose of intervention.

They have made a major, long-term commitment on the Asian mainland, which is bound to reduce their concern for Europe and may lead to reduction of their forces there, without consulting their European allies. As a result, they have undermined the confidence of these allies at a critical moment: The number of West Europeans who privately echo General de Gaulle's doubts about America's reliability has greatly increased. While most of them continue to recognize that they have no alternative to the Atlantic Alliance, its bonds have been further weakened—to the common danger of Western Europe and the United States.

The United States has bombed the territory of a foreign state, not indeed without provocation, but without declaration of war, in defiance of the U.N. Charter, and in open disregard of "world opinion,"—in a manner comparable to no action by any Western power since the ill-conceived Suez adventure. As a result, they have not only further weakened the United Nations and alienated many neutrals, but have probably undone some of the effect achieved by previous American administrations in seeking to "educate" the Soviets to the observation of certain "ground rules" in the conduct of power conflicts.

Last, not least, they have created a crisis of conscience for many loyal American citizens. The people who now oppose the war in Vietnam are certainly a minority, but they are by no means confined to the usual fringe of pacifists and left-wing extremists; most of them, from university teachers and students to churchmen and other community leaders, are the same kind of democratic idealists who have been the backbone of many liberal causes, from foreign aid to racial integration. The fact that normally they are unable to propose a practicable alternative policy does not diminish the symptomatic importance of their protest, for theirs is primarily a moral reaction to an unaccustomed climate of official cynicism. The airy contempt with which some unofficial defenders of official policy treat such "sentimental" considerations as international law, neutral opinion, or even the wishes of the unfortunate people of Vietnam is indeed something new in responsible American circles; to one European who had just spent a year in the United States, it sounded ominously similar to the notorious *"Realpolitik"* of Imperial Germany, while the protesters seemed to embody the American democratic tradition. But it is not possible for a great modern democracy in the long run to call on its young men to fight and die for a cause that bears no intelligible relation to its professed ideals. Any loyal American will defend the security of his country, but a war against "Communism" in far distant lands only makes sense if it is a struggle for the right of peoples to determine their own form of government. It is no trifling matter for the leaders of a free country to undermine the faith of their young generation in the righteousness of its cause.

Assuming the U.S. Administration came to realize the dangers of the present course—could they still reverse it? Their spokesmen truthfully point out that Peking is obstinately opposed to negotiation on any terms and urges the Vietnamese to fight on until a complete American withdrawal—not, presumably, because the Chinese consider such a military victory likely, but because a protracted war fought by Americans on Asian (but not on Chinese) soil suits their political aims. It is true, too, that under Peking's pressure, the Hanoi Government has failed to respond to various overtures for negotiating. Pending such a response, the Administration says, holding on in Vietnam is the only alternative to unilateral withdrawal, that is, to an unacceptable military defeat.

On this last point, they are right. Having involved America's military power and prestige in an ill-chosen issue, the United States cannot simply withdraw and abandon the South Vietnamese leaders and forces allied to them without catastrophic international effect.

A political defeat due to the unique history of Vietnam could be confined to that country; an American military defeat could not. The practical question, therefore, is this: What could the United States still do, beyond the repeated proclamation of its readiness for "unconditional" negotiations, to strengthen the presumptive supporters of such negotiations in Hanoi aganst their opponents?

It must be recognized that, due largely to the errors committed so far, there is not much scope left for changes between the present policy and an unacceptable capitulation. Yet there are still a very few steps that the United States could, and therefore should, take to facilitate negotiation. While holding on in South Vietnam, it could stop the bombing of the North, which has clearly reduced the chances of negotiation with Hanoi without achieving much military effect. It could make it clear publicly that it is prepared to accept the Vietcong, or the "National Liberation Front," as a negotiating partner in its own right—not only under some diplomatic disguise —at any peace conference. Above all, it could and should state that it is not committed to maintain the "independence of South Vietnam" as a state, still less the American military presence there, but only the right of the South Vietnamese to decide their own future in the absence of all foreign troops. In other words, it could even now put itself on the basis of the Geneva agreement of 1954.

If negotiation comes about on such a basis, it should aim at the best possible terms for making a free popular decision possible, and for ensuring the safety of those Vietnamese who have fought the Communists. If it succeeds, the first step will have been taken for extricating the United States from an overextended military commitment at a bearable price.

If, on the other hand, negotiation continues to be refused by the Vietnamese Communists even after all these steps have been taken, the Americans will have to hold on until their opponents change their mind, and the continued suffering of the Vietnamese people will be the sole responsibility of the Communists. But even in that case, the wider concept of the American role in Southeast Asia will have to be revised to prevent an increasing involvement in conflicts on politically unfavorable ground, to allow the neutral Asian powers to play their natural role in balancing Chinese Communist influence, and thus to restore the world-wide freedom of action of the United States.

It has been suggested that it is doubtful whether the United States has the "capacity to deal successfully with a political war against the Communists in a non-Western area." The hypothetical example of a Communist coup against an unpopular Shah has been chosen to ask whether it would be politic to "let Iran go down the drain." It has been argued that the United States should use military force in favor of any government threatened by the Communists, regardless of that government's popular support. "What," it has been asked, "has a government's popularity to do with whether we ought to help its *people* resist Communist subversion or invasion?" But does it not matter whether the people *want* to be helped in this way?

Here, I believe, we reach the core and center of our debate, and it involves the very nature of our conflict with the Communist powers. For some of the defenders of U.S. policy, that conflict is like a world war. Once you are involved in it, your national survival is at stake; and in a war you fight to deny strategic territory to the enemy regardless of the wishes of its inhabitants (as the Americans sought to deny Indochina to Japan regardless of anti-French feeling there). The House of Representatives recently applied the same reasoning in proclaiming the right of the United States to intervene against any attempt to set up a Communist government in the Western hemisphere (thus providing *ex post facto* justification for President Johnson's action in Santo Domingo). It has even been claimed elsewhere that President Kennedy's handling of the Cuban missile crisis is an example supporting this outlook. Faced with Khrushchev's missiles, it has been said, Kennedy "did what comes naturally to an industrial-military power: he threatened to use that power and didn't bother to set up a 'cohesively organized and popularly based political force' in Cuba."

At this point the fallacy becomes tangible. Cuba became a threat to the security of the United States when the missiles were implanted there; and because there was such a threat, the use of American power to remove it was justified and necessary. But once the missiles were removed, the Communist regime in Cuba was no longer a "clear and present danger" to American security, only a potential one; and a potential danger did not justify, in President Kennedy's eyes, the use of actual military action. Conflict with Cuba, as with other Communist regimes, has continued since; but that conflict is now different from "real" war, because national survival is no longer at stake in it.

The confusion arises from the intermingling of power politics and ideological passions that constitutes the essence of the Cold War. The Soviet Union and China are both, on different levels, great powers, and both, in different degrees, are ideologically hostile to the West. But while Communist ideology is both a major motivation and one of the weapons of their hostility, it is not that ideology as such that threatens the survival of the advanced Western countries. A threat to our security arises only if a hostile great power either gets hold of a place that is of vital importance in itself (by its strategic position or indispensable resources), or if it scores a political success of a kind that would indirectly but crucially change the world balance of power (e.g., by causing the disintegration of the Western alliance). To forestall either kind of hazard has long been the major task of Western—and, above all, American —military power and diplomacy, as last exemplified in preventing the Soviets' military implantation in Cuba and their attempted political breakthrough at Berlin.

But the world-wide ideological conflict is not confined to such life-and-death issues, and outside such crises it is primarily a contest for the minds of men. To prevent the expansion of Communist totalitarian regimes in countries where Western security and the balance of world power are not directly involved is also a *legitimate* Western concern, particularly where the Communists operate by organized terrorism and civil war. But it is not a *vital* Western concern, to be pursued regardless of cost and of the attitude of the people whose future is at stake. The United States quite rightly did not desire the Castro regime to turn Communist, but since they failed to prevent that, they have found that they can live with a Communist Cuba that is not an outpost of Soviet military power —just as they have lived with a Communist North Vietnam since 1954, and just as they could live with a Communist South Vietnam, particularly if the latter ceased to be dependent on Chinese military power.

Let me repeat that I regard both world-wide political, ideological, and economic competition against Communist influence and military aid to nations threatened by Communist force as a necessary part of Western policy. I even hold that American intervention in South Vietnam was reasonable so long as there was a chance of political success. Yet my crucial point is that where vital security issues are not involved, the decisive stake of the contest is not the control of territory but the allegiance of a people. That is why in such cases Western intervention makes no sense unless it takes place in support of a "cohesive political force."

Nor do I share the pessimistic view that Americans are generally unable to match the Communist powers in political warfare in non-Western areas. Since the rise of Communist China, Vietnam and Cuba have been the only countries to come under Communist control, despite the considerable expenditure of both Russian and Chinese efforts on the conversion of the Third World. These efforts have on the whole been frustrated neither by Western military action (which proved necessary only in Korea and Malaya), nor by the attractions of Western democracy and liberal economics (which are often inapplicable in underdeveloped countries), but by the growth of a great variety of indigenous nationalist and even national-revolutionary regimes and by increasing Western, including American, flexibility and realism in supporting such regimes despite their different political and economic institutions and their anti-imperialist declarations. To cooperate with such indigenous forces of national mobilization and modernization is the only form of "matching" Communist political warfare open to the West in the Third World, and the West has learned it remarkably fast. Nor can American inexperience be blamed for the unfortunate fact that in some countries, including Vietnam, such forces do not exist. But where their absence has given a native Communist movement a decisive advantage, it seems to me a wiser course, in the present age of Communist pluralism, to encourage its independence from the Communist great powers by coming to terms with it rather than to cement its dependence on them by trying to bomb it out of existence.

President Johnson's "peace offensive" at the turn of 1965–66, the interruption and resumption of the bombing of North Vietnam, and the hearings of the Foreign Relations Committee of the U.S. Senate have thrown further light on the situation. As a result of these events, it has become obvious that the principal obstacle to a negotiated end of the fighting is the question of who should represent the people of South Vietnam at the conference table. The official American position appears still to be that only the Saigon Government can speak for its subjects, and that the Vietcong or its political arm, the National Liberation Front, are nothing but an extension of the North Vietnamese Government and a tool of its aggression; hence they could take part in a peace conference only as a kind of appendix to the delegation of the latter. Conversely, the official position of the North Vietnamese Government and the Vietcong is that the Saigon Government is nothing but a puppet of the American imperialists, and that only the National Liberation Front should take part in a peace conference on behalf of the people of South Vietnam.

In view of the evident fact that both the army of the Saigon Government and the Vietcong contain large numbers of South Vietnamese fighting with conviction for their respective causes (in addition to considerable numbers of unwilling recruits on either side who desert at the first opportunity), both positions are obviously unrealistic. Yet they are being maintained despite the fact that Communist as well as American hopes of a decisive military victory have by now clearly faded: Each side now proclaims its belief that it can wear down its opponent in a test of endurance.

In the case of the Vietnamese Communists, this hope takes the form of a mistaken expectation that the growth of opposition to the war in the United States will eventually force a unilateral American withdrawal, despite the fact that none of the responsible and representative critics of the Administration advocates such a step. The Communists' hope is naturally fed by their Chinese allies, who are interested in the continuation of the war rather than in an independent, united, and neutral Vietnam, even if it be a Communist Vietnam. But Hanoi's will to fight on is not being counteracted by the Soviet Government either—though it seems unlikely that the Soviets would share the illusions of their Vietnamese comrades. One reason for this—the only one stressed by official American analysts—is the Soviet desire to compete with the Chinese for influence on North Vietnam and therefore to avoid exposing themselves to the charge of "appeasing the imperialists"; but another, no less important reason is presumably the Soviet discovery that the American involvement in Southeast Asia, by withdrawing American attention and initiative from Europe, serves Soviet interests in a vital area—at least as long as there is no serious danger of major escalation.

It is more difficult to discover on what the American Administration's hopes of eventually wearing down the Vietcong are based; there is no obvious reason why the Communists should not be able to match any foreseeable increase in the American forces in Vietnam, and thus to prevent any serious application of the reform plans which Saigon has now adopted, about ten years too late, on American prompting. More plausibly, President Johnson is reluctant to offer in advance of negotiations the few concessions he can still make short of a unilateral withdrawal—such as acceptance of the Vietcong as a negotiating partner and willingness to agree to the formation of a coalition government that includes the Communists to supervise elections. Yet as a result of the initial mistake of widening the American commitment, the granting of the first concession and the implied offer to grant the second seem now the only means—and not even sure means—for changing the balance of wills in Hanoi in favor of a negotiated peace; and the lessons of the past year have only reinforced the argument that, from the point of view of American, and generally Western interests, in Vietnam, negotiation from a position of political weakness is now preferable to an indefinite continuation of the war.

II. Soviet Policy in the Underdeveloped Countries: Changing Behavior and Persistent Symbols

JOHN H. KAUTSKY

. . . as in private life one distinguishes between what a man thinks and says of himself and what he really is and does, still more in historical struggles must one distinguish the phrases and fancies of the parties from their real organism, . . . their conception of themselves from their reality.

—KARL MARX, *The Eighteenth Brumaire of Louis Bonaparte.*

THE DECADE of the 1960's opened with what seemed to some observers to be renewed Soviet concern for Communist Party strength, leadership, and ultimately control in underdeveloped countries. There was discussion in Soviet and Soviet-sponsored journals and meetings of the relation of the working class (virtually a synonym for the Communist Party) to the national bourgeoisie, of the leading role of the working class, and of a "noncapitalist" path of development and the future transition to socialism.[1] All this culminated in the doctrine of "national democracy," as formulated in the Moscow Declaration of December, 1960, of the Conference of Eighty-one Communist Parties[2] and embodied in the Program of the Communist Party of the Soviet Union of 1961.[3]

However, if we distinguish between what the Soviet Government says and what it does, between its symbols and its behavior, we find that in fact no major change in Soviet policy toward the underdeveloped countries took place in the early 1960's. There may, indeed, have been renewed emphasis on some of the more traditional symbols of Communism in response perhaps to domestic developments and probably to Chinese Communist pressure,[4] but

[1] See excerpts from an international seminar held in Leipzig in May, 1959, on "The National Bourgeoisie and the Liberation Movement," in *World Marxist Review*, II, No. 8 (August, 1959), 61–81, and No. 9 (September, 1959), 66–81; Walter Z. Laqueur, "Communism and Nationalism in Tropical Africa," *Foreign Affairs*, XXXIX, No. 4 (July, 1961), 610–21, which reprints a few excerpts from *The African Communist*, a journal founded in London in the fall of 1959, evidently to stimulate the organization of Communist parties in Africa; and *World Trade Union Movement*, No. 7 (1960), reprinting a resolution of the General Council of the World Federation of Trade Unions, 1960, on the "Struggle Against Colonialism."

[2] Reprinted in Dan N. Jacobs (ed.), *The New Communist Manifesto and Related Documents* (Evanston, Ill.: Row, Peterson & Co., 1961); see particularly pp. 31–33. For comments and references to Soviet elaborations, see Laqueur, "Towards National Democracy: Soviet Doctrine and the New Countries," *Survey*, No. 37 (July–September, 1961), pp. 3–11; and William T. Shinn, Jr., "The 'National Democratic State': A Communist Program for Less-Developed Areas," *World Politics*, XV, No. 3 (April, 1963), 377–89. For a discussion of "national democracy" in the general context of Soviet policy in underdeveloped countries, see Richard Lowenthal, "'National Democracy' and the Post-Colonial Revolution," in Kurt London (ed.), *New Nations in a Divided World* (New York: Frederick A. Praeger, 1963), pp. 56–74. The same article, slightly changed and abbreviated, appeared as "On 'National Democracy': I. Its Function in Communist Policy," *Survey*, No. 47 (April, 1963), pp. 119–33.

[3] Reprinted in Jan F. Triska (ed.), *Soviet Communism: Programs and Rules* (San Francisco: Chandler Publishing Co., 1962); see especially p. 58.

[4] The Conference of Eighty-one Parties was, after all, called to reconcile differences between Moscow and Peking. It may be noted, however, that the Chinese Communists never accepted the concept of national democracy, preferring their own formula of "new democracy." The difference is not merely verbal, for the former involves rule by the "national bourgeoisie," the latter rule by the Communist Party.

the trend, initiated a decade earlier, toward Soviet support for non-Communist neutralist regimes in underdeveloped countries and toward the convergence of Communist parties with modernizing nationalist movements in these countries has, apart from mostly verbal zigs and zags, been continuing down to the present.[5]

This trend cannot be fully understood unless it is traced from its beginnings in the post-World War II period, but, rather than to repeat this oft-told story[6] here, I will summarize it only briefly. I will then offer some possible explanations for the departure of Soviet policy from what is still commonly thought of as Communist

[5] I have tried to place this trend in a broader perspective of the politics of underdeveloped countries and an interpretation of the Russian Revolution as a movement in one such country in my "Essay in the Politics of Development," in Kautsky (ed.), *Political Change in Underdeveloped Countries: Nationalism and Communism* (New York: John Wiley & Sons, 1962), pp. 1–119. For an excellent critique of this essay, see Richard Lowenthal, "Communism and Nationalism," *Problems of Communism*, XI, No. 6 (November–December, 1962), 37–44. On the point most relevant here, Professor Lowenthal wrote that, far from marking the "assimilation of the Communists in underdeveloped countries to other movements of the nationalist intelligentsia, as Professor Kautsky assumes, the new strategy of 'national democracy' heralds a renewed Communist bid for leadership of the national fronts in rivalry to the established nationalist movements" (*ibid.*, p. 40). However, by 1965, Professor Lowenthal thought that "the new strategy" had been abandoned as a failure in the summer of 1963 and been replaced by "nothing less than the deliberate renunciation of independent Communist parties, publicly acting as such, in a number of countries" ("Russia, the One-Party System, and the Third World," *Survey*, No. 58 [January, 1966], p. 43). I prefer to think of the changes between 1959 and 1963 as merely verbal, since in fact there was continuing Soviet aid to the countries in question and Communist parties did not challenge their governments, but admittedly the line between "words" and "facts" is never too clear, for policy often consists of as much of the former as of the latter.

[6] Among numerous contributions on the subject, the following are particularly relevant here: Bernard S. Morris and Morris Watnick, "Current Communist Strategy in Non-Industrialized Countries," *Problems of Communism*, IV, No. 5 (September–October, 1955), 1–6; and Morris, "Recent Shifts in Communist Strategy," *Soviet Survey*, No. 16–17 (June–July, 1957), pp. 40–44 (these two articles are reprinted in Kautsky [ed.], *op. cit.*, pp. 282–303); Hugh Seton-Watson, "The Communist Powers and Afro-Asian Nationalism," in Kurt London (ed.), *Unity and Contradiction* (New York: Frederick A. Praeger, 1962), pp. 187–206; and Donald S. Carlisle, "The Changing Soviet Perception of the Development Process in the Afro-Asian World," *Midwest Journal of Political Science*, VIII, No. 4 (November, 1964), 385–407. I traced the early phases of the change in Soviet policy in some detail in my *Moscow and the Communist Party of India* (New York: John Wiley & Sons, 1956), and indicated some later ones in "Russia, China, and Nationalist Movements," *Survey*, No. 43 (August, 1962), pp. 119–29.

policy. And, finally, I will suggest why Soviet and Communist statements do not reflect this departure.

In the late 1940's, with the onset of the Cold War between the Soviet Union and the United States, the Soviet Government, for the first time, ceased to claim that it represented exclusively an anti-capitalist proletarian or at least lower-class movement. Even in the popular and national fronts of the late 1930's and early 1940's, Communists had only sought alliances with the bourgeoisie but never claimed to represent it. But now, in a search for anti-American allies, Communist parties, following instructions from Moscow, began to declare that they represented the interests of all classes, quite explicitly including the "national bourgeoisie," that is, the capitalists, not just the interests of the so-called exploited. The enemy now became not capitalism, but imperialism, that is, American foreign policy. This was the beginning of the end of the class struggle and of proletarianism in Communist mythology.

In their attempt to unite all classes under the leadership of some intellectuals against foreign imperialism and also in favor of rapid industrialization, Communist parties in underdeveloped countries became quite similar to the non-Communist nationalist movements in terms of the support they solicited, the social background of their leadership, and the character of their program. At that time, though, they were still strenuously opposed to such movements and denounced them and their policy of neutralism as serving the interests of imperialism.

In the early 1950's, however, and especially after Stalin's death in 1953, the Soviet Government evidently recognized that neutralist nationalists in underdeveloped countries could be genuinely anti-Western. Communist parties were therefore pushed by Moscow to support the foreign policies of their "bourgeois" governments. Then the Soviet Union began to provide substantial aid to the industrialization efforts of some of these governments, and Communist parties were now expected to support their domestic development policies as well. Gradually, by the late 1950's, they were urged more and more by Moscow to give up their independent role and follow the lead of the non-Communist nationalist movements.

During the very period when these major changes in Soviet policy took place, Soviet leaders and writers frequently repeated the old doctrines from which Soviet policy was now in fact departing. To cite only one instance, at the Twentieth Congress, in 1956, Khrushchev asserted that "in all the forms of transition to socialism, an absolute and decisive requirement is political leadership of the working class, headed by its vanguard. The transition to socialism is impossible without this."[7] Authoritative Soviet commentaries on the doctrine of national democracy of the early 1960's, too, dealt with this newly invented stage of history as a transitional one leading ultimately to "socialism," that is, rule by the Communist Party. In fact, however, the doctrine had been evolved in order to account for the new situation in which the so-called bourgeoisie in underdeveloped countries pursued Moscow-approved anti-imperialist policies. The definition of a national democracy in the Moscow Declaration of the Eighty-one Parties makes very clear that to qualify for inclusion in this category, a country must, above all, pursue "anti-imperialist," that is, anti-Western policies. National democracies are explicitly recognized to be under the rule of "bourgeois," that is, non-Communist nationalists and not to be attempting the construction of so-called socialism. Indeed, in three of the four countries then described[8] as approximating national democracies—Guinea, Ghana, Mali (the fourth one is Indonesia)—there are no Communist parties. Nevertheless this stage is characterized by Soviet theoreticians as both a long-lasting one[9] and a highly desirable one from the Soviet point of view.

7 N. S. Khrushchev, "The Central Committee Report," in Leo Gruliow (ed.), *Current Soviet Policies—II: The Documentary Record of the 20th Party Congress and Its Aftermath* (New York: Frederick A. Praeger, 1957), p. 38.

8 B. N. Ponomarev, "On the National Democratic State," *Kommunist (Communist;* Moscow), No. 8 (May, 1961), pp. 33–48; condensed translation in *The Current Digest of the Soviet Press*, XIII, No. 22 (June 28, 1961), 3–7. Ponomarev, who specifically rejects the classification of states as belonging or not belonging to the category of national democracy as "schematic and harmful," also mentions Cuba, but Cuba was soon promoted to the status of a country building socialism. See Shinn, *op. cit.,* pp. 383–84.

9 As E. Zhukov, a leading Soviet expert on underdeveloped countries, had written a few months before the concept of national democracy had been formulated: "For many lagging countries of Asia, and especially Africa . . . the central task . . . remains for a *comparatively long period* of time that of 'struggle not against capital but against survivals of the Middle Ages.' From this stems the possibility of the cooperation *over a long period* of the workers, peasants and

In recent years, Soviet writers have also spoken with approval of the "socialism" of non-Communist nationalist movements in under-developed countries. To be sure, on this point, too, there have also been reassertions of the old doctrine associating the building of socialism solely with the Communist Party. Still, it has now been recognized by Soviet writers that the old Marxist category of the bourgeoisie is inapplicable to the present leaders of nationalist movements and that these are, rather, intellectuals.[10] This, in turn, makes it easier for Moscow to proclaim that the present non-Communist regimes of certain underdeveloped countries are bringing about the transformation to socialism, that is, that they are doing what according to one of the firmest Leninist articles of faith could only be done under the leadership of the Communist Party.[11]

By now it is clear, then, that the doctrine of national democracy was but another step in the subordination of Communists to the leadership of non-Communist nationalist movements rather than

---

intelligentsia . . . with that part of the national bourgeoisie which is interested in independent political and economic development of its country and is ready to defend its independence against any encroachments by the imperialist powers." Zhukov, "Significant Factor of Our Times. On Some Questions of the Present-Day National-Liberation Movement," *Pravda*, August 26, 1960, pp. 3–4; condensed translation in *The Current Digest of the Soviet Press*, XII, No. 34 (September 21, 1960), 18–19 (italics added).

[10] Cf. Carlisle, *op. cit.*, pp. 401–3, and the Soviet sources cited there.

[11] For a well-documented discussion of statements by Khrushchev and some Soviet writers in 1963 and 1964 that certain non-Communist-ruled countries, especially Algeria and Egypt, were "embarked upon the road of socialist development" and of opposition to this thesis by other Soviet figures and by Arab Communists, especially the anti-Nasserite Syrian Khaled Bagdash, see Uri Ra'anan, "Moscow and the 'Third World,'" *Problems of Communism*, XIV, No. 1 (January–February, 1965), 22–31. Georgi Mirsky, "The Proletariat and National Liberation," *New Times* (Moscow), No. 18 (May 1, 1964), pp. 6–9, states very bluntly that "if the conditions for proletarian leadership have not yet matured, the historic mission of breaking with capitalism can be carried out by elements close to the working class. Nature abhors a vacuum." The vacuum is filled, on the one hand, by the "revolutionary-democratic leaders," with Ben Bella given as an example, and, on the other hand, by the Soviet Union, for "the socialist world system is performing the functions of proletarian vanguard in relation to imperialist-oppressed nations" (*ibid.*, pp. 8–9). For a recent Soviet statement sharply characterizing as "absurd" suggestions that Marxists-Leninists "deny the socialist aspirations of national-democratic parties," see A. Iskenderov, "The Developing Nations and Socialism," *Pravda*, June 4, 1965, p. 3; excerpt translated in *The Current Digest of the Soviet Press*, XVII, No. 22 (June 23, 1965), 16–17.

a new strategy aiming at Communist leadership. In the three
African countries once named as approaching the state of national
democracy, there was no working-class leadership and no Communist Party was permitted, but the Soviet Union, far from seeking
to organize such parties, supported the existing regimes[12] and designated their single parties as "national democratic parties." In Indonesia, the large Communist Party has recently been brutally suppressed, but Soviet relations with Indonesia do not appear to have
deteriorated and, according to one press report, the Soviet Government even let it be known to the military masters of Indonesia
that it had no objections to their crack-down on the PKI.[13] Other
governments of underdeveloped countries never recognized as national democracies, too, have continued to receive Soviet support
and economic and military aid, though they opposed or even
banned and suppressed their local Communist parties. This has
been the story in India ever since the 1950's, and in Iraq under
Kassem in the early 1960's.[14] Ben Bella was made a Hero of the

[12] In late 1961, Sékou Touré accused alleged Communists in the Guinea
Teachers' Union of planning to overthrow his government and implied that they
were in contact with the Soviet Embassy. It is not clear whether the accusations
were justified, but the Soviet Ambassador was replaced with an expert on foreign
trade; early in 1962 Anastas Mikoyan visited Conakry to stress Soviet promises
of noninterference, and Soviet and East European aid and trade have continued
to flow to Guinea. See Alexander Dallin, "The Soviet Union: Political Activity,"
in Zbigniew K. Brzezinski (ed.), *Africa and the Communist World* (Stanford,
Calif.: Stanford University Press, 1963), pp. 33–35; and Alexander Erlich and
Christian R. Sonne, "The Soviet Union: Economic Activity," *ibid.*, pp. 72–73.

[13] "Sukarno Warns Public to Halt Campaign Against Communists," Associated
Press dispatch, Singapore, October 23, 1965, *St. Louis Post Dispatch*, October
24, 1965.

[14] On this period in Iraq, see Manfred Halpern, "The Middle East and North
Africa," in Cyril E. Black and Thomas P. Thornton (eds.), *Communism and
Revolution* (Princeton, N.J.: Princeton University Press, 1964), pp. 304–11. In his
excellent conclusions on Communism in the Middle East in general, Halpern
finds that "the U.S.S.R., through the requirements of its foreign policy, has
become a major brake on Communist revolutions in the Middle East and North
Africa" and that "it can cement government-to-government relations in this
highly nationalist region only at the cost of minimizing its support and encouragement for the Communist Party" (*ibid.*, pp. 324 and 326). See also the rather
desperate attack by an Iranian Communist leader on "the verbal subterfuge
according to which an improvement in relations between Iran and the Soviet
Union can only prejudice the revolutionary movement" (I. Eskandari, "Iran:

Soviet Union by Khrushchev while the Communist Party was out-lawed in Algeria. Nasser was closest to Moscow while the Egyptian Communists were in jail,[15] and even when Khrushchev voiced his disapproval of the suppression of the Egyptian and Syrian Communists, Soviet aid continued. As Khrushchev said at the Twenty-first Party Congress, putting first things first: "We do not conceal the fact that we and some leaders of the U.A.R. have different views in the ideological field, but in questions of struggle against imperialism . . . our positions coincide. . . . Differences in ideological views must not hinder the development of friendly relations between our countries and the cause of the common struggle against imperialism."[16] Since then, Nasser, too, has become a Hero of the Soviet Union traveling the road of noncapitalist and/or socialist development.[17]

Present Situation and Perspective," *World Marxist Review,* VIII [May, 1965], 75). Eskandari rejects not only this Chinese view but also, much more briefly and weakly, turns against the Soviet position of making "the class struggle . . . dependent on peaceful coexistence with the socialist countries," so that "the party of the working class would be a passive factor waiting to see how world events develop before deciding on its own policy" (*ibid.,* p. 76).

15 A recent Soviet article devoted mainly to Egypt, after noting "a phase of worsened relations with the Soviet Union" during the period of the Syrian-Egyptian union (1958–61), proudly states that "economic cooperation between the Soviet Union and the United Arab Republic developed continuously, and the agreement on Soviet economic and technical assistance in building the first stage of the High Aswan Dam was signed at a time when the strain caused by political divergences was at its highest (December 1958)" (K. Ivanov, "National-Liberation Movement and Non-Capitalist Path of Development," *International Affairs* [Moscow], No. 5 [May, 1965], p. 64).

16 N. S. Khrushchev, "On the Middle East," in Alvin Z. Rubinstein (ed.), *The Foreign Policy of the Soviet Union* (New York: Random House, 1960), p. 401. Cf. also the Soviet explanation that their aid was being granted "to the former colonies on an intergovernmental basis rendering it to nations and not to some classes within them," since they were engaged not chiefly in an internal class struggle but a common struggle against imperialism (L. Stepanov, "Soviet Aid—and Its 'Critics,'" *International Affairs,* No. 6 [June, 1960], pp. 20–26).

17 Ra'anan, *op. cit.* Khaled Bagdash, "Some Problems of the National-Liberation Movement," *World Marxist Review,* VII, No. 8 (August, 1964), 50–58, in what amounts to a weak defense of Communist Party interests against Soviet policy, reluctantly admits that "there is no denying . . . that a number of progressive steps" had been taken by Nasser (*ibid.,* p. 53), but decries a "tendency to belittle the role of the working class both at the present stage of the national-liberation movement and in the future, and to exaggerate the role of the intelligentsia, the officers, and other members of the petty-bourgeoisie who profess to be for socialism" (*ibid.,* p. 55).

How is one to explain the evolution of Soviet and Communist policy in the course of less than two decades from Communist parties serving as indispensable instruments both of Soviet foreign policy and domestic revolution to the virtual abandonment by Soviet foreign policy of both revolution and of the Communist parties?

This change is really startling only if we assume, like many people, including Communists themselves, that Communism is an unchanging and unchangeable phenomenon, that, for instance, one can learn about its present problems and policies by reading Lenin or even Marx. Once we recall the tremendous changes the world —and particularly the Soviet Union—has undergone in the last few decades, it would be far more startling if Communism had remained the same since the 1920's and 1930's.

Communist parties and the myth of the proletarian world revolution were important instruments of Soviet foreign policy when it had few other instruments. The early Soviet republic was weak as compared to other European powers; it was isolated diplomatically, having no allies and not even membership in the League of Nations; it was certainly weak economically and could not offer any foreign aid to anyone, nor did it have the propaganda strength the Soviet Union could later derive from its successful industrialization. No wonder the Soviet Government concentrated on one asset it did have in international affairs: the support of some disciplined followers of the Communist parties throughout the world who looked to Moscow for leadership and dreamed of overthrowing the many regimes hostile to the Soviet Union. Being unable to deal with existing foreign governments to its satisfaction, the Soviet Government looked forward to their overthrow by Communist parties and hence emphasized the goal of world revolution.

All this is now changed. In the past decade or two, the Soviet power position in world affairs has become an utterly different one from that of the 1920's and 1930's. Today the Soviet Union can powerfully influence non-Communist governments by means of military pressure or offers of military aid. It has allies and governments in sympathy with it and it is a strong member of the United Nations. It can give substantial amounts of foreign aid to developing countries and has in some cases provided more aid than the

United States. The success of its own program of industrialization, which turned a backward country into one of the most powerful and advanced ones, provides it with great propaganda appeal to intellectuals in underdeveloped countries, who are now in leading positions and are committed to similar programs.

As these military, economic, diplomatic, and propaganda weapons became available to her foreign policy, the Soviet Union could more and more influence non-Communist governments, and the more this became true the less was the Soviet Government interested in replacing such governments with Communist ones. Why bother to wait till established non-Communist governments can be overthrown when they can be influenced in the present? Why, for instance, wait for the weak Egyptian or even the stronger Indian Communist parties to grow strong enough to capture their governments, when their present non-Communist governments can be induced to serve some Soviet purposes by grants of military aid and by massive economic and technical assistance? To be sure, if Moscow followed such a policy it could then not expect to control these governments, but, after all, Moscow has not been able to control Communist governments either, particularly if they came to power without the aid of the Soviet Army, like those of Yugoslavia, China, North Vietnam, and Cuba. Soviet support thus shifted from the Communist parties in underdeveloped countries to their non-Communist and often anti-Communist governments, and it is for this reason that the Communist parties were, as we noted, instructed to support these governments.

Communist parties can continue to serve a useful function for the Soviet Government, on the one hand, by putting pressure on their own governments on behalf of pro-Soviet policies and, on the other, by keeping quiescent—in a manner to be discussed below— people who might otherwise cause trouble for governments cooperating with the Soviet Government and by absorbing at least some of the support that might otherwise go to a party sympathetic to the Chinese Communists. If they fail to do so, if they, either independently or at the behest of the Chinese Communists, turn against the non-Communist nationalists, then, from the Soviet point of view, they become a nuisance interfering with good relationships on the governmental level.

The logical end of the development traced here might well be the dissolution of those Communist parties that the Soviet Union can control and their merger with the non-Communist nationalist movements.[18] It may not come to this in many countries for quite some time, but it is worthwhile to note that in a few places this has in fact occurred and that it may be the beginning of a trend.

In Cuba, this development has been obscured, because the non-Communist nationalist movement itself was declared to be Communist, but the fact remains that the official pre-Castro Communist Party (the PSP—Popular Socialist Party) merged with that movement and is not, as such, in power today.[19] In Algeria, the leaders of the outlawed Communist Party have cooperated with the government of the FLN and have merged their newspaper, the most widely read in the country, with that of this single party.[20] In Ghana, Guinea, and Mali, there were no Communist parties to merge, but, as we noted, none have been created, and the official single parties have in some ways, been treated as substitutes for them. Thus, their delegates attended the Twenty-second Soviet Party Congress in October, 1961. The most striking case is that of Egypt, where the Communist Party officially dissolved itself in April, 1965, with a statement declaring that Nasser's single party was the only organization capable of carrying on the revolution.[21] Nothing could be more indicative of the trend under discussion than Communists stating that only their jailers can carry on their revolution.

It is evident, then, that ever since the 1950's, the Soviet Government has come to feel that its goals could be pursued more effectively through cooperation with nationalist governments of

[18] Lowenthal, "Russia, the One-Party System, and the Third World," pp. 50–58, believes that the Communists are pursuing a policy of "licensed infiltration" vis-à-vis one-party regimes in underdeveloped countries and he recognizes that the main advantage of this policy for the Soviet Union is the "reduction of the grounds for possible diplomatic friction" (*ibid.*, p. 57) with the one-party states rather than any accretion to Soviet strength through a growth of Communist Party strength.

[19] For a careful analysis of Castroite-Communist relations, see Theodore Draper, *Castroism: Theory and Practice* (New York: Frederick A. Praeger, 1965), pp. 3–56.

[20] "Red Paper to Join with Ben Bella's," *The New York Times,* June 6, 1965, p. 28.

[21] "Party Dissolved by Reds in Cairo," *The New York Times,* April 26, 1965, p. 16.

underdeveloped countries than through their overthrow and replacement by Communist parties. This change of attitude really involves an imperceptible change in the goals of Soviet foreign policy itself. It has been a change from Communist revolution as a rather immediate policy objective—whether it was regarded as desirable in itself or for the protection of the Soviet Union—to the postponement of revolution to the indefinite, far-off future in favor of more immediate measures to strengthen the Soviet Union. This, in turn, in the period of the Cold War, meant also weakening the United States, and for that purpose, cooperation with non-Communist nationalist movements and governments of many underdeveloped countries whose anti-colonialism predisposed them against the Western powers, quite apart from any Soviet influence, proved more fruitful than the old pro-Communist policies.

This change of attitude toward world revolution resulted from a development parallel and related to the changing power position of the Soviet Union, namely, the evolution of Soviet society and leadership. The people who came to power in Russia in 1917 were revolutionary intellectuals. They had spent their lives dreaming, plotting, and making the revolution, and they were not going to stop being revolutionaries simply because they had succeeded. As is the case with all revolutionaries, to them the revolution had to go on, and world revolution was hence an important policy. This generation of revolutionary intellectuals was replaced during the Stalinist period of industrialization by technically trained bureaucratic and managerial intellectuals.

Today, the Party is neither the Leninist one of professional revolutionaries nor the Stalinist one enforcing immense sacrifices to achieve rapid industrialization. The new intelligentsia has become a new upper class demanding more consumer goods. They inherited the benefits of the revolution, and hence the revolution lies for them in the past, not in the present or the future. Thus, the 1961 Program of the Communist Party of the Soviet Union proclaims the final victory of socialism and the end of the class struggle in the Soviet Union.[22] To the new Soviet elite, the word "revolution" has become a symbol of conservatism, like the term "American Revo-

22 Triska, *op. cit.*, pp. 24 and 31–32.

lution" to the Daughters of the American Revolution. Soviet leaders
have hence lost interest in the revolution abroad and sympathy with
revolutionary groups abroad and have shifted their interests to
developing the Soviet system of production. Indeed, the 1961 Party
Program characterizes this concern with Soviet domestic development as "the Soviet people's great *internationalist* task."[23]

If the foregoing analysis is valid, Soviet policy in the underdeveloped countries should, in the future, have little to do with the
advancement of Communism. This has, of course, been true for
quite some time, concealed only by the constant repetition of old
myths both in the East and the West. The Soviet Union has supported some Communist parties and has sacrificed others (and
ignored many); her allies and friends include Communist governments as well as anti-Communist ones, both of the traditional
variety, as in Afghanistan and Ethiopia, and of the modernist
variety, as in Egypt and India; and she has among her enemies
both anti-Communist governments and Communist ones, especially
China. In the period of governmental instability that lies ahead
for much of the underdeveloped world, Soviet policy will no doubt
seek to gain or maintain its influence with those in power regardless of their attitude toward the domestic Communist Party. Thus,
in the Algerian coup of June, 1965, Moscow was quick to cooperate
with Boumedienne, who had eliminated its erstwhile friend Ben
Bella, and after October, 1965, as already noted, a similar development took place in the anti-Communist upheaval in Indonesia. The
Soviet Government, after some grumbling in the press, has tried
to maintain friendly relations with the new government of Ghana,
despite the overthrow of the Convention People's Party that Moscow had recognized as a kind of surrogate Communist Party.

More and more, it becomes necessary for an understanding of
Soviet policy to distinguish between the fate of the Soviet Union
and that of Communist parties abroad. Just as Communist Party

[23] *Ibid.*, p. 25. The same point was more recently made in *Pravda:* "The
Socialist countries' course of building socialism and Communism, far from
retarding the revolutionary initiative of the working people of the capitalist
countries, is the most effective means for its all-round development" ("The
Supreme Internationalist Duty of the Socialist Country," *Pravda*, October 27,
1965; translated in *The Current Digest of the Soviet Press*, XVII, No. 43
[November 17, 1965], 8).

defeats, like those in Egypt and Iraq and more recently in Indonesia, have not necessarily been Soviet setbacks, so Soviet advances are not necessarily Communist advances. Currently the growth of Soviet power in Asia, as demonstrated in Moscow's role as peacemaker in the Indian-Pakistani dispute and potential role as a peacemaker in Vietnam, is often being noted. It is interesting to reflect that this growth of power rests on Soviet economic, diplomatic, and military strength rather than on Communist Party strength. Far from relying on the Communist parties in the areas concerned or advancing their cause, Soviet policy may well tend to weaken them.

Thus, Soviet success on the governmental level may be accompanied by a loss of Soviet influence over Communist parties. Though this is not necessarily tantamount to a gain in Chinese influence— for there is also the third possibility of growing independence of Communist parties—the long-range trend with respect to influence on parties may well be in favor of the Chinese. Communist parties in underdeveloped countries may feel resentful of Moscow as Soviet policy has more and more supported their non-Communist governments and thus effectively helped keep them out of power. Initially, Soviet cooperation with non-Communist governments was anti-American. Now that the Soviet Union would seem to seek stabilization and even some accommodation with the West, it may find it even harder to compete for the allegiance of Communist parties and even non-Communist nationalist movements with China, whose strident anti-Westernism appeals to many nationalist intellectuals of underdeveloped countries. More generally, the Soviet Union may gradually lose out to China in its attempts to continue to identify itself with aspirations of the revolutionary intelligentsia in underdeveloped countries. The very success of Soviet industrialization, which once made her so attractive to this intelligentsia, may now have gone so far as to make the Soviet model with its shift from producers goods to consumer goods and its declining growth rate less relevant to their needs than the Chinese one with its emphasis on heavy industry.

In effect, just as the class struggle was given up by Communist parties in the late 1940's, when they began to claim to represent the national bourgeoisie, so world revolution, too, has now been dropped as an objective of Soviet policy. But why, then, the continued use by the Communists of not only class struggle or "proletarian" terminology, but also of world-revolutionary verbiage?

Terms like "the proletarian revolution," "socialism," and the very word "Communism" itself have never, in Communist usage, meant what they seemed to suggest. Some have been myths all along, from their Marxian and pre-Marxian beginnings, but all of them became myths when transferred from their Western European origins to underdeveloped Russia and subsequently to other underdeveloped countries, where the Marxian vision of an advanced industrial proletariat converting highly developed private capitalism into socialism and Communism simply did not apply.[24] This does not mean the Communist words are meaningless, but that they have been meaningful not as predictions but as myths. What has happened over the years, then, is not that they have lost their meaning, but that the function these myths have served has changed.

At one time, the Communist myths, like those of class struggle and world revolution, were calls to action; they urged those to whom they were addressed to rise up and change the *status quo*. In recent years, their function has become one of inducing not action but quiescence. They now serve to reassure those who are attracted to the old symbols, who have an interest in radical change, that their interests will be taken care of.[25] The more the Chinese Communists still use the same myths as calls to action and the more Communist parties are attracted to them, the more must Soviet voices, in order to prevent or delay this process, appeal to these myths that suggest that the Soviet government is still mainly concerned with Communist Party strength, leadership, and ultimate victory.

[24] I have dealt with the phenomenon of Western analytical concepts becoming myths in underdeveloped countries in "The Western Word and the Non-Western World," *The American Behavioral Scientist*, VII (April, 1964), 25–29, and have tried to analyze its complex results with respect to Communism in "Myths, Self-Fulfilling Prophecy, and Symbolic Reassurances in the East-West Conflict," *The Journal of Conflict Resolution*, IX, No. 1 (March, 1965), 1–17.

[25] On the concept of symbolic reassurances, see Murray Edelman, *The Symbolic Uses of Politics* (Urbana, Ill.: University of Illinois Press, 1964), especially chap. II.

However, this is not to imply that the Soviet leaders consciously use Communist symbols and myths as myths, that is, as lies. Rather, the leaders themselves believe in the myths, though to what extent it is impossible to establish and no doubt varies among individuals. They cannot dispense with the revolutionary mythology—or even with their belief in it—for they derive their legitimacy from a revolutionary tradition. Their symbols reassure them that they remain faithful to this tradition.

Thus symbols assure everyone that there has been no change— no so-called basic or fundamental change—and paradoxically thus leave the policy-makers free in fact to change their policies. Soviet leaders could not have maintained themselves in power nor could they have kept their consciences quiet as they supported anti-Communist governments in a number of countries even against Communist parties, and also as they withdrew missiles from Cuba, sent war planes to India to be used against Communist China, backed, for quite some time, a neutralist against a Communist faction in Laos, and signed the test-ban treaty with the United States and perhaps advised the Vietcong to stop fighting, had they announced that they were abandoning the goal of world revolution. They are free to *do* all these new things only because they *say* that they continue to pursue the old policy.[26]

The Sino-Soviet conflict is, of course, an integral part of the story of Soviet policy in underdeveloped countries. To be sure, it could be argued that it has chiefly served to reinforce tendencies that can be explained from changes in the internal and international position of the Soviet Union, both the tendency to cooperate with non-Communist governments in underdeveloped countries and the

[26] That words remain the same while policies change, probably because old words provide symbolic reassurance, that "environmental stimuli and even the substantive content of one's world view may vary more than his verbal output: policy changes more dramatically than prayers or vocabularies" is interestingly demonstrated by William John Hanna, "Environmental Change and Verbal Stability," *The Journal of Communications*, XV, No. 3 (September, 1965), 136, who subjected Soviet delegates' speeches to the U.N. Security Council from 1946 to 1960 to a thematic intensity content analysis and found "that the Soviet delegates' formal political communications did not basically change during the years 1946–1960" in spite of major changes in the domestic and international environments of the Soviet elite and probable changes in its world view (*ibid.,* p. 147).

tendency to continue to describe these new policies in terms of the old symbols of Communism. In any case, there is no need here to deal at any length with the Sino-Soviet conflict as such, but some light can perhaps be thrown on it in the present context.

Unlike the present Soviet leaders, the Chinese Communist leaders are not conservatives, for they do not have much to conserve yet; they are not the heirs of a successful revolution, they *are* the revolutionaries themselves and, like all revolutionaries, they regard their revolution as still unfinished.[27] Not only are their experiences and quite possibly their personality needs different from those of the present Soviet leaders, but the power position of their country is very different from that of the Soviet Union, too. Much like Lenin's and unlike Khrushchev's and Brezhnev's Russia, China has few allies and no representation in international bodies and only enough military strength to threaten her own immediate neighbors, no economic strength to provide any substantial foreign aid to developing countries, and no obvious success of her industrialization program to use as propaganda appeal.[28] The Chinese Communists, then, like the early Soviet Government, cannot hope to influence many non-Communist governments, though in a very different world situation they have been trying to do so with some limited success, not only around the Chinese borders but also in Africa.[29] Mao, like Lenin and Stalin, and unlike Khrushchev and Brezhnev, still relies heavily on foreign Communist parties and hopes that they will capture power.[30] Hence the sometimes diametrically oppo-

[27] On the differences between Chinese and Soviet societies and the attitudes of their leaders contributing to the Sino-Soviet conflict, see T. H. Rigby, "The Embourgeoisement of the Soviet Union and the Proletarianization of Communist China," in London (ed.), *Unity and Contradiction,* pp. 19–36.

[28] However, as has been noted, the unsolved problem—though not the failure —of Chinese industrialization may be more appealing to some intellectuals in underdeveloped countries than the success of Soviet industrialization.

[29] See Lowenthal, "China," in Brzezinski (ed.), *Africa and the Communist World,* pp. 142–203; and William E. Griffith, "Africa," in "International Communism: The End of an Epoch," *Survey,* No. 54 (January, 1965), pp. 185–87.

[30] In practice the distinction is not so sharp, because it is becoming more and more difficult to define what constitutes a Communist party, especially from the Chinese point of view. Where Communist parties are nonexistent, as in much of Africa, or are under Soviet domination, as in Northern Africa, the Chinese have sought contacts with non-Communist anti-imperialist groups, whether in power or not, including some of the governments whom the Soviet Communists also

site policies the Soviet and Chinese Communists urge on the Communist parties in underdeveloped countries, notable in India, where the Chinese Communists want Communists to oppose and eventually replace the very government that the Soviet Union wants Communists to support,[31] and the consequent splits of Communist parties in a number of countries. Chinese and Soviet Communists use the same symbols, and this gives the superficial appearance of agreement that has deceived both people in the West and the Communists themselves. Yet words that are calls to action for one side are calls to quiescence for the other.[32]

It should be made clear that the development analyzed here is merely a tendency. Since myths can, to some extent, be self-fulfilling prophecies and can therefore have concrete consequences, and since the symbols producing quiescence are difficult to distinguish from those calling for action, this development evolves in the form of a zig-zag line rather than a straight one.

It should also be added that the argument presented here is such that it cannot be satisfactorily proved by quotations from Soviet statements. Such statements sometimes hint at the change, but they cannot fully admit it. It is in the nature of a myth that it is never

---

cultivate, like Ben Bella's and by late 1963 even Nasser's. They have even suggested that any group or leader—for example, Ben Bella—regardless of class and regardless of party, can, like Castro, declare himself to be and thus become a "Marxist-Leninist." As Chou En-lai remarked in 1963, "Marxism-Leninism cannot be the monopoly of the Communist Party." Quoted by Benjamin Schwartz, "The Polemics Seen by a Non-Polemicist," *Problems of Communism*, XII, No. 2 (March–April, 1964), 106, who excellently sums up this remarkable stretching of Communist dogma, which the Soviet Communists had, in effect, accepted earlier in the Cuban case, as follows: "Thus, the essence of the true proletarian class nature is now not only detached from the industrial proletariat, it is even detachable from constituted Communist parties. It is now a completely free-floating fluid which may find its embodiment where it listeth."

31 For the positions of the two Indian Communist parties, as outlined from a pro-Soviet point of view after the split, see G. Adhikari, "The Problems of the Non-Capitalist Path of Development in India and the State of National Democracy," *World Marxist Review*, VII, No. 11 (November, 1964), 35–42.

32 For an excellent brief analysis of the different Soviet and Chinese attitudes toward the underdeveloped countries as a function of "different needs of Communist parties ruling societies in different stages of economic and social development," see Lowenthal, "Preface to the American Edition," *World Communism: The Disintegration of a Secular Faith* (New York: Oxford University Press, 1964), pp. ix-xv.

described as such by those who believe in it, and it is in the nature of symbols leading to quiescence and inaction that they sound as if they were calls to action. This is unfortunate, because both academic experts on the Soviet Union and also, paradoxically, those anti-Communists who insist that the Communists' words cannot be trusted have a long tradition of relying on these very words, sometimes including the ancient ones of Lenin and even Marx, to prove their points about Soviet policy. The Communists' words can, indeed, not be trusted, and the Communists do deceive others—but they also deceive themselves, for their calls to revolutionary action are really symbols of reassurance. If policy speaks louder than words, if one considers what the Soviet Government and Communist parties, insofar as they follow Soviet policy, do and not what they say, it becomes clear that their policy has not for a long time been one of either class struggle or world revolution. It has in short not been the policy that we have for half a century been accustomed to calling "Communism."

What, then, is Communism in underdeveloped countries today, as distinguished from the intellectual-led nationalist and modernizing movements in these countries? The answer, difficult as it is to accept for those who cling to the old meaning of the word Communism, is simply that Communism *cannot* be sharply distinguished from them, as Soviet policy has sought to identify Communism more and more with these movements. Indeed, it can be argued that Communism itself has all along been a modernizing movement in underdeveloped countries, including Russia,[33] though its use of Western proletarian symbols concealed that character from Communists and non-Communists alike.

The difficulty of drawing the distinction between Communist and non-Communist modernizing movements is well illustrated by recurring debates in the West over whether certain nationalist-modernizing movements are Communist or not. Castro conveniently, but not really satisfactorily, resolved this question when he himself declared that he was a Marxist-Leninist. But were Lumumba and Gizenga Communists? What about Sékou Touré and Jomo Kenyatta and

[33] Cf. Theodore H. von Laue, *Why Lenin? Why Stalin? A Reappraisal of the Russian Revolution, 1900–1930* (Philadelphia: J. B. Lippincott Co., 1964).

even Sukarno? Were the revolution of 1964 in Zanzibar and the uprising in 1965 in Santo Domingo Communist or not? To what degree are the Vietcong Communist? Such questions have been debated time and time again, and similar ones are bound to arise in the future as modernizing nationalists in underdeveloped countries employ symbols similar to the traditional Communist ones and receive the support, verbal and even material, of the Soviet Government.

Both sides to these questions can always produce evidence, yet neither can prove its case, because the debates themselves rest on the false assumption that any man or any movement or revolution must either be Communist or non-Communist.[34] In fact, the Communists have come to support the non-Communists, or, to put it even more paradoxically, Communists have gone non-Communist. Clearly, the very concept of Communism has become a source of confusion. It is hence useless for analytical purposes, useful as it remains as a myth to both those who support and those who oppose whatever they choose to regard as Communism.

[34] On the use of nationalist-modernist symbols by Communists and the role of the concept of national democracy in this connection, see Justus van der Kroef, "The Vocabulary of Indonesian Communism," *Problems of Communism*, XIV, No. 3 (May–June, 1965), 1–9.

12. The Two Alliances: Conflict and Interdependence

ADAM BROMKE[*]

THE POSTWAR period is commonly regarded as a completely novel chapter in international relations. World War II brought about the two developments that revolutionized the entire pattern of world politics. First of all, the multipolar system of balance of power—the traditional "concert of Europe" involving several great powers, one of them occupying the position of the holder of balance —finally came to an end. In its place a bipolar system—with centers in Moscow and Washington—emerged. At the same time, the production of the atom bomb and its immediate military use marked the beginning of the nuclear era. The two events appeared mutu-

* The author is indebted to the Canada Council for a grant in aid of research that enabled him to visit several countries in both the eastern and western parts of Europe in the spring of 1966.

ally to reinforce each other. The two major victors in World War II, the United States and the Soviet Union, soon became the only two nuclear superpowers in the world.

By the 1950's, the new pattern of world politics seemed to be well entrenched. The dominant trend in the international sphere was the rivalry between the two coalitions—each grouped around one of the two nuclear superpowers—here engaged in a diplomatic wrangle, there in economic competition, and elsewhere even in a limited military struggle. The chasm between the two blocs was deepened by the respective ideologies. Moscow openly proclaimed its ambition to spread Communism throughout the world. Washington, if only in response, strove to formulate its own universalist aspirations. "Each side, for quite different reasons, developed oversimplified and emotionally colored stereotypes of the other, which obscured the real nature of the conflict."[1]

The ideological rivalry pushed both the United States and the Soviet Union toward seeking allies among the hitherto noncommitted nations. The scope of the conflict between the two superpowers was widened, while the role of the smaller states was reduced. On their own, the smaller countries counted for little in a global struggle; and when they joined one or the other side, they were overshadowed by the leaders of their respective alliances.

Paradoxically, the division of the world into two blocs, engaged in a bitter conflict, resulted in the close interdependence of developments on both sides. In a bipolar structure the interdependence worked virtually in a hydraulic-like fashion: "each group [responding] to the actual and anticipated activity from outside itself and [being] limited in its actions by the presence, actual or imputed, of these activities."[2] The increased pressure from one side usually led to the closing of ranks on the other side. The growing integration on the second side, in turn, was interpreted as an increasing

[1] Marshall D. Shulman, *Beyond the Cold War* (New Haven, Conn.: Yale University Press, 1966), p. 2.

[2] David Easton, *The Political System* (New York: Alfred A. Knopf, 1953) p. 178. Shulman, in discussing the impact of the EEC upon CEMA, prefers to compare the process to electrodynamic induction, where "it is possible for a charged body to induce an electrical or magnetic current in a nearby body without physical contact" ("The Communist States and Western Integration," *International Organization*, XVII, No. 3 [Summer, 1963], 659–60).

threat to the first. Thus, the Communist takeover of Eastern Europe in the immediate postwar years brought about the defense pact between Western Europe and the United States. The growing cooperation in the West, in turn, prompted the Communists to consolidate their position by establishing the Cominform and CEMA. Similarly, the Berlin Blockade in the late 1940's and the Korean War in the early 1950's resulted in the increased integration of the Atlantic Alliance and the rearmament of Germany. The inclusion of the German Federal Republic in NATO, however, led to the signing of the Warsaw Treaty in 1955 by the Communist states. At each step the gulf between the two blocs widened.

It was also in the 1950's, however, that the first cracks in the bipolar structure—unnoticed by many[3]—appeared. In the long run, the postwar system proved to be self-defeating. In various ways it produced its own antidotes. First of all, the mutually reinforcing relationship between bipolarity and the nuclear era broke down. With the steady progress by the Soviet Union in developing its own nuclear arsenal it reached the position vis-à-vis the United States that led to the mutual "balance of terror." By the close of the decade, each side possessed sufficient destructive means to assure that even if first exposed to attack, it could still retaliate by dealing a crippling blow to its opponent. In these circumstances, the possession of nuclear weapons acquired new meaning. They were no longer viewed as an instrument for the conduct of war, but on the contrary, as a deterrent against the outbreak of war.

In the new situation, both superpowers gradually became aware that war between them was simply no longer a rational proposition. Consequently, efforts to mitigate the conflict between the United States and the Soviet Union were undertaken. Two attempts at a *détente*—the first at the time of the Geneva Conference in 1955, and the second at the time of Khrushchev's visit to the United States in 1959—were made.

The search for some workable *modus vivendi* between the two

[3] As early as 1954, George F. Kennan wrote: "Let us remember that the dominant characteristic of our present international situation is the passing of the phenomenon people have called bipolarity. . . . Yet many of us seem not to be aware of this" (*Realities of American Foreign Policy* [Princeton, N.J.: Princeton University Press, 1954], p. 100).

superpowers proved to be an arduous and tedious task. Its achievement was hindered by various factors. The negotiations between the two sides repeatedly ran into the ideological barrier. Each side spoke a different diplomatic language and used a different conceptual framework. Neither trusted the good faith of the other. Agreement, moreover, was made difficult by the nature of the nuclear stalemate itself. There was the fear of a surprise attack. There was the risk of a resort to nuclear brinkmanship with the danger of pushing the conflict beyond the point of no return. There was the apprehension of a technological breakthrough that would give one side a decisive advantage over the other. All of these features of the nuclear stalemate not only prevented any effective steps being taken towards disarmament, but led to a continued arms race where both sides, if only as a precautionary measure, strove to achieve not merely parity but superiority in nuclear weapons.

The attainment of some broad Soviet-American compact, above all, was prevented by the fact that their community of interest was still extremely narrow. It was virtually confined to a single, essentially negative, factor: the fear of mutual nuclear annihilation. And by itself the nuclear stalemate could do "no more than to prevent open warfare; it clearly [could] make no positive contribution to the resolution of conflict."[4] The periods of *détente*, thus, were interspersed by periods of renewed hostility, such as the one starting with the Hungarian and Suez conflicts in 1956, and continued through the Middle East and the Far East crises in 1958 into the renewed friction over Berlin early in 1959, and another one starting with the U-2 incident in the spring of 1960 and culminating in the crises in Berlin in 1961 and in Cuba in 1962.

It was not only that throughout the 1950's bipolarity and the nuclear era ceased to reinforce each other, but at the same time the bipolar system itself began to create its own antidotes. The simultaneous quest for allies among the noncommitted nations on the part of both superpowers brought about largely an opposite effect. It enabled these countries to play one side against the other and, in this way, to preserve their nonalignment. The efforts by the two

[4] J. W. Burton, *International Relations: A General Theory* (Cambridge: Cambridge University Press, 1965), p. 99.

superpowers to strengthen the coalitions with each of them had similar effects. By helping the weaker partners to regain strength, they were at the same time creating potential rivals in their own ranks.

The conditions of the nuclear stalemate, thus, were particularly conducive to the revival of the role of the smaller states. The growing realization that both the United States and the Soviet Union mutually neutralized their power, and yet were unable to act in unison, bolstered the confidence of nonaligned and aligned countries alike. The moves toward nonalignment gathered momentum, climaxing in the attempt, at the Belgrade conference in 1961, to forge the movement into a coherent Third World force. The incipient centrifugal forces were also revealed in both alliances. The attempt of the Hungarians in 1956 to leave the Warsaw Treaty and adopt neutrality was unsuccessful; but in the same year Poland, although remaining in the Communist bloc, managed to win from the U.S.S.R. a measure of genuine autonomy. And in the late 1950's, the first signs of the Sino-Soviet rift came to the surface. Similarly, the attempt of Britain and France to act on their own at the time of the Suez crisis in 1956 failed; but with De Gaulle's accession to power in France, friction between Paris and Washington erupted anew. All in all, in the second half of the 1950's, "the two-bloc system [was] in the process of loosening but not of breaking up."[5]

The event that drastically accelerated the erosion of the bipolar system was the eruption in the early 1960's of the Sino-Soviet dispute. While in the 1940's the emergence of the Communist bloc had triggered the chain reaction toward the rigid polarization, now the disarray in the Communist alliance set in motion the opposite trend toward depolarization.

The changes in the Communist orbit brought about by the Sino-Soviet rift were far-reaching.[6] For all practical intents and purposes,

[5] Hans J. Morgenthau, "America and Soviet Alliance Policies," *Confluence*, VI, No. 4 (Winter, 1957). Reproduced in Ivo D. Duchacek (ed.), *Conflict and Cooperation Among Nations* (New York: Holt, Rinehart, and Winston, 1960), p. 423.

[6] For a comprehensive discussion of the impact of Sino-Soviet dispute upon the Communist orbit, see Bromke (ed.), *The Communist States at the Crossroads* (New York: Frederick A. Praeger, 1965); and Leopold Labedz (ed.), *International Communism After Khrushchev* (Cambridge, Mass.: M.I.T. Press, 1965).

the alliance between the Soviet Union and China came to an end, to be replaced by bitter rivalry. It was Communist strategy toward the West that provided the major bone of contention between the Russians and the Chinese. The Chinese, ignoring the nature of the nuclear stalemate, were critical of Soviet attempts to seek a *détente* with the West. When Khrushchev, especially after the fiasco of the Cuban missile gamble, intensified his efforts to reach some *modus vivendi* with the United States, Soviet and Chinese policies openly diverged. In 1963, Peking denounced the Moscow nuclear test-ban treaty and energetically forged ahead with its own nuclear program. Russian attempts to bring the Chinese into line, undertaken first by Khrushchev and intensified by his successors, proved to be futile. Even serious aggravation of the struggle between the Communists and the Americans in Vietnam has failed to bring the Soviet Union and China together. With North Korea and particularly North Vietnam trying to steer a middle course between Peking and Moscow, there has been a growing variety in the policies of the Communist countries in Asia.

The impact of the Sino-Soviet split went beyond Asia and had significant repercussions in Europe.[7] In their rivalry with the Russians for the leadership of the Communist bloc, the Chinese appealed to the nationalist sentiments of the East Europeans. They denounced the U.S.S.R. for restricting the sovereignty of the smaller Communist states and encouraged them to seek emancipation from Moscow's hegemony. The Chinese line found response in at least two countries in Eastern Europe. Albania severed its ties with Moscow and openly sided with Peking. In exchanging the Soviet Union for distant China as its patron, the Albanian Communist regime gained a considerable measure of independence, even though this was used to preserve the Stalin-like dictatorship at home. Romania exploited the rift between the two Communist giants in a more

[7] For a comprehensive review of the political developments in Eastern Europe in the mid-1960's, see Brzezinski, *Alternative to Partition* (New York: McGraw-Hill Book Co., 1965); John C. Campbell, *American Policy Toward Communist Eastern Europe* (Minneapolis: University of Minnesota Press, 1965); Ghita Ionescu, *The Break-up of the Soviet Empire in Eastern Europe* (Baltimore, Md.: Penguin Books, 1965); Bromke, *Eastern Europe in a Depolarized World* (Toronto: Baxter Publishing Co., 1965); and J. F. Brown, *The New Eastern Europe: The Khrushchev Era and After* (New York: Frederick A. Praeger, 1966).

subtle manner. She took what amounted to a neutral stand in the conflict and shrewdly played one side against the other. In this way, Bucharest managed to win a considerable degree of independence from both Moscow and Peking. In the domestic sphere the Romanians adopted the policy of "Romanization"—emphasizing their own national heritage—and pursued a course of industrialization largely independent of CEMA. And, at least in some aspects of foreign policy, notably their criticism of all military blocs, they moved close to nonalignment. Khrushchev's efforts to arrest these developments were of no avail. His attempts to browbeat tiny Albania back into line ended in a spectacular fiasco. The Soviet leader took a more conciliatory stand vis-à-vis Romania. This, however, helped him little, for apparently it encouraged the Romanian Communist regime to seek further concessions from Moscow.

The Sino-Soviet rift also affected relations between Moscow and those Communist states in Eastern Europe that remained loyal to it. They were now elevated to the rank of junior, but, nevertheless, genuine partners of Russia. In exchange for their support of Moscow against Peking, they were given greater leeway in domestic, and in a limited way even in external affairs. Thus, especially after the extensive "de-Stalinization" undertaken by Khrushchev in 1961, the policies of the different East European countries were adjusted to fit their own peculiar circumstances. Poland continued to refrain from collectivization of agriculture; Hungary widened the scope of cultural freedom; and Czechoslovakia undertook a sweeping reform of its economic system. All in all, there was a marked trend toward polycentrism in Eastern Europe.

By the mid-1960's, the internal cohesion of what had remained of the Communist bloc after the defection of China and her allies had been seriously impaired. Various developments have contributed to the erosion of Moscow's authority. First of all there has been a marked decline in the role of Communist ideology. The growth of doctrinal pluralism in turn bred incipient pragmatism. The continued adherence of the different Eastern European regimes to the Communist ideology has increasingly assumed the form of mere rationalization to ensure their continuance in power. Side by side with the erosion of ideology, there has been a noticeable growth of nationalism. Apparently, in Eastern Europe "the original national identities have not been destroyed by the temporary domination exercised by the Soviet Union."[8] The different Communist governments in the region have become increasingly concerned with their national interests. Finally, there has been the gradual restoration of Eastern Europe's traditional bonds with the West. To a greater or lesser degree all the countries in the area have expanded their economic, cultural, and even political contacts with the Western world.

The growing disarray among Moscow's own supporters was clearly not to the liking of Khrushchev. He tried, therefore, to arrest the spread of polycentrism by forging anew some multilateral bonds among the Communist states. He emphasized the need for closer cooperation among the Communist states adhering to the Warsaw Treaty and the CEMA, and to foster this objective he called for an international Communist meeting. Khrushchev's plan, however, proved to be unattainable. Even some Communist states that firmly sided with the Soviet Union in the dispute with China had little taste for the restoration of an international Communist organization. As a result the meeting was postponed several times, and when it took place in March, 1965—after Khrushchev had already been removed from power—it accomplished very little. Apparently the new Soviet leaders recognized that at least at this stage the situation was not conducive to promoting multilateral cooperation among the Communist states.

Two major factors now hold the Communist states in Eastern Europe together. First, there are the vested interests of the ruling Communist elites. A too abrupt discarding of Communist ideology and, above all, of its cardinal tenet of firm bonds with the Soviet Union could place in serious doubt the legitimacy of the Communist retention of power. This seems to be particularly true with respect to the badly beleaguered Ulbricht regime in East Germany. Second, in the case of some other countries, there exists a genuine unity of national interests with Russia. This is particularly true with regard to Poland and Czechoslovakia, which feel threatened by the revived power of West Germany and, consequently, look to Russia for protection from their Western neighbor. Thus, at least

[8] Raymond Aron, "On Polycentrism," *Survey*, No. 58 (January, 1966), p. 12.

in one aspect, relations between the U.S.S.R. and the East European countries have returned to the normal pattern of international politics, where the conduct of foreign policy of the different countries is primarily determined by their national interests.

The new Soviet leaders seem to be aware of the realities of the situation in Eastern Europe, because at least for the time being they have abstained from advancing any new plans for comprehensive integration of the area.[9] Instead, they have fostered bilateral ties with the individual countries in the region, in each case striving to exploit the peculiar aspects of the local situation in binding them most effectively to the U.S.S.R. In some cases, as for instance in Soviet-Polish relations, consultations at the highest level have become a regular feature, amounting virtually to a special relationship between the two Communist states.[10]

Barring some drastic change in political trends in the Communist orbit as a whole, the special relationship between the Soviet Union and the various East European countries seem to be the pattern for the future. In an increasingly polycentric situation, the network of such special relationships—some close and some loose, some ideological and some national, some political and others economic—appears to be the most effective, and, indeed, perhaps the only feasible way for the U.S.S.R. to preserve its influence in the area.

The impact of the changes in the Communist orbit was soon felt in the outside world. The areas most directly affected by the Sino-Soviet split, naturally enough, were South Asia and the Far East. When, in the fall of 1962, China invaded India, the two superpowers moved spontaneously to contain Peking. New Delhi received support, including military equipment, both from Washington and Moscow. China countered this by courting the favor of

9 For a discussion of the situation in Eastern Europe following the ouster of Khrushchev, see J. F. Brown, "East Europe: The Soviet Grip Loosens," *Survey*, October, 1965.

10 The communiqué issued after the Brezhnev-Gomulka conference in September, 1965, stressed that this was "a normal meeting in line with the regular contacts between the Polish and Soviet Parties" (*Trybuna ludu* [*People's Tribune*; Warsaw], September 13, 1965). And indeed, from Brezhnev's ascendancy to power until the end of 1965, the two leaders met five times: in October, 1964, January, April, September, and October, 1965.

India's traditional enemy, Pakistan—notwithstanding its member-ship in the anti-Communist SEATO and CENTO alliances. By endorsing Pakistan's claim to Kashmir, Peking soon achieved a close rapport with Rawalpindi. Thus, when, in the fall of 1965, the war over Kashmir broke out between Pakistan and India, the Chinese openly supported the Pakistanis. The two superpowers stepped in and brought the conflict to an end. With the active support of both the United States and the Soviet Union, a cease-fire was arranged by the United Nations. At the same time an important change took place in other areas in Asia. In the mid-1960's, Soviet-Japanese relations, notwithstanding Tokyo's contin-ued close bonds with Washington, showed signs of a marked improvement.

The parallel policies of the United States and the Soviet Union on the Indian subcontinent and in the Far East, revealing a single objective—the containment of China—introduced a novel element into relations between the two superpowers. Their community of interest was no longer confined to a single, essentially negative factor: fear of mutual nuclear annihilation. Another more tangible element, bringing together America and Russia, entered into the picture. Washington and Moscow now had an adversary in common. This opened up new vistas for a *détente* between the two super-powers, not only in Asia but in the world at large. In the summer of 1963, at the very time when formal negotiations between the Russians and the Chinese to mend their rift ultimately broke down, the first major step toward reducing the armament race between the United States and the Soviet Union was taken. The nuclear test-ban treaty was signed in Moscow. Agreements not to orbit nuclear weapons in outer space and to cut back the production of fissionable explosives followed. At the same time, both sides re-frained from aggravating tensions in the areas where they con-fronted each other, notably in Berlin and Cuba. All of those developments markedly improved the climate of relations between Washington and Moscow. Late in 1964 and still early in 1965, plans were discussed for President Johnson's visit to the U.S.S.R.

The improvement in American-Soviet relations in 1963–64, how-ever, represented at best a prelude to, but not as yet a genuine *détente*. The community of interest of the two superpowers, even after their adoption in some instances of a parallel course on China, was apparently still too limited to bring about their reconciliation on a global scale. The American-Soviet *semi-détente* thus was more in the nature of a cease-fire than a genuine truce. The measures toward disarmament were half-hearted—they did not strike at the roots of the arms race. In areas where the Americans and the Russians confronted each other, tensions were reduced, but no progress to remove their sources was made. Above all, in the main theater of American-Soviet conflict—Central Europe—an agreement between the two superpowers was nowhere in sight. In Asia, the gradually increased conflict in Vietnam marred progress toward a real *détente* between the United States and the Soviet Union, and by 1965 brought it to a standstill.

Although the improvement in relations between the two superpowers in 1963–64 was restricted, it had a considerable impact upon the Western coalition. The reduction of tensions in Europe contributed to the loosening of the internal cohesion of the Atlantic alliance. Feeling more secure, the various member countries placed their national objectives over those of NATO. Serious disagreements concerning not only its current policies but the very purpose of the alliance were revealed, especially between the United States and France.[11]

The debate on the future of NATO testified to the close interdependence between the events in the East and the West. A good many differences between Washington and Paris stemmed from their divergent evaluation of the changes in the Communist orbit.[12] The Americans argued that despite the reduction of East-West

[11] For a comprehensive discussion of the impact of the changes in East-West relations upon the Atlantic alliance in the mid-1960's, see Arnold Wolfers (ed.), *Changing East-West Relations and the Unity of the West* (Baltimore, Md.: The Johns Hopkins Press, 1964); Edgar S. Furniss, Jr. (ed.), *The Western Alliance: Its Status and Prospects* (Columbus, Ohio: Ohio State University Press, 1965); Karl H. Cerny and Henry W. Briefs (eds.), *NATO in Quest of Cohesion* (New York: Frederick A. Praeger, 1965); Henry A. Kissinger, *The Troubled Partnership* (New York: McGraw-Hill Book Co., 1965); also see the special January, 1966, issue of *Survey* on "Foreign Policy in a Polycentric World."

[12] On the East European implications of the Western debates, see an illuminating paper by Pierre Hassner, "Polycentrism, West and East," delivered at the Fifth International Conference on World Politics in Noordwijk, Holland, in September, 1965.

tensions, the task of the Atlantic alliance to bring about a genuine settlement in Europe was not completed and, therefore, its dismantling would be premature. Indeed, they claimed that the preservation of NATO was essential for the encouragement of continued changes in the Communist orbit, for as former Secretary of State Dean Acheson put it: "If through a revival of nationalist rivalries in the West . . . the alliance should fall apart, the Soviet Union would have little incentive to act with moderation or restraint."[13] The French countered the American thesis with the argument that, as the Gaullist deputy Jean de Lipkowski put it: "An independent Europe can propose the original solutions that the United States, paralyzed by the equilibrium with the Soviet Union, is not able to propose." Therefore, he suggested that it was not in the interest of the West to remain a monolithic bloc while in the East polycentrism destroyed Communist unity.[14]

The French put their strategy into practice. They opposed the American plan to revitalize the alliance by creating a multinational nuclear fleet, and instead proceeded to develop their own nuclear force. Early in 1966, France, despite bitter opposition from the United States, decided to withdraw completely from NATO's integrated defense system. Even though the Americans managed to extract a pledge of continued cooperation from the other fourteen members of the alliance, not all of them gave it with equal enthusiasm. The Portuguese, the Greeks, and the Scandinavians clearly were not eager to censure De Gaulle, and even the Germans were reluctant to make an outright condemnation of the French. The effects of France's decision, thus, have gone beyond the mere weakening of NATO's military structure. At the political level a serious source of friction has been created among the Western allies, which, if it does not lead to their piecemeal falling apart, will almost certainly reduce their multilateral cooperation to the lowest common denominator.

The strains on the Atlantic alliance, however, were not confined to the Franco-American dispute. Centrifugal forces appeared in other areas too. The eastern flank of NATO was ruptured by the

13 Dean Acheson, "Decision or Drift," *Foreign Affairs*, XLIV, No. 2 (January 1966), 205.
14 *The New York Times*, March 25, 1965.

bitter dispute between Greece and Turkey over Cyprus, with the threat in mid-1964 of an outbreak of war between the two countries. In the south, Portugal has been estranged because of the lack of support that she has received from the Atlantic allies in her stubborn efforts to cling to colonial possessions in Africa. And in the north, Norway and Denmark have been giving new thought to the possibility of entering a Scandinavian pact with neutral Sweden, should NATO fall apart. And lastly, the growing American involvement in the war in Vietnam has aroused little enthusiasm in Europe. The French have been openly critical of the United States and serious reservations have also been raised in other countries. The Europeans have been increasingly worried that American preoccupation with Asian affairs would divert attention from trying to resolve what to them are the most important European problems.

By the mid-1960's, NATO unity had been seriously impaired. The crisis perhaps has not been so serious as in the East, for the Western alliance has never striven to attain the character of an ideological monolith, as has the Communist bloc. It has been somewhat easier for the West, therefore, to preserve the external façade of unity. Yet a certain degree of similarity to developments in Eastern Europe has been present in Western Europe. First of all there has been a marked revival of nationalism. There came "the discovery that the confident announcements of [the] obsequies . . . of the European nation state . . . that echoed through the political speeches in the late 1940's were, to say the least, premature."[15] Moreover, there has been a growing interest in the concept of a united Europe—"from the Atlantic to the Urals." The marked increase in contacts by the West European states with both the U.S.S.R. and Eastern Europe soon followed.

In 1964, Franco-Soviet relations underwent a rapid improvement. The *détente* was preserved even after the new deterioration of American-Soviet relations. If anything, throughout 1965, Moscow-Paris cooperation was steadily widened, culminating in President de Gaulle's visit in the U.S.S.R. in mid-1966. France has also developed extensive contacts with the various Communist states in East-

---

15 Max Beloff, "Polycentrism in the West," in Evan Luard (ed.), *The Cold War: A Re-Appraisal* (New York: Frederick A. Praeger, 1964), p. 268.

ern Europe, most notably Poland. At the same time there took place several changes in relations between the Soviet Union and other members of the Western alliance. The Cyprus crisis had the effect of pushing first Greece, and then Turkey, toward seeking Soviet support. As a result, there was a considerable relaxation of tensions between Moscow and Ankara in 1965. Norway and Denmark maintained fairly extensive contacts with the Soviet Union and some of the East European countries. More recently, the tendency toward improving relations with the Communist world has also been manifested in the "Northern Tier" of Middle Eastern states that are members of the CENTO pact. There has been discernible improvement in relations between Iran and the U.S.S.R. and—after the debacle of the Chinese-backed war against India—between Pakistan and the Soviet Union.

Today two main factors hold the Western alliance together. First there is the long-standing commitment of the ruling elites in the different countries to the idea of Atlantic unity. "Many European leaders . . . have built their political careers on close ties to the United States. Their domestic opponents would surely construe a public criticism of U.S. policies as an admission of failure."[16] Second, in the case of some countries there exists a genuine unity of interests with America. This is certainly true of West Germany, which feels that it needs U.S. protection to hold its own against the Soviet Union, and particularly to maintain its precarious position in West Berlin. To a large extent it is also true of Britain, which shares with America common interests east of Suez and has been traditionally linked to the United States by a special relationship.

Indeed, it is the web of special relationships between the United States and some of its Atlantic partners with whom it has strong common interests, which seems to be gradually replacing the old multilateral framework of NATO. If this trend continues it might well lead to the emergence of "quite novel patterns . . . among the nations of the Atlantic and European area, with frameworks vary-

[16] Kissinger, "Strains on the Alliance," *Foreign Affairs*, XLI, No. 2 (January, 1963).

ing from function to function—now loose, now tight, now comprehensive, now limited to a core of states—and thereby leaving open
the door for such presently undreamed of forms as may later
manifest themselves for our emerging pluralist yet interdependent
world."[17]

The simultaneous disarray in the ranks of both great coalitions
has resulted in the gradual but unmistakable erosion of the ideological line dividing the world. Each of the two superpowers, while
striving to preserve the cohesion of its own alliance, has endeavored
to spread disarray in the ranks of its opponent. The West has
favored the growth of polycentrism in the East, and vice versa.
Each side strove to counteract this by encouraging the dissidents in
the opposing ranks. In 1964, the United States announced the policy
of "building bridges" to Eastern Europe aimed, at least in part, at
assisting those countries to strengthen their independence from
Russia. The American-Romanian agreement of May, 1964, extending to Bucharest—in recognition of its more independent course
—exceptionally favorable trading terms, emphasized this Washington objective. In the same year, Khrushchev undertook diplomatic
maneuvers vis-à-vis West Germany, which might have been an
attempt to weaken Bonn's ties with Washington, while his successors have worked hard to widen the gap between France and
America.[18]

Parallel to the efforts of the two superpowers, the smaller countries on each side have moved to expand the contacts with their
counterparts on the other side. Thus, in recent years, relations between Bulgaria and Greece, Romania and West Germany, Poland
and France[19] have shown considerable improvement. These developments in part have been encouraged by the leaders of each alli-

[17] Lawrence W. Martin, "Europe and the Future of the Grand Alliance," in
Roger Hilsman and Robert C. Good (eds.), *Foreign Policy in the Sixties* (Baltimore, Md.: The Johns Hopkins Press, 1965), p. 22.

[18] For a penetrating discussion of the Soviet policy toward France after the
fall of Khrushchev, see Richard Lowenthal, "The Soviets Change Their Foreign
Policy," *The New York Times Magazine,* April 4, 1965.

[19] For an evaluation of the prospects and limits of Franco-Polish cooperation,
see Bromke, "Poland and France: The Sentimental Friendship," *East Europe,*
February, 1966.

ance, as part of the policy of splitting the other side; in part, however, they have arisen from the genuine initiative of the middle powers, as an expression of their bolder posture in international affairs.

The increased contacts among the smaller countries belonging to the opposite alliances have been particularly significant as an indication of new trends in the international sphere. By diluting the bonds in each bloc and replacing them with ties cutting across the ideological boundary, these contacts contribute directly to the decline of the bipolar system. They blur the distinction between the aligned and nonaligned states. As such, they offer the best evidence that "the era of frozen hierarchic blocs has gone [and that] the tide runs strongly toward flexibility and occasional interpenetration."[20]

The nature of relations between the United States and the Soviet Union, which has been characterized as a state of "neither war nor peace,"[21] appears to be encouraging the spread of polycentrism in both the East and the West. The combination of the nuclear stalemate and bipolarization produces a situation where the two superpowers can resolve their differences neither by force nor by settlement.

The mutual balance of terror prevents both Russia and America from resorting to force. And without the actual threat of war, the gradual erosion of the two alliances is inevitable. The trend, of course, could be reversed. One sure way to revive NATO would be by restoring the Soviet Union's tight grip over Eastern Europe. With an increased threat to Western Europe, even France would close ranks with the United States. There is no reason to doubt the sincerity of President de Gaulle's statement of 1963 that "as long as the Soviets threaten the world [the Atlantic] alliance must be maintained."[22] Conversely, any renewed effort at the integration of the West is likely to lead to the restoration of the cohesion of

[20] Furniss, "A Personal Evaluation of the Western Alliance," *The Western Alliance* . . . , p. 174.

[21] The phrase, borrowed from Trotsky, was used by Hugh Seton-Watson as the title of his book on the political developments in the post-war world: *Neither War Nor Peace* (New York: Frederick A. Praeger, 1960).

[22] Quoted in Wolfers (ed.), *op. cit.*, p. 175.

the Soviet bloc. Feeling that they have nothing to gain by continued de-Stalinization, the Russians might reverse it and try to restore their influence in Eastern Europe by force. As Premier Kosygin put it in 1965, "any unification of forces in [the Western] camp must be directed against us. It compels us to muster our own forces and react to what you do."[23] Thus, there is a growing realization on both sides that there exists a penalty for trying to arrest the spread of polycentrism in its own ranks. It only leads to similar measures on the other side that virtually cancel any benefits. The over-all effect of such developments is that of aggravating the conflict and reviving the specter of the nuclear holocaust both sides are eager to avoid.

The hydraulic-like interdependence between the two blocs, thus, seems to be working in the direction of a gradual erosion of a bipolar structure and its replacement by a multipolar system. The alternation in American-Soviet relations, between the periods of hostility and of *détente,* by no means invalidates this trend. For as Jean-Baptiste Duroselle observed, "if there is an intensification of the Cold War, then the allies will faithfully close ranks. But if the Cold War becomes less important . . . then the diverging national interests reappear."[24]

The United States and the Soviet Union are also unable to reach a genuine settlement of their conflict. They cannot possibly agree to divide the world into two spheres of influence, each of them retaining the dominant position in its own part. This is so because where there exist only two superpowers their rivalry is unavoidable. Even with the emergence of a common threat to them from China, their community of interest is too narrow. China is still too weak to bring America and Russia effectively closer together. This could be brought about only by a realignment of forces in the international sphere resulting in the emergence of a rival equally threatening to each of them. As Herbert S. Dinerstein put it, the United States and the Soviet Union can reach a *détente* but not an *entente,* "they can only become more friendly, they cannot become friends . . . unless and until [they] perceive a threat from a power of equal

---

23 *The New York Times,* December 8, 1965.

24 Jean-Baptiste Duroselle, "De Gaulle's Designs for Europe and the West," in Wolfers (ed.), *op. cit.,* p. 182.

rank . . . the necessary basis for conversion of *détente* to *entente* . . . does not exist."[25] Thus, even if both superpowers are opposed to the emergence of new power centers, it is just what they need in order to reach more lasting accommodation. In the bipolar system the very logic of their position pushes them in the direction of a multipolar structure.

It is exactly at this point that the two trends, the spread of polycentrism in both alliances and the search for a *modus vivendi* between the two superpowers, merge. For if the trend toward reassertion of the smaller countries continues it might well go beyond nonalignment and produce a realignment of forces on the world scene. In the end it might lead to the emergence of the third force that is needed to bring about the settlement of Soviet-American rivalry.

Whether or not such a third force will actually come into being will largely depend on the progress of the smaller states' nuclear programs. "France and China, the countries most dedicated to the overthrow of the system of polarisation of power, clearly see the construction of their own nuclear armouries as one of the bases of their policies."[26] Each of them hopes that the acquisition of nuclear weapons would provide it with a means to emerge as leaders of new groupings of states, comparable in strength with that of either of the superpowers.

There exist, of course, powerful forces in the world that hinder the replacement of a bipolar system by a multipolar structure. There is the residue of the old ideological commitments. There are vested interests in the existing political and military structures. There are the conflicting national objectives of the smaller states. There is, above all, the gap in strength between the superpowers and the smaller countries. Yet it seems that the pattern of the post-war international politics is unmistakable. At each consecutive stage of striving for a *détente* between the two superpowers, the strength

[25] Herbert S. Dinerstein, "The Transformation of Alliance Systems," *The American Political Science Review*, LIX, No. 3 (September, 1965), 596. Shulman introduces a similar distinction between what he calls "an atmosphere of *détente* and a *rapprochement*" (*Beyond the Cold War*, p. 58).

[26] Erasmus, "Polycentrism and Proliferation," *Survey*, No. 58 (January, 1966), p. 70.

of the centrifugal forces in both alliances is enhanced. Certainly the strength of polycentric tendencies in the 1960's has far exceeded that of the 1950's. If the trend were to be arrested once again, the likelihood is that it will reassert itself with greater force in the 1970's. For inherent in the very nature of a bipolar system are the seeds of its own destruction.

Notes on the Contributors
and the Editors

WILLIAM E. BAUER is a member of the Canadian Department
of External Affairs. He has had extensive experience in various
areas of Asia, including Vietnam, and attended the Geneva Conference on Laos in 1962.

ADAM BROMKE is a member of the Department of Political Sci-
ence and former Chairman of the Soviet and East European
Studies Program at Carleton University. He is the author of
Poland's Politics: Idealism vs. Realism and recently edited *The
Communist States at the Crossroads*.

JEAN ETHIER-BLAIS is a member of the Department of French
at McGill University and a former member of the Canadian Department of External Affairs.

JOHN H. KAUTSKY is Chairman of the Committee on International and Area Studies at Washington University, St. Louis. He
edited *Political Change in Underdeveloped Countries*.

RICHARD LOWENTHAL is Professor of International Relations
at the Free University of West Berlin and a board member of its
Eastern Europe Institute. He is the author of a number of books,
including *World Communism*.

PEYTON V. LYON is Chairman of the Department of Political
Science at Carleton University. From 1953 to 1959, he served with

the Canadian Department of External Affairs, holding posts at Ottawa and Bonn. He is the author of *The Policy Question*, a book on Canadian foreign policy.

PAUL MARTIN has been a member of the Canadian Parliament since 1935. As Secretary of State for External Affairs in the Canadian Government, he has headed the Canadian delegation to NATO ministerial meetings, the United Nations General Assembly, and the United Nations Conference on Trade and Development.

HENRY B. MAYO is a Senior Professor and Head of the Political Science Department in Middlesex College at the University of Western Ontario. He is the author of several books, including *Democracy and Marxism*.

FRANZ MICHAEL is Professor of International Affairs and Associate Director of the Institute for Sino-Soviet Studies at George Washington University. From 1934 to 1938, he was a professor at the National Chekiang University in Hangchow. He has written several books, including *The Far East in the Modern World* (with George E. Taylor).

BERNARD S. MORRIS, a member of the Department of Government at Indiana University, served for fifteen years in the Bureau of Intelligence and Research of the State Department. He is the author of *International Communism and American Policy*.

HARALD VON RIEKHOFF is a member of the Department of Political Science at Carleton University. In 1964–65, he was Defence Research Fellow for the Canadian Institute of International Affairs.

H. GORDON SKILLING is a member of the Department of Political Economy and Director of the Center for Russian and East European Studies at the University of Toronto. He is the author of several books including *Communism National and International: Eastern Europe after Stalin*.

PHILIP E. UREN has served with the Canadian departments of External Affairs and Defence and is now a member of the Department of Geography at Carleton University and Managing Editor of *Canadian Slavonic Papers*. He recently edited a symposium entitled *East-West Trade* for the Canadian Institute of International Affairs.

Index